P9-BVG-765

Yale Studies in English
Richard S. Sylvester, Editor
Volume 176

DICKENS AS SATIRIST

by Sylvia Bank Manning

New Haven and London, Yale University Press

1971

Library of Congress catalog card number: 70–115374
International standard book number: 0–300–01342–6
Designed by John O. C. McCrillis,
set in Baskerville type,
and printed in the United States of America by
The Carl Purington Rollins Printing-Office of
the Yale University Press, New Haven, Connecticut.
Distributed in Great Britain, Europe, and
Africa by Yale University Press, Ltd., London;
in Canada by McGill-Queen's University Press,
Montreal; in Mexico by Centro Interamericano de
Libros Académicos, Mexico City; in Australasia
by Australia and New Zealand Book Co., Pty.,
Ltd., Artarmon, New South Wales; in India by
UBS Publishers' Distributors Pvt., Ltd., Delhi;
in Japan by John Weatherhill, Inc., Tokyo.

To my mother,
in memory of my father.

"The name of Merdle is the name of the age."

Contents

Preface

The original form of this book was a doctoral dissertation for Yale University. It was directed by Martin Price, and whatever is good in my approach to novels I owe to him. In my understanding of Dickens there is also an immeasurable debt to an admirable body of criticism, beginning with G. K. Chesterton and Edmund Wilson, that will be apparent to all familiar with the subject. I tender special thanks to the anonymous reader of my dissertation whose plentiful comments were most helpful in rewriting; to California State College at Hayward for a quarter's special leave to write this book; and to my husband Peter, whose undying hostility to Dickens provided an invaluable sounding board.

PART I

Dickens as Satirist

CHAPTER I

Characteristics of Dickensian Satire

When Martin Chuzzlewit comes to the United States, a new acquaintance soon tells him:

> I believe no satirist could breathe this air. If another Juvenal or Swift could rise up among us to-morrow, he would be hunted down. If you have any knowledge of our literature and can give me the name of any man, American born and bred, who has anatomised our follies as a people, and not this or that party, and who has escaped the foulest and most brutal slander, the most inveterate hatred and intolerant pursuit; it will be a strange name in my ears, believe me. In some cases I could name to you, where a native writer has ventured on the most harmless and good-humoured illustrations of our vices and defects, it has been found necesary to announce, that in a second edition the passage has been expunged, or altered, or explained away, or patched into praise. [*Martin Chuzzlewit,* chap. xvi][1]

Dickens was apparently drawing on his recent experience with *American Notes,* less satiric though the book was, both in tone and observation, than the American section of *Chuzzlewit.* One suspects that the much-needed anatomizer will now be Martin-Dickens, protected by not being "American born and bred." A letter to C. C. Felton, then professor of Greek literature at Harvard, seems to corroborate this. On their disagreement concerning a "certain Chuzzlewitian question," Dickens wrote that he is "contenting myself with this prediction, that one of these

1. All quotations from Dickens's novels are from the *New Oxford Illustrated Dickens* (London, 1948–58), but reference will be made by chapter and, where applicable, book.

years and days, you will write or say to me: 'My dear Dickens, you were right, though rough, and did a world of good, though you got most thoroughly hated for it.' "[2]

The conception of satire presented in the passage from *Martin Chuzzlewit* is formal and traditional: satire is a literary genre devoted to the anatomizing of follies. With the same sense of a literary mode, Dickens had written to Cruikshank in May 1836:

> When you have a spare half hour or so, one of these days, I should like to spend it with you in talking over the idea you suggested sometime since relative to a little satire on the class of pieces usually presented at the Theatres in these times. I think I could turn it to the account you desire. [*Letters,* I, 72]

In 1839 Dickens told Forster that he intended writing a series of "satirical papers" for a periodical to begin the following year, and in 1855 that he had an idea for a "fine little bit of satire" for *Household Words.* Some years later he described the work of Swift and Voltaire as "satirically" humorous *(Letters,* I 219; II, 622; III, 360).

The plans of 1839 and 1855 bore issue, though it was not very distinguished. The earlier proposals led to *Master Humphrey's Clock,* which soon was diverted from satire; the 1855 idea became "The Thousand and One Humbugs" in *Household Words,* April 21, April 28, and May 5 of that year. On the theme he discussed with Cruikshank, Dickens incorporated a comic attack into the theatrical chapters of *Nicholas Nickleby* (see especially Nicholas's account in chapter xxiv of the play he is "adapting" from the French for the Crummles company). Much later, in *Household Words,* March 30, 1850, his article "The Amusements of the People" described in a mocking, satiric tone a play called *May Morning,* or *The Mystery of 1715, and the Murder.* In the April 30th issue of that year he described a play about Lady Hatton, who has sold herself to the powers of darkness, and another called *Eva the Betrayed,* or *The Ladye of*

2. *The Letters of Charles Dickens,* ed. Walter Dexter, 3 vols. (London, 1938), 1:534; hereafter cited in the text as *Letters.*

Lambythe. The mocking of 1850 is quite conceivable; the parody in *Nicholas Nickleby,* which itself exhibits a plot hardly less ludicrous, presents something of an anomaly. Nonetheless, that satire is certainly intentional, in the traditional sense of the anatomizing proposed in *Martin Chuzzlewit* for the contemporary Juvenal or Swift.

Very early in his career, however, Dickens begins to demonstrate another conception of satire, one which is rather difficult to define. Illustration may serve better, and relevant passages from the early novels are cited in appendix A. A particularly apt example occurs in the essay "An Old Stage-Coaching House," in *The Uncommercial Traveller.* Describing how the place has changed from the bustling yard it once was, Dickens writes:

> A "Scientific Shoeing-Smith and Veterinary Surgeon," had further encroached upon the yard; and a *grimly satirical* Jobber, who announced himself as having to Let "A neat one-horse fly, and a one-horse cart," had established his business, himself, and his family, in a part of the extensive stables. [italics mine]

Here "satire" seems to be a sort of ironic commentary, generally revealing an unpleasant or bitter truth and therefore often "grim," like the Jobber. The satire is not a verbal attack; it can be an ironic statement, but it is more frequently a presence, an incident, or an incongruous fact.

The concept is somewhat clarified by its use in *David Copperfield.* David has just told Traddles how Creakle has become the tenderest of magistrates: "Traddles shrugged his shoulders, and was not at all surprised. I had not expected him to be, and was not surprised myself; or my observation of similar *practical satires* would have been but scanty" (chap. lxi; italics mine). Here the aspect of a bitter, ironic turn is dominant. Later uses make the revelation of painful truth central. In *Bleak House* Esther admits that Caddy's complaints against her mother contain much "bitterly satirical truth" (chap. xiv); in *The Mystery of Edwin Drood,* Edwin decides that since he and Rosa have broken their engagement the jewels he has bought for her are "but a sign of broken joys and baseless projects; in their very beauty they were . . . almost a cruel *satire* on the loves, hopes, plans, of humanity, which are able to forecast nothing, and are so much brittle dust" (chap. xiii; italics mine).

It is apparent that for Dickens satire is not necessarily literary: it is any form of truthful, ironic, and often bitter commentary upon life. He had always noticed such comment embodied in various odd incidents or incongruous juxtapositions; that he could also create the embodiment, in the total vision of a literary work, seems to have become clearer to him as he wrote his later novels. One such creation was *Hard Times,* which he described in a letter to Charles Knight as "my satire" *(Letters,* II, 620). Book I, chapter xx of *Little Dorrit* opens with this speculation:

> If Young John Chivery had had the inclination, and the power, to write a satire on family pride, he would have had no need to go for an avenging illustration out of the family of his beloved. He would have found it amply in that gallant brother and that dainty sister, so steeped in mean experiences, and so loftily conscious of the family name; so ready to beg or borrow from the poorest, to eat of anybody's bread, spend anybody's money, drink from anybody's cup and break it afterwards. To have painted the sordid facts of their lives, and they throughout invoking the death's head apparition of the family gentility to come and scare their benefactors, would have made Young John a satirist of the first water.

The achievement is far beyond the unfortunate Young John, but it is only a part of what Dickens accomplished in this novel —"painted the sordid facts" of life about him. Dickens's "dark" of the "loves, hopes, plans" that might be. The ironic truth of novels combine a grim vision of what is with a yearning glimpse the later works consists in the relations between the two visions each novel presents and in turn between them and the world that we, the readers, live in. It is far from mimesis and in fact depends upon incongruity.

Dickens knew the classic English satirists and Juvenal and Horace as well, but he did not see himself as the inheritor of their tradition. Whatever influence he may incidentally have felt, formal relations to them are weak. Classical satire is a highly literary genre whose practitioners are very conscious and proud of its long tradition. In this regard, Dickens's work is not satire.[3] In the sense, however, of the term *satire* as a mode of vision, defined less formally by tone and attitude, the work does have fundamental affinities with what is accepted as traditional satire, exhibiting significant satiric traits that in the later novels become dominant. Take the following quotation:

> On first appearance it is heavy, formless, and directionless, a vague slipping, oozing movement like a sliding sea of mud going in any and all directions. . . . But though the spread is without guiding purpose and therefore moves in a random fashion, it is still relentless and never-ceasing. . . . It flows on and on, covering all that it encounters, and in the end it has spread over everything; all that is rational and useful is buried beneath it.

This might almost be a critic's description of the fog in *Bleak House;* in fact, it describes the progress of dullness in *The Dunciad.*[4] The essential movement in the two works is the same: a world full of dunces, weighed down by its own hopeless machinery, grinds to a halt that is the death of all that is vital and meaningful. Dickens's work exhibits the "standard configurations" Alvin Kernan describes as characteristic of the satiric "scene"—"massive amounts of foolishness and villainy, and a jumble of material things pressing in a disorderly fashion upon, and threatening to obliterate, the remnants of sanity and decency"[5]—but the differences in form, particularly in the extent to which Dickens develops the novelistic interests of his books, have tended to obscure or distract from the fundamental community of vision between Dickens's and earlier satire.

3. See appendix B for a fuller discussion of this relation.
4. Alvin Kernan, *The Plot of Satire* (New Haven, 1965), p. 109.
5. Alvin Kernan, *The Cankered Muse* (New Haven, 1959), p. 251.

Dorothy Van Ghent defines "the principle of relationship between things and people" in Dickens's novels as the tendency of things to assume human attributes and, reciprocally, of the animate, particularly the human, to become things. What remains is "a world visibly disintegrated into things"; given such a world, one way to find coherence in it is to mention everything: "Hence the indefatigable attention to detail."[6] From this point of view, the striking quantity and discreteness of details in Dickens's novels are the means by which the novelist tries to comprehend the world before him. J. Hillis Miller offers a similar analysis, defining the special quality of Dickens's imagination as "his assumption that he can get behind the surface by describing all of it bit by bit."[7] But the detail is not only an aspect of the writer's attempt to understand the world he sees; it is equally, and more certainly, a central quality of that world—a function not of the writing but of the vision. To transcribe into words a world crowded with matter is to write in infinite detail, just as to transcribe that world into picture would be to fill the canvas with a multitude of objects.[8] And this cluttered world is typically satiric:

> The scene of satire is always disorderly and crowded, packed to the very point of bursting. . . . The scene is equally choked with things. . . . [Characteristic qualities are] density, disorder, grossness, rot, and a hint of an ideal. . . . [The] satiric scene remains fundamentally the same picture of a dense and grotesque world of decaying matter moving without form in response only to physical forces and denying

6. Dorothy Van Ghent, "The Dickens World: A View from Todger's," *Sewanee Review* 58 (1950): 419–26.

7. J. Hillis Miller, *Charles Dickens: The World of His Novels* (Cambridge, Mass., 1958), p. xvi.

8. Mario Praz thus compares Dickens both to Hogarth and to Cruikshank. Hogarth's "satirical portraits and his impressions of the London slums" anticipate the descriptions of Dickens. The animated landscapes and rich expression of faces in Hogarth are not yet in Fielding or Smollett, but they are found in Dickens. Dickens and Cruikshank are "like translations of the same range of humour into two different media" *(The Hero in Eclipse in Victorian Fiction,* trans. Angus Davidson [Oxford, 1956], pp. 13–14, 18).

> the humane ideal which once molded the crowd into a society and the collection of buildings into a city.[9]

If one can differentiate between rhetorical and dramatic uses of incident in works of literature—one to develop a thesis, the other to create an imitation of life—and accept that formal satire chooses the first of these and drama and the novel mainly the second,[10] a primary difficulty of Dickens becomes apparent. The plots of Dickens's novels are satiric, but—to use E. M. Forster's distinction—the stories are not, and Dickens presents this combination of satire and the novel, of thesis and imitation, with overlapping sets of incidents. Coincidence or perverse fortuity, in the mimetic novel, tends to appear crude; in satire it is incidental and acceptable or even meaningful; in the satiric novel it is a question of emphasis. The same can be said of other breaches of novelistic realism (such as the use of emblematic proper names).

The incidents of a Dickens novel, then, may be used simultaneously to tell a sentimental or romantic story and to plot a satiric vision of society. In much the same way the characters may serve a double purpose: they may be simultaneously dramatic (or novelistic) and rhetorical (satiric counters), or they may move from one mode to the other. More often the characters are divided into two groups, one dramatic and one rhetorical (with possibly a third group of those who are or can be both), and the difficulty is the incongruity of their appearance together in the same fictional world. This conjunction of at first seemingly incongruous modes can also occur in the use of incident: somehow in the same world we have Krook's explosion by spontaneous combustion and Richard's slow neurotic disintegration. In *Bleak House* this strange mixture is carried even into the narrative voice: the third-person narrator is the angry satirist; Esther, though at times the innocent exposer, is painfully accepting. Such bifurcation is fundamental to Dickens's satire. Frye defines *satire* as "irony which is structurally close to the comic: the comic struggle of two societies, one normal and the

9. Kernan, *Cankered Muse*, pp. 7–8, 14.
10. Kernan, *Plot of Satire*, p. 98.

other absurd, is reflected in its double focus of morality and fantasy." The fantasy is "a content which the reader recognizes as grotesque."[11] In Dickens the absurd society is the caricatured world; the normal society is the world that the dramatic characters are struggling to achieve and that modern taste often rejects as falsely sentimental or impossibly contrived.[12]

It is important that the dramatic or more novelistic elements do not blind us to the special nature of the satiric. One might have to admit that Ruth Pinch is a colorless, saccharine failure in what is supposed to be a representation of reality; but Pecksniff, and for that matter most of the characters in *Martin Chuzzlewit,* cannot be approached with any such standards of realism. Pecksniff and Sarah Gamp are no more "real" in that sense than Flimnap and the Empress of Lilliput, and the relation of their world to the "real" one—much more like that of *Gulliver's Travels* than, say, *Middlemarch*—is oblique: reflective and satiric. Santayana's defense of Dickens's characters has often been quoted:

> When people say Dickens exaggerates, it seems to me they can have no eyes and no ears. . . . The world is a perpetual caricature of itself; at every moment it is the mockery and the contradiction of what it is pretending to be. . . . Humour is the perception of this illusion, the fact allowed to pierce here and there through the convention, whilst the conven-

11. Northrop Frye, *Anatomy of Criticism* (Princeton, 1957), p. 224.

12. This is truer of the later novels. George Ford, following Edwin Muir's analysis in *Structures of the Novel* of the two kinds of traditional plots used by Dickens—episodic and dramatic—distinguishes similarly between static and dramatic characters and points out that in the later novels

> an attempt was made . . . to make the best of two traditions. *Dombey and Son,* for example, consists in part of a ballet sequence in which assorted groups of static characters are projected in successive scenes, throughout which they behave typically, and in part of a foreground story of Florence and Walter, who are separated by some extraordinary and improbable accidents and coincidences. . . . But these foreground scenes, in which change occurs, are usually not so convincing as the more static background. [*Dickens and his Readers* (New York, Norton, 1965), pp. 140–41].

> tion continues to be maintained, as if we had not observed its absurdity. Pure comedy is more radical, cruder, in a certain sense less human; because comedy throws the convention over altogether, revels for a moment in the fact, and brutally says to the notions of mankind, as if it slapped them in the face, There, take that! That's what you really are! At this the polite world pretends to laugh. . . . It does not like to see itself by chance in the glass, without having had time to compose its features for demure self-contemplation.[13]

The defense might have been clearer had Santayana spoken, rather than of "pure comedy," of satire. For he who tears off the mask to reveal the shabby reality beneath and who revels in so doing is the satirist; and it is satiric form that, in Swift's famous preface, has almost preempted the metaphor of itself as a mirror of truth: "Satyr is a sort of Glass, wherein Beholders do generally discover every body's Face but their Own" *(The Battle of the Books)*. There is of course a great difference, for whereas Swift's people try to see everyone but themselves, Santayana's see themselves but refuse recognition and denounce the mirror as false. Still, it is essentially the same mirror: the mirror that, according to the satirist or apologist, shows the unpleasant truth, and yet in fact works by exaggeration, by distortion, and by caricature, with truth that is truth in a special, intensified sense. Santayana insists that "there *are* such people" as Quilp and Squeers; there may well be, but as the men who propose the *Argument Against Abolishing Christianity* or tell *A Tale of a Tub* are, not as Anna Karenina or even Emma Woodhouse are. The two modes are equally valid, but the realities they offer far apart. Sarah Gamp and Jeremiah Flintwinch are creations as preposterous as the Modest Proposer and the Brobdingnagian dwarf; William Dorrit and Eugene Wrayburn have a more psychologically based, but still qualified, reality.

The critics who are the implied opposition to Santayana's defense might have found Dickens's grotesques easier to accept

13. George Santayana, "Dickens," *Soliloquies in England and Later Soliloquies* (New York, 1922), pp. 65–66.

when considered in a matrix of satire rather than with reference to the novelistic tradition, triumphant by the end of the century, of George Eliot. In the latter, the grotesque is inadequate (witness the discomfort caused by the presence of the Dickensian Raffles in *Middlemarch);* in satire, it is a widely accepted method of characterization. This is not to say that Dickens deliberately confined his characters to caricature for conscious satiric purpose and refrained from making them fully developed and rounded. What Dickens might have done is in any case beside the point, for what was important to creation and what remains important to understanding is the happy conjunction of Dickens's genius for caricature with the requisites of satire, his primary mode. The nature of Dickens's characters can be justified by the explanation that his novels are largely satiric, but that contention itself is induced in good part by the presence of grotesque and caricature.

Dickens's own defenses of his characters vary from the explanation designed mainly to appease a hostile critic to more general analyses of greater perception and validity. His argument in defense of Mr. Squeers in the preface to *Nicholas Nickleby* turns toward the neoclassic purpose of universality:

> Mr. Squeers is the representative of a class, and not of an individual. Where imposture, ignorance, and brutal cupidity, are the stock in trade of a small body of men, and one is described by these characteristics, all his fellows will recognize something belonging to themselves, and each will have a misgiving that the portrait is his own.

One might object that there is significant difference between the selected representative and the universal type, but the central consideration is Dickens's insistence that his so-called eccentric creation is the embodiment of general and widespread qualities. His defense of the Watertoast Association in *Martin Chuzzlewit* lacks this theoretical reach:

> When this book was first published, I was given to understand, by some authorities, that the Watertoast Association and eloquence were beyond all bounds of belief. Therefore

> I record the fact that all that portion of Martin Chuzzlewit's experiences is a literal paraphrase of some reports of public proceedings in the United States (especially of the proceedings of a certain Brandywine Association), which were printed in *The Times* Newspaper in June and July 1843, at about the time when I was engaged in writing those parts of the book; and which remain on the file of *The Times* Newspaper, of course. [*Martin Chuzzlewit,* preface]

Here Dickens is close to the type of factual argument that gave rise to the ridiculous interchange with G. H. Lewes on the subject of spontaneous combustion in *Bleak House.* Distinction between imaginative and actual reality is forgotten. In the paragraph that precedes this one, Dickens is somewhat more candid about his characters, although he makes havoc of terminology:

> The American portion of this story is in no other respect a caricature, than as it is an exhibition, for the most part, (Mr. Bevan excepted) of a ludicrous side, *only,* of the American character—of that side which was, four-and-twenty years ago, from its nature, the most obtrusive, and the most likely to be seen by such travellers as Young Martin and Mark Tapley.

The exhibition of "a ludicrous side *only*" is exactly what caricature is, but Dickens skirts the definition and refuses to accept the term; rather than defend it and deny the denigration it usually implied, he prefers to disown it and to call his work something else. He shows again the satirist's claim to essential truth, but he also affirms and accepts the limited nature of his presentation. In so doing he is on the way to the realization of possible oblique relations between art and reality as commonly perceived that he implied when he wrote to Forster of the "fantastic fidelity" to their originals of his characters in *The Lazy Tour of Two Idle Apprentices* (written with Collins). He insists on fidelity, but he admits, with pleasure, that it is fantastic. There are ways of telling truth that are more effective than literal transcription: "It does not seem to me to be enough to say of any description that it is the exact truth. The exact truth must be there; but the merit or art in the narrator, is the manner of stating the truth."[14]

Generally, however, Dickens rested his defense on the same argument Santayana used: if you say I exaggerate, it is because you are blind in real life to the deeper, truer lines I see and reproduce in art. He tended to maintain a concept of one constant reality perceived at varying depths—the deepest being that of the writer of genius—rather than to argue for the validity of deliberate limitation or distortion. This is suggested at the opening of the preface to *Martin Chuzzlewit:*

> What is exaggeration to one class of minds and perceptions, is plain truth to another. That which is commonly called a long-sight, perceives in a prospect innumerable features and bearings non-existent to a short-sighted person. I sometimes ask myself whether there may occasionally be a difference of this kind between some writers and some readers; whether it is *always* the writer who colours highly, or whether it is now and then the reader whose eye for colour is a little dull?

It is asserted more definitely in an article for *All the Year Round,* July 27, 1867, called "The Spirit of Fiction" (which, like all other articles in this and in *Household Words,* if not written by Dickens was certainly printed under his editorial supervision and with his approval as reflecting his own opinions):

> To different authors, according to their capacities and dispositions, the facts present a different appearance and receive a different interpretation. . . . Greater differences still exist between the common observer and the writer of genius. The former accuses the latter of intentional exaggeration, substitution, addition, and has never been able in society to see the startling phenomena which he condemns in the romance as melodramatic and unnatural. The reason is, that such an individual has never developed the

14. John Forster, *The Life of Charles Dickens,* 2 vols. (New York, Everyman, 1966), 2:278.

> sense required for seeing such things; and, because he is partially blind, he accuses his informant of wilful invention.

The writer here is defending the romance, but the thesis is the same as the one Dickens used to defend satire in *Martin Chuzzlewit.* It is not great theory, but the satirist can seldom afford to confess the distortion central to his art.

Just as the scene, plot, and characters of Dickens are often essentially satiric, so is his rhetoric. Much has been made of his advice to Wilkie Collins:

> You know I always contest your disposition to give an audience credit for nothing, which necessarily involves the forcing of points on their attention, and which I have always observed them to resent when they find it out—as they always will and do. . . . The three people who write the narratives in these proofs have a DISSECTIVE property in common, which is essentially not theirs but yours; and that my own effort would be to strike more of what is got *that way* out of them by collision with one another, and by the working of the story. [*Letters,* III, 145]

But although his own narration may avoid the "dissective" tendency (yet one recalls with discomfort John Harmon's meditative monologue), it is equally coercive of the audience. The outburst upon the death of Jo in *Bleak House* is a well-known instance: "Dead, your Majesty. Dead, my lords and gentlemen. Dead, Right Reverends and Wrong Reverends of every order. Dead, men and women, born with Heavenly compassion in your hearts. And dying thus around us every day" (chap. xlvii). If direct apostrophe of this sort is relatively rare (and to be effective it must be), the obviously rhetorical style of the narrator is pervasive and continues through Dickens's latest work. The following example is from *Our Mutual Friend:*

> Mr. and Mrs. Veneering were bran-new people in a bran-new house in a bran-new quarter of London. Everything about the Veneerings was spick and span new. All their furniture was new, all their friends were new, all their

> servants were new, their plate was new, their carriage was new, their harness was new, their horses were new, they were as newly married as was lawfully compatible with their having a bran-new baby, and if they had set up a great-grandfather, he would have come home in matting from the Pantechnicon, without a scratch upon him, French polished to the crown of his head. [Bk. I, chap. ii]

Newness is to be the salient quality of the Veneerings, and Dickens demonstrates no reticence in making this point clear. The manner may be inimical to the Jamesian novel, but it is regular to satire. As Kernan remarks, "If *ars est celare artem,* even the greatest satirists have consistently been failures."[15]

Dickens's narrator presents the targets of satire and often embodies the qualities they lack. Because he defines the standpoint and the norm from which the attack is justified, his presence in the foreground of the work is both as central and as legitimate as that of the speaker in Pope's satires and moral epistles. The character of this narrator-persona is virtually identical with Dickens's image of the ethical man he wanted—and often believed himself—to be, and he is more free from bourgeois aspiration or reaction than the author was in actual life. For example, in *Bleak House* the third-person narrator speaks through Esther (a slip Dickens could detect in Wilkie Collins but commit himself) to deride Richard's public-school education (chap. xiii); yet Dickens was pleased when with the help of Miss Coutts he was able to send his eldest son to Eton. (Charley did withdraw from Eton at Christmas, 1852, when *Bleak House* was about half written; however, he did so not at his father's urging, but because he himself had decided to go into business.) The narrator of *Great Expectations,* describing in chapter xxxii Pip's visit to Newgate, sounds, as Philip Collins points out, very much like Bounderby in *Hard Times* (Bk. I, chap. xi). Collins explains that "in the 1840's Dickens' opinions on prison-discipline had been, on the whole, enlightened; by the '50's and '60's he was running level with, or even

15. Kernan, *Plot of Satire,* p. 17.

behind, public opinion, let alone progressive opinion, in this field."[16] Yet *Little Dorrit,* written in the latter '50s (1855–57), demonstrates that prisons not only cripple the weak and depress the innocent (Dorrit and Clennam) but furthermore fail to hinder the truly criminal (Rigaud): for its narrator, prison is a univalent symbol of evil. Generally, however, the persona of the novels is very close to the author.

The nature of the narrator-persona is not constant throughout the novels and in fact undergoes significant development. *Pickwick Papers* pretends to be the collation of an editor whose tone and manner show the influence of Fielding (particularly *Tom Jones)* but who also may owe something to the relationship between "editor" and subject in *Sartor Resartus.* The book opens with a bombastic presentation of the "Transactions of the Pickwick Club," "which the editor of these papers feels the highest pleasure in laying before his readers, as a proof of the careful attention, indefatigable assiduity, and nice discrimination, with which his search among the multifarious documents confided to him has been conducted" (chap. i.) The editor is not particularly important, but from time to time he makes his presence felt. He suffers the historian's limitations of knowledge in discomfort aggravated by his admiration for his hero: "It would afford us the highest gratification to be enabled to record Mr. Pickwick's opinion of the foregoing anecdote. We have little doubt that we should have been enabled to present it to our readers, but for a most unfortunate occurrence" (chap. iii). His self-consciousness continues to show itself, and sometimes he plays with the reader: "It is not unlikely that the inquiry may be made, where Mr. Weller was, all this time? We will state where he was in the next chapter" (chap. xxxvi).He prefaces the final remarks with a last word on the conventions of fiction:

> It is the fate of most men who mingle with the world, and attain even the prime of life, to make many real friends, and lose them in the course of nature. It is the fate of all authors or chroniclers to create imaginary friends, and lose them in the course of art. Nor is this the full extent of their

16. Philip Collins, *Dickens and Crime* (London, 1962), p. 19.

> misfortunes; for they are required to furnish an account of them besides.
>
> In compliance with this custom—unquestionably a bad one—we subjoin a few biographical words, in relation to the party at Mr. Pickwick's assembled. [chap. lvii]

Although the effects, especially in the opening chapters, are often simply of heavy parody or technical crudity, the editor does attain some degree of personality. He is lively, interested, eager, and occasionally facetious or irreverent. He has the self-consciousness and distance to use the first-person plural.

In *Oliver Twist* the narrator presents himself simply as "I." The book opens:

> Among other public buildings in a certain town, which for many reasons it will be prudent to refrain from mentioning, and to which *I* will assign no fictitious name . . . on a day and date which *I* need not trouble *myself* to repeat. . . .
>
> Although *I* am not disposed to maintain that the being born in a workhouse, is in itself the most fortunate and enviable circumstance that can possibly befall a human being, *I do mean to say* . . . . [chap. i; italics mine]

Later he intrudes, particularly in thematic asides, with phrases such as "I need hardly beg the reader to observe" or "if I wanted any further proof" (chap. xii). When formality does enter it is to assist sarcasm:

> As it would be no means seemly in a humble author to keep so mighty a personage as a beadle waiting . . . the historian whose pen traces these words—trusting that he knows his place, and that he entertains a becoming reverence for those upon earth to whom high and important authority is delegated—hastens to pay them that respect which their position demands. [chap. xxvii]

The chapter heads and occasionally the narrator's remarks retain a Fielding-like tone. At other points the narrator comments in a more impersonal voice, and in the last chapter he proceeds to the conventional summing-up without protest: "The fortunes of those who have figured in this tale are nearly closed. The little that remains to their historian to relate, is told in few and simple words" (chap. liii). Although he enters again in the first person to linger fondly over his characters through the last paragraphs, his relation to the story as a whole remains less formal, less defined, and finally less important than was the editor's to the *Pickwick Papers.* One result of this is that his personality becomes even less immediate to the audience.

This tendency grows in the novels that follow. *Nicholas Nickleby* is told by a narrator who maintains a third-person voice, even in the opening and closing chapters. In *The Old Curiosity Shop,* the strange narrator who walks by night and loves children and whose odd character gives the opening of the tale a peculiar note of its own formally leaves the story at the end of chapter iii: "And now, that I have carried this history so far in my own character and introduced these personages to the reader, I shall for the convenience of the narrative detach myself from its further course, and leave those who have prominent and necessary parts in it to speak and act for themselves." Although there continues to be a distinct narrative voice, it becomes impersonal in the sense that it is not attached to any nameable or otherwise definable character. In this novel, as in *Nicholas Nickleby* and *Barnaby Rudge,* the tone of which the modern reader is most acutely aware is, unfortunately, the special cute and enthusiastic voice Dickens reserves for his good characters in their happier moments, to exclaim upon their joys or to gush over their virtues. This voice is heard again in *Martin Chuzzlewit* in reference to Tom and Ruth Pinch, but after that it pretty much disappears from the novels. It persists longer in the Christmas stories. With *Chuzzlewit,* however, and then increasingly from *Dombey and Son* on, the sterner tones of the impersonal voice become dominant. This voice is an undefined third person who mocks, denounces, and offers at significant points appropriate pronouncements of moral standards. The voice can be pathetic or poetic too but is most impressive as that of the mocking or bitter moralist.

It is a voice, however, rather than a person. Pope, who knew and was known by his audience, could present a persona who was his own moral exemplar by standards that were understood on both sides. The wider and more diverse the audience and the greater the distance between it and the poet, the more the poet has to describe the persona. Pope could name a defendant "P" and imply a good deal by that alone; Churchill had to spend many more lines descanting upon himself, though he retained the first person; and Byron's narrator in *Don Juan* is still someone who can interrupt his narrative to tell the reader that he has a headache. With Dickens we see the gradual disappearance of this particularized narrator and his replacement by a voice that is more a body of moral precepts than a conceived character. The attempt is to place the standard in some objective realm in which it can be widely accepted. The break is clear in *Bleak House,* where the personalism, along with the enthusiasm and coyness of the earlier narrators, is relegated to Esther, whose contrast points up the more distant and harsher quality of the third-person narrator. *Great Expectations,* narrated—like *David Copperfield*—by its hero, is an experiment in a different mode. The other later novels are all presented by this stern, satiric voice that offers frequent rhetorical expositions of its moral principles.

Despite this impersonalization, the narrator-persona was still close—certainly in the minds of the contemporary audience—to the moral character of the author himself. This was probably emphasized somewhat after 1853, when Dickens gave his first public readings for the benefit of the Birmingham and Midland Institute, and even more so after 1858, when the professional readings began. It may in part explain the very strong need Dickens felt to justify to the public his separation from Catherine and then to keep secret from them his relationship with Ellen Ternan.

The satirist's rhetoric is generally the servant of his anger. Dickens, as we have seen, puts his at the service of other effects as well, most notably the pathetic. One result is that, although in passages of pure denunciation or castigation the anger is at maximum intensity, in the effect of almost any given chapter and certainly of a book as a whole there is a softening of the angry or satiric Dickens with admixtures of the jolly or sentimental. Denunciation, however, is not the most successful—or the primary—technique of Dickens's satire. Far more important is what he achieves through character and drama. Yet here too there is a balance, stronger than any requirements and most manifestations of a satiric norm, of good characters and praiseworthy actions. In a work like *The Chimes* this opposition is all too painfully clear and, furthermore, was quite deliberate: Dickens described the work to Macready as "my little Christmas book, in which I have endeavoured to plant an indignant right-hander on the eye of certain wicked Cant that makes my blood boil, which I hope will not only cloud that eye with black and blue, but many a gentle one with crystal of a finer sort" *(Letters,* I, 646). Earlier, when he was still only thinking about the story, he had written to Forster: "In my mind's eye, Horatio, I like more and more my notion of making, in this little book, a great blow for the poor. Something powerful, I think I can do, but I want to be tender too, and cheerful" *(Letters,* I, 627). Modern taste revolts at the tenderness and cheer, but Macready cried unabashedly.

Dickens's general principle seems to have been that beauty and caricature are compatible, and he resisted the severance of the two that many considered aesthetically necessary. In a review for *The Examiner* (December 30, 1848) of a series of drawings from *Punch* by John Leech, he wrote:

> Now, besides that it is a poor device to represent what is being satirised as being necessarily ugly—which is but the resource of an angry child or a jealous woman—it serves no purpose but to produce a disagreeable result. There is no reason why the farmer's daughter in the old caricature who is squalling at the harpsichord . . . should be squat and hideous. The satire on the manner of her education, if there be any in the thing at all, would be just as good if she were pretty. Mr. Leech would have made her so.

Dickens's own practice does not demonstrate this: Fanny Squeers, Miggs, and Charity Pecksniff are certainly not pretty. Rather, they are balanced by beautiful and unsatirized opposing characters: Madeline Bray, Dolly Varden, and Mary Graham.

The technique is crude, but a selective and thereby softened vision is achieved. Later, Dickens was able to use the contrast more tellingly: in *Bleak House* for instance, the sweetness-and-light of Esther Summerson darkens and embitters by its counterpoint the voice of the third-person narrator. Later still Dickens's technique changed further as his novels became more concerned with continuous character and action—less, that is, like the picaresque adventures or the string of incidents common to satire, and closer to the later nineteenth-century idea of a novel—and as perhaps he himself gained a more complex understanding of humanity. Bella Wilfer, after all, must have the same pretty face when she is a self-willed materialist as she will have as the lovable and loving Mrs. John Harmon. But even beyond such circumstantial necessities, a more sympathetic perception begins in the later work to prevent simplistic division between good and bad. While Coodle, Doodle, and Foodle can be treated with unqualified derisive contempt, Sir Leicester Dedlock, though only a secondary character, escapes from the satiric mold. Through his generosity to his wife and his collapse at her flight from him, he becomes an object of pity and even of sympathy. The novel has brought Dickens too close to Sir Leicester for the maintenance of satiric distance: Sir Leicester is not absolved, but he is somehow forgiven. A lesser but similar tolerance is allowed Merdle in *Little Dorrit*. His swindle is thoroughly criminal, but as the victim of the Chief Butler and in his disappointment and discomfort in the "Society" he has striven for, he is as much an object-lesson to be regarded with a mixture of pity and laughter as he is a cheat to be hated. This is an appreciable advance from an earlier large-scale confidence man, Montague Tigg of *Martin Chuzzlewit,* who even as the murder victim of Jonas Chuzzlewit remains quite unsympathetic.

In the earlier books, the satire is generally very close to comedy and its anger diverted to laughter, though this does not make the exposure less complete or the contempt engendered less pure. Mrs. Gamp is an example. Later the tone changes. There is less humor and a strong undertow of bitterness in a character like Mr. Vholes. His own distance from humanity is frightening, but the full horror lies in his being but part of an extensive network of evil that threatens to strangle all forces opposing it. For other figures, conversely, this vision of evil as diffuse tends to diminish the individual guilt, allowing developments of character that become transformations somewhat expiatory. Mr. Gradgrind's belated understanding and remorse and Mrs. Clennam's saving confession are movements in the moral direction urged by the satire which soften considerably the judgments made upon these characters. The ultimate shaft of satiric lightning glances off—in the former instance onto Bounderby, in the latter onto Flintwinch and Rigaud. This final clemency, like the sympathy accorded Sir Leicester or Mr. Merdle, is alien to traditional satire. Moderation of this sort is the product partly of the times and partly of the satirist's peculiar sensibility, as is the balancing by goodness, pathos, or cheer. It is also, however, an evolution closely involved with literary form, for its essence is a blending of the impulses of satire and of the novel in a union that mixes without dissolving. And to present an effective indictment of evil with this moderation, Dickens needed extension and flexibility, with plenty of room for both narrative denunciation and sentimentalizing, mockery and praise, for dramatic interchange, multiple plots, and enough characters so that the lightning could glance off some and land on others. The total vision was too full of complex variety and detail for containment in a moderately long poem or squib, or even for a novel that would satisfy later standards of unity and consistency.

CHAPTER 2

Satire and Social Reform

Like Jonson and the Augustans, Dickens often defended his satire against critical attack on the basis of the satirist's moral responsibilities and the freedom of expression consequently necessary. He differed from them in his greater emphasis on the practical cause of social reform. In the 1850 preface to *Oliver Twist,* he furiously attacked Sir Peter Laurie, an alderman who turned to laughter the Metropolitan Sanitary Association's discussions on the sanitation of Jacob's Island (which the Bishop of London noted had been described in *Oliver Twist)* by pointing out that the cost of proposed improvements would be remarkably cheap because Jacob's Island existed only in a work of fiction. Dickens quotes *The Observer*'s account of this and then continues with surprisingly Swiftian parodic logic:

> When I came to read this I was so much struck by the honesty, by the truth, and by the wisdom of this logic, as well as by the fact of the sagacious vestry, including members of parliament, magistrates, officers, chemists, and I know not who else listening to it meekly (as became them), that I resolved to record the fact here as a certain means of making it known to, and causing it to be reverenced by, many thousands of people. Reflecting upon this logic and its universal application; remembering that when Fielding described Newgate, the prison immediately ceased to exist; that when Smollett took Roderick Random to Bath, that city instantly sank into the earth; that when Scott exercised his genius on Whitefriars, it incontinently glided into the Thames; that an ancient place called Windsor was entirely destroyed in the reign of Queen Elizabeth by two Merry Wives of that town, acting under the direction of a person

> of the name of Shakespeare; and that Mr. Pope, after having at a great expense completed his grotto at Twickenham, incautiously reduced it to ashes by writing a poem upon it —I say, when I came to consider these things, I was inclined to make this preface the vehicle of my humble tribute of admiration to Sir Peter Laurie. But I am restrained by a very painful consideration—by no less a consideration than the impossibility of *his* existence. For Sir Peter Laurie having been himself described in a book (as I understand he was, one Christmas time, for his conduct on the seat of justice), it is but too clear that there CAN be no such man!

One sees here a likeness to such bitter parody of the logic of irresponsibility as that in *A Modest Proposal.* Dickens's main purpose, however, is not to show the wickedness or stupidity of Sir Peter Laurie or many others like him—though that is made very clear on the way—but to show the immediate importance of sanitary reform:

> I was as well convinced then as I am now, that nothing effectual can be done for the elevation of the poor in England until their dwelling-places are made decent and wholesome. I have always been convinced that this reform must precede all other Social Reforms . . . and that, without it, those classes of the people which increase the fastest must become so desperate, and be made so miserable, as to bear within themselves certain seeds of ruin to the whole country.

One might compare this to the *Bickerstaff Papers,* where an analogous *reductio ad absurdum* is performed, with the object, however, not to purge a metropolitan area but to propagate knowledge and belief. Yet it must be remembered that Dickens's defense is contained in a preface written more than ten years later than the novel itself; the novel is not so narrowly directed. The 1841 preface (to the third edition) states that "the stern and plain truth . . . was a part of the purpose of this book" and finds precedents in Fielding, Defoe, Goldsmith, Smollett, Richardson, Mackenzie, and above all Hogarth. In opposition to a work like Gay's "witty satire" *(The Beggar's Opera* makes the life of the rogues more enviable than otherwise), Dickens insists on the moral necessity to show the "miserable truth" of the underworld. The general claim to truth-telling, though it may here be an honest biographical profession as well, is traditional to satire and as such almost a device constant to the genre.[1] While this claim is again part of a later preface and does not describe the whole novel (which is indeed as close to the morality play as to satire), the vision of wretchedness, though not sustained, is strong and significant in the book and an early rendering of what in the later novels will become dominant and ineluctable.

Dickens's emphasis on social problems rather than on individual morality and on reform rather than mere exposure and castigation is related to the rising concern in the nineteenth century for social philanthropy and legislation. Yet, paradoxically, as long as social reform is a clear answer (that is, in the earlier work), vice is seen largely in terms of individual crime; in the later work, when the satiric vision deepens, there is more and more "mere exposure and castigation" as social maladies come increasingly to appear but one form of deep, pervasive, and strangely self-perpetuating evil that reform can barely touch. The dark world is present in all the novels, even in *Pickwick,* but in the early books the light world more or less triumphs: the law is Dodson and Fogg, two men who might be made to lose a case, and Serjeant Buzfuz, who can be stopped short by Sam Weller; prison is a depressing place, but one that can be quitted; hunger and cold are cruelties allowed by stupid Bumbles and careless Boards of Directors or inflicted by greedy Squeerses; economic persecution with a touch of sadism is prac-

1. "In short, the satirist makes every effort to repudiate the Muse and to emphasize the down-to-earth quality of himself and his work, but the very vigor of these efforts and their continuous appearance in satire suggest that they are themselves stylistic devices used in a perfectly conventional manner to establish the character and tone traditionally thought appropriate for the satiric genre" (Kernan, *Cankered Muse,* pp. 3–4). This of course does not mean that Dickens's assertions cannot also be perfectly sincere. Certainly he was not a traditional satirist.

ticed by a demonic dwarf appropriately deformed in all aspects of body and mind. In the later work, the toll upon the light world becomes heavier and the resolution more difficult: the law is the enormous machinery of Chancery or the Circumlocution Office; prison is a state of soul; cruelty can be inflicted by the most oppressed victims in the very act of freeing themselves from hunger and cold; money is the obsession of an entire society, and the powerful usurer can be a weak would-be dandy operating through an innocent Jew. By this very complexity the light world is finally reduced to a few rays glimpsed through almost universal darkness. In *The Mystery of Edwin Drood* the light world is, through the person of Jasper, almost totally the false mask of the dark—but with *Drood* we have moved from satire to horror.

Although Dickens's satire at its best incorporates a good deal of specific social criticism, and although reformism was a point he used in self-justification, generally the more topical the reformatory purpose of his satire, the less effective it is. *The Chimes* offers a prime example in Dickens's attempt to ridicule Sir Peter Laurie (as Alderman Cute) in a narrative voice as self-congratulatory as the object it derides. Yet the one sustained exception to this generalization is another attack on the inhumanity of utilitarianism: *Hard Times* is probably as much a favorite of modern criticism as *The Chimes* is anathema. Aside from its brilliant narrative style (the tone of *The Chimes* seems geared to an audience of affected six-year-olds), *Hard Times* benefits by an expanded vision. Its indictment is not of one or two pompous hypocrites but of all—Gradgrindery, ugliness, selfishness, or political demagogy—that destroys the life of the imaginative and generous. Thus the satire transcends its topical targets. Alderman Cute refers to a particular person; although Gradgrind and Bounderby also have reference to contemporary misdoers, the reference is reflective—to a whole political class rather than a specific individual—and is itself only part of their broader function as representatives of a type of mind. In a letter to Charles Knight, Dickens explained both motives but stated the more general one first:

> My satire is against those who see figures and averages and nothing else—the representatives of the wickedest and the most enormous vice of this time—the men who, through long years to come, will do more to damage the real useful truths of political economy than I could do (if I tried) in my whole life; the addled heads who would take the average of cold in the Crimea during twelve months as a reason for clothing a soldier in nankeens on a night when he would be frozen to death in fur, and who would comfort the labourer in travelling twelve miles a day to and from his work, by telling him that the average distance of one inhabited place from another in the whole area of England, is not more than four miles. Bah! What have you to do with these? [*Letters,* II, 620]

That the problem is less one of specific ills than of a general defect of character, and that the only help for it seems to be a persistent mirroring of this darkness until it is recognized, is the tenor of a letter to Austen Henry Layard written some months before *Little Dorrit* was begun:

> There is nothing in the present time at once so galling and so alarming to me as the alienation of the people from their own public affairs. . . . So, every day, the disgusted millions with this unnatural gloom and calm upon them are confirmed and hardened in the very worst of moods. . . . But you can no more help a people who do not help themselves, than you can help a man who does not help himself. And until the people can be got up from the lethargy which is an awful symptom of the advanced state of their disease, I know of nothing that can be done beyond keeping their wrongs continually before them. [*Letters,* II, 651–52]

A letter to Macready a few months later shows that this work refers not only to the more immediate, practical efforts of *Household Words* but to the novels as well. After a long and gloomy paragraph on the present state and future hope of England, Dickens turns to his progress on *Little Dorrit:* "In No. 3 of my new book I have been blowing off a little indignant steam which would otherwise blow me up" *(Letters,* II, 695). The preface to *Little Dorrit* asserts that the events and characters do have verifiable specific reference:

> If I might offer any apology for so exaggerated a fiction as the Barnacles and the Circumlocution Office, I would seek it in the common experience of an Englishman, without presuming to mention the unimportant fact of my having done that violence to good manners, in the days of a Russian war, and of a Court of Inquiry at Chelsea. If I might make so bold as to defend that extravagant conception, Mr. Merdle, I would hint that it originated after the Railroad-share epoch, in the times of a certain Irish Bank, and of one or two other equally laudable enterprises. If I were to plead anything in mitigation of the preposterous fancy that a bad design will sometimes claim to be a good and an expressly religious design, it would be the curious coincidence that such fancy was brought to its climax in these pages, in the days of the public examination of late Directors of a Royal British Bank.

The paragraph ends, however, with a strange, weary about-face: "But, I submit myself to suffer judgment to go by default on all these counts, if need be, and to accept the assurance (on good authority) that nothing like them was ever known in this land." The tone of this sentence is hard to ascertain. Dickens may simply be tired of argument and too weary to care, or, more probably, this may be heavy sarcasm at the expense of the "good authority." In either case, the statement contains an important implication: the topical specificity is ultimately less important than the deeper fidelity to a far more general experience of abuse. This experience alone will maintain the truth of the fictional instances; contemporary references are only supplementary.

As satirist, Dickens matured as he learned to integrate his satire upon particular objects with the whole of the work that contained it. With this integration came a broadening, generalizing tendency, and that in turn usually meant some shift in focus from the social to the moral or ethical, from practical problems to questions of character and ontology. Even from the satire on the Poor Law in *Oliver Twist* to that on the Yorkshire schools in *Nicholas Nickleby,* there is a slight advance in this direction. The poorhouse is a less aggressive evil than Squeers's school: it stays put, whereas Squeers follows and seeks to retrieve his victims. The death of little Dick in *Oliver Twist* is a gratuitous addition of pathos; the death of Smike is the result and evidence of the power of Squeers in the world. The poorhouse and London sections of *Oliver Twist* can be allegorized into a social tract with a single, unifying message (neglect of the paupers leads to vice and crime) or understood as two sides of a single coin,[2] but the book remains divided, despite critical exegesis. As Nicholas allows Smike to join his adventures, he literally carries the shadow of the school through them. The satiric theme is thus maintained until the final breaking-up of Dotheboys at the end of the novel, and the evil the school represents is a continuous thread in the fabric of the plot.[3]

In both *Nickleby* and *Oliver,* however, the essential satire attacks, at a deeper level, not the specific social phenomenon at issue but the violation of humanity—the "offense against life"[4] —that underlies it. In this light, charges such as G. H. Ford's that the satire on the Poor Law is unfair become irrelevant.[5] What distinguishes such satire from interpolated journalism is the pervasion, simultaneous with the humor, of a sense of deep-lying, unpardonable evil.

The glory of *Pickwick Papers,* on the other hand, is its easy triumph into comedy. Dickens wrote to Carlyle in 1863: "I

2. See William F. Axton, *Circle of Fire* (Lexington, Ky., 1966), pp. 84 ff., for an excellent reading on this interpretation.

3. This is not to say that *Nickleby* is by any means a fully integrated book; indeed, much of its satire is not only isolated and topical but dragged in at the expense of all probability. Nicholas's sudden tirade in chapter xlviii against stolen dramatic adaptations of current novels, for instance, is an outburst of Dickens's anger about his own difficulties, and it is unjustifiably out of place in the novel.

4. Steven Marcus, *Dickens from Pickwick to Dombey* (New York, 1965), p. 59.

5. Ford, *Dickens and his Readers,* p. 42.

should be very glad if you would come to one of my Readings one night. I think if you would come some evening when I read the trial from Pickwick, you would find a healthy suggestion of an abuse or two, that sets people thinking in the right direction" *(Letters,* III, 348). But although Bardell vs. Pickwick was based upon an actual case, the satire is not upon that case but upon legal thinking and procedure, and its absurdity is consistently hilarious.

Two modes of transcendence from journalism to literature, then, are an undertone of tragedy and an overtone of comedy; a third is envelopment by irony. Dickens's verbal irony is generally poor, particularly in his earlier writing. Its sarcasm tends to a repulsive cuteness, and even when in the later works it succeeds by participation in a broader tonal bitterness, it is often excessive. Irony of vision, however, is the signal quality of these later novels. By the impulse of an ironic perception of the nature of man and the state of society, Dickens was led, when he might have parodied some specific governmental department, to create instead that paradigm of bureaucracy, the Circumlocution Office. It is an ironic distillation that reaches through the visible facts of society to its essential experience. The Marshalsea, sum and substance of prison, works in much the same way, as both its topical outdatedness and its reflections within the novel in the mental prisons of various characters should emphasize. The problem is social in dimension but moral in essence. This is the achievement of Dickens's mature satire: not social criticism in the sense of propaganda for particular social reforms (though this is never entirely forgotten), but the rendering of a darkened world and commitment to the living cry for regeneration.

PART II

Toward Satire

CHAPTER 3

Satiric Vision: *Pickwick Papers* to *Barnaby Rudge*

The primary satire of Dickens is not in the obvious local or topical attacks one could label satire with little opposition—though with perhaps equally little enthusiastic response—but in something far less specifiable. There is a somber autumn coloration underlying the earlier work and dominant in the later that seems to arise from the sense of a world somehow dying, with life and vitality yielding to torpor, rigidity, or death. The best description of full vitality is the whole of *Pickwick Papers*. This first novel celebrates life; the later books tend increasingly to attack whatever defiles it, tramples on it, or seeks to confine it. With each novel the concept of demonic power changes significantly, always in the direction of increased complexity and, at least until *Great Expectations* and *Our Mutual Friend,* of increased hopelessness. What remains constant is that the demonic power is a force of death as death-in-life, of stagnation that suppresses vitality in all forms. When the vision becomes total, it is an autumnal world of satire that the novels portray, winter that they resist, and spring and summer to which they yearn to return. The desire for return is expressed first in sentimental reminiscence, then in outraged recall.

In the earlier novels the stagnating force is embodied chiefly in characters whom the author can isolate, set up as comic butts, and overcome in satiric deflation, and over whom the other characters in the novel can triumph through intelligence, luck, or the powerful intervention granted true virtue. In the later or dark novels this force is seen as a vast social mechanism or as a sort of mental disease of epidemic proportion, difficult to isolate and perhaps impossible to defeat. In the last novels—*Great Expectations, Our Mutual Friend,* and *The Mystery of Edwin*

Drood—there appears a strong tendency to return to individual responsibility, both for blame and for hope.

Between the two extremes, of life in its fullest vitality on the one hand and living death on the other, there is a range of intermediary stages of torpor or rigidity. The very word *rigidity* brings to mind Henri Bergson's essay on laughter; application of his theories to Dickens's work is unavoidable. Laughter, Bergson suggests, arises at the spectacle of something mechanical encrusted on the living, some rigidity or other applied to the mobility of life, against which that laughter is a corrective mockery. About two-thirds of the way through the essay he summarizes:

> The comic is that side of a person which reveals his likeness to a thing, that aspect of human events which, through its peculiar inelasticity, conveys the impression of pure mechanism, or automatism, of movement without life. Consequently it expresses an individual or collective imperfection which calls for an immediate corrective. This corrective is laughter, a social gesture that singles out and represses a special kind of absent-mindedness in men and in events.[1]

Bergson's theory has been criticized as a negative vision of comedy, particularly in its inadequacy in terms of such comedy as Shakespeare's. Limitation of this sort there surely is: Bergson's concluding remarks on the bitter aftertaste of brine show that he believes laughter to have a fundamentally negative bent. Yet for the many situations he treats and for the particular types of comedy he cites as instances (Molière and Labiche are the two favorite examples), the theory is remarkably viable. As for Dickens's work, much of it could be offered as an illustrative appendix to the essay; and for an understanding of Dickens's satire the theory is an invaluable aid, whatever its range of further applicability. Bergson's persistent conception of laughter in social terms (social signification being one of the three essential conditions for it, along with human relevance and

1. For the convenience of ready availability I have used the translated text of the Doubleday Anchor edition, *Comedy*, with an introduction by Wylie Sypher (New York, 1956), pp. 61–190. This reference, p. 117.

absence of emotion) fits the dominantly social—rather than intellectual or aesthetic—concerns of Dickens's novels. Especially in the earlier books, Dickens's laughter is very clearly what Bergson suggests all laughter is at its base: the corrective response of a social group toward one of its members or toward a subgroup of members (notably the professions) whose behavior is eccentric to the interests of the society. This somewhat explains Dickens's failure to attack outrightly the fundamental values of his audience, a reticence severer moralists have deplored. Whether or not he in fact shared their assumptions, the most effective position for evoking such a response was one which would not antagonize the reader but rather court his assent by a feeling of alliance with the narrator against the comic butts. Finally, the idea of laughter as corrective contains an inherent satiric bias (though Bergson does not deal with satire) that is present in the comedy of Dickens too, with increasing strength as the novels proceed. Let me make clear, however, that my use of Bergson here is not intended to imply advocacy of his theory as the full and final explanation of laughter or comedy. I use the theory because it helps immensely in explaining the aspect of Dickens that concerns this study. In fact, the essential perceptions shared by Dickens's vision and Bergson's theory become in Dickens's later novels less and less laughable.

Two of the laws Bergson states are:

> 1. The attitudes, gestures, and movements of the human body are laughable in exact proportion as that body reminds us of a mere machine.
>
> 2. We laugh every time a person gives us the impression of being a thing.

Our mental state, like life, is ever changing; if our gestures were true to it, they would never be repeated. Consequently, they can only be imitated "in their mechanical uniformity, and therefore exactly in what is alien to our living personality." The gesture repeated to the point of automatism is the action of a machine. The face that is fixed is the face of a doll. The living, human countenance is mobile; a comic face is one that appears to be in permanent grimace:

> This is the reason why a face is all the more comic, the more nearly it suggests to us the idea of some simple mechanical action in which its personality would for ever be absorbed. . . . But this effect gains in intensity when we are able to connect these characteristics with some deep-seated cause, a certain *fundamental absentmindedness,* as though the soul had allowed itself to be fascinated and hypnotized by the materiality of a simple action.[2]

Compare these formulae with the introduction of Miss Tox in *Dombey and Son:*

> The lady thus specially presented, was a long lean figure, wearing such a faded air that she seemed not to have been made in what linen-drapers call "fast colours" originally, and to have, by little and little, washed out. But for this she might have been described as the very pink of general propitiation and politeness. From a long habit of listening admirably to everything that was said in her presence, and looking at the speakers as if she were mentally engaged in taking off impressions of their images upon her soul, never to part with the same but with life, her head had quite settled on one side. Her hands had contracted a spasmodic habit of raising themselves of their own accord as in involuntary admiration. Her eyes were liable to a similar affection. She had the softest voice that ever was heard; and her nose, stupendously aquiline, had a little knob in the very center or key-stone of the bridge, whence it tended downwards towards her face, as in an invincible determination never to turn up at anything. [chap. i]

Miss Tox begins by having been manufactured, like something inorganic, rather than born. Furthermore, she is so automatic that she appears to have ossified. This vision of the triumph of matter over spirit is echoed in the narrator's play upon the keystone of the bridge of her nose, verbal comedy that Bergson analyzes as the calling of attention to the material aspect of a metaphor. Miss Tox will complete her development to a per-

2. Bergson, *Comedy,* p. 146.

fect automaton when she displays her unfailing reliability in completing Mrs. Chick's clichés. This is Bergsonian rigidity incarnate, one of many examples in Dickens's gallery of characters. Like most in the earlier novels and some in the later ones, she is very funny.

But with *Dombey and Son* the satiric bias, almost full-fledged, is beginning to take precedence. The evolution of Dickens's work from Christmassy to dark can in fact be described as a movement from the perception of rigidity in life through laughing comedy to the rendering of the same tendencies with feelings of revulsion and repudiation that demand serious satire. In the earlier novels, when the bright world of vitality is dominant and rigidity is scarcely a threat, the vision is comic and the satire latent; in the later, dark novels, when rigidity has become so pervasive and powerful that living death is truly a menace if not an actuality, the vision is ironic and its mode primarily satiric. As laughter attacks mechanical rigidity or the failure to keep up with life's infinite changefulness, "the comic expresses, above all else, a special lack of adaptability to society."[3] Rigidity of all sorts is mocked from the standpoint of society's image of itself in ideal elasticity. But if this is taken a step further until the whole of society begins to exhibit such rigidity, from what point of view—other than the divine—can laughter or mockery come? This is what happens in Dickens's dark novels: the whole of society is seen through some metaphor of rigidity, and the narrator who reveals the irony speaks as a disembodied voice from a point above the world he exposes. He is no longer the spokesman of a group—to which the reader too belongs—enjoying the humor of its eccentrics; he is a detached critic of the group itself.

From the aspect of rigidity as the body taking precedence over the soul, Bergson expands to "the manner seeking to outdo the matter, the letter aiming at ousting the spirit." The first illustration he offers is the excessive respect to outward formalities that in comedy often dominates a profession: "And so we find the means substituted for the end, the manner for the mat-

3. Bergson, *Comedy,* pp. 75–87 passim.

ter; no longer is it the profession that is made for the public, but rather the public for the profession."[4] Compare this passage on the law in *Bleak House:*

> The one great principle of the English law is, to make business for itself. There is no other principle distinctly, certainly, and consistently maintained through all its narrow turnings. Viewed by this light it becomes a coherent scheme, and not the monstrous maze the laity are apt to think it. Let them but once clearly perceive that its grand principle is to make business for itself at their expense, and surely they will cease to grumble. [chap. xxxix]

This passage is as apt an illustration of professional rigidity as the description of Miss Tox is of rigidity of character, but it is not nearly so funny. The irony is much closer to bitter satire than to the laughter of comedy. The law in *Pickwick Papers* was just as rigid, but in *Pickwick* it was a profession of individuals one could stand away from and oppose—as both Mr. Pickwick and his faithful Sam did. In *Bleak House* it is an enveloping force that threatens to impose its will upon all of society. Hence there is no external point from which to laugh at it; involvement is unavoidable, and therefore so is emotion. With emotion, as Bergson insists, laughter disappears, and satire becomes bitter. In *Hard Times* and *Little Dorrit,* rigidity is again seen on a wide scale—rationalistic, anti-poetic, utilitarian thought, then multifaceted imprisonment—and again the satire in these books is harshly ironic and bitter, the comedy isolated in moments and even then of strongly satiric bent. Comedy or light satire either celebrates vitality or mocks the rigidity of an individual or group of individuals within a society; when the individual must repudiate the society itself for nurturing that very rigidity, as when society espouses the principles of Chancery, strict utilitarianism, or the Circumlocution Office, then the satire is dark and tends to be bitter.

Whether the satire is so light that one hesitates over the boundary between it and comedy or so intense that humor is

4. Bergson, *Comedy,* pp. 94–95.

lost, the root perception remains the same: rigidity—innate or imposed—leading to lethargy, torpor, and eventually living death. The spirit of rigidity is embodied in a variety of forms, against which are opposed appropriately corresponding standards of vitality. In addition, one referent is continuous: Dickens's own energy. The flexibility and above all the enormous vitality of the satiric style constitute an ever-present contrast to the joylessness of automatism and repression. The world that the novels envision is never again so full of delight as it was in *Pickwick*, but the exuberance of the Pickwickian style remains, and the widening gap between the two becomes one measure at least of how diminished the world has become.

I should now like to trace the variations upon this satiric theme from *Pickwick Papers* through *Barnaby Rudge*. Because in these early novels the sense of a stagnating, deathlike force is manifest almost exclusively in satirical characters, my discussion will necessarily do violence to the works as wholes. The limited nature of this inquiry makes the concentration upon satire artificial until, in the later novels, the satire becomes Dickens's main emphasis as well.

The brightness of the world of *Pickwick Papers* allows hardly a need for struggle against darker forces. This may be due at least in part to the compression and isolation of evil into the interpolated tales,[5] but it is also the confessed bias of the narrator. Just before the conventional summing-up he suggests:

> Let us leave our old friend in one of those moments of unmixed happiness, of which, if we seek them, there are ever some, to cheer our transitory existence here. There are dark shadows on the earth, but its lights are stronger in the contrast. Some men, like bats or owls, have better eyes for the darkness than for the light. We, who have no such optical powers, are better pleased to take our last parting look at the visionary companions of many solitary hours,

5. Cf. Edmund Wilson, "Dickens: The Two Scrooges," in *The Wound and the Bow*, rev. ed. (London, 1952).

> when the brief sunshine of the world is blazing full upon them. [chap. lvii]

The dark world is not unrecognized, but this work is dedicated to a celebration of the bright.

The satire on scientific associations and on parliamentary procedure at the opening of this book is rather a failure, and it is actually as eccentric to the whole of the novel as the political satire in the story of Prince Bladud is shown to be by its undisguised interpolation into the narrative (chap. xxxvi). The excessive boobiness of Pickwick at the beginning is also at odds with the later development and seems to be rejected as the character grows to fullness. Pickwick remains in a light of gentle irony (somewhat sharpened again in chap. li when he farcically intervenes between two fighting editors only to receive the blows of both), but such perspective is a sign of health: we rejoice in Pickwick and love him even as we see him being ridiculous. G. K. Chesterton described this change: "Dickens went into the Pickwick Club to scoff, and Dickens remained to pray."[6] Yet what appears to be a change may have continuous meaning. The Samuel Pickwick who delivers bombastic speeches, who as antiquarian interposes too much "learning" between himself and the object to be able to decipher the engraving "Bill Stumps his mark," and who as scientist earnestly transfers into his notebook the glorious fictions of a coachman upon his horse, is marked mainly by that notebook. His relation to life is through this, through theory, and through observation. Later, when the ridiculousness has practically disappeared and he has made his amazing gain in dignity, the notebook is dropped. In the Fleet he may attempt to cut off direct experience by locking himself in his room, but what he learned during the trial has made him a different man, and the misery of the debtors penetrates nonetheless. His relation to life is now immediate.

A number of characters are satirized as they stand in opposition to the joy of life, but the final turn is usually positive. Such opposition and suppression is the crime of false piety, as the novel's 1847 preface makes clear:

6. *Charles Dickens,* ed. Steven Marcus (New York, 1956), p. 96.

> Lest there should be any well-intentioned persons who do not perceive the difference . . . between religion and the cant of religion, piety and the pretence of piety, a humble reverence for the great truths of Scripture and an audacious and offensive obstrusion of its letter and not its spirit in the commonest dissensions and meanest affairs of life, to the extraordinary confusion of ignorant minds, let them understand that it is always the latter, and never the former, which is satirized here.

Dickens protests against those who have "just enough religion to make them hate, and not enough to make them love, one another." It was in the name of the simple reliefs of a hard life, particularly for the poor man, that he repeatedly refused support to the temperance societies that solicited his aid. Advocates of temperance, like the puritans who would close the cheap theatres and forbid all Sunday entertainments, fail to see the people as individual, suffering human beings. This divorce from felt life is the basis of Dickens's attack on the Brick Lane branch of the United Grand Junction Ebenezer Temperance Association, in which Mr. Stiggins is active. Their report is well received by the membership:

> "H. Walker, tailor, wife, and two children. When in better circumstances, owns to have been in the constant habit of drinking ale and beer. . . . Is now out of work and penniless; thinks it must be the porter (cheers) or the loss of the use of his right hand; is not certain which, but thinks it very likely that, if he drank nothing but water all his life, his fellow workman would never have stuck a rusty needle in him, and thereby occasioned his accident (tremendous cheering). . . .
>
> "Betsy Martin, widow, one child, and one eye. Goes out charing and washing, by the day; never had more than one eye, but knows her mother drank bottled stout, and shouldn't wonder if that caused it (immense cheering). Thinks it not impossible that if she had always abstained from spirits, she might have had two eyes by this time (tremendous applause). . . .

> "Thomas Burton. . . . Has a wooden leg; finds a wooden leg expensive, going over the stone; used to wear second-hand wooden legs, and drink a glass of hot gin and water regularly every night—sometimes two (deep sighs). Found the second-hand wooden legs split and rot very quickly; is firmly persuaded that their constitution was undermined by the gin and water (prolonged cheering). . . ." [chap. xxxiii]

There is no distinction between wooden and animate legs. Still, the absurdity is so grotesque that the attack cannot become virulent. Dickens castigates Mr. Stiggins himself somewhat more severely. In his sermon:

> Mr. Stiggins did not desire his hearers to be upon their guard against those false prophets and wretched mockers of religion, who, without sense to expound its first doctrines, or hearts to feel its first principles, are more dangerous members of society than the common criminal; imposing, as they necessarily do, upon the weakest and worst informed, casting scorn and contempt on what should be held most sacred, and bringing into partial disrepute large bodies of virtuous and well-conducted persons of many excellent sects and persuasions. [chap. xlv]

But if Stiggins is no better as shepherd than Mr. Chadband as vessel, he is not allowed to terrorize so direfully street boys and demented servants or to ally himself with anyone so effectively pernicious as Grandfather Smallweed. The missionary spirit he urges Sam Weller to emulate is an early taste of Borrioboola Gha: " 'Oh, my young friend, who else could have resisted the pleading of sixteen of our fairest sisters, and withstood their exhortations to subscribe to our noble society for providing the infant negroes in the West Indies with flannel waistcoats and moral pocket handkerchiefs?' " (chap. xxvii). Unlike Mrs. Jellyby's zeal, however, it results in no family calamities and is hilariously undercut by the irrepressible Sam. With Mrs. Jellyby we chafe; with Mr. Stiggins, Dickens releases all tension in laughter.

Traditional professional rigidity is displayed by the medical students Benjamin Allen and Bob Sawyer, who are satirized in their treatment of patients as surgical specimens (see, for example, their conversation in chap. xxxii). But although they are not very pleasant characters, such satire is rather commonplace, and in this novel its emphasis is always jocose. Dodson and Fogg, who consider their clients purses to be squeezed, are more harshly exposed; the abuses of the law and its practitioners appear early in Dickens's writings as principal instruments of oppression. The tale of the cobbler who has been ruined in a Chancery suit upon a disputed will (chap. xliv) is already as bitter as will be its development into the plot of *Bleak House,* and the narrator is in deadly earnest about the unfair treatment of prisoners:

> We no longer suffer them to appeal at the prison gates to the charity and compassion of the passers by; but we still leave unblotted in the leaves of our statute book, for the reverence and admiration of succeeding ages, the just and wholesome law which declares that the sturdy felon shall be fed and clothed, and that the penniless debtor shall be left to die of starvation and nakedness. [chap. xlii]

Here *Pickwick* temporarily darkens. The satire upon the Eatanswill election, in contrast—the Blues and the Buffs—is broad, humorous, and never very serious, a grotesque spoof of social absurdity (one might compare the Veneering election in *Our Mutual Friend*). It is somewhat heavier when turned directly upon Mr. Pott, editor of the *Eatanswill Gazette,* for his Blue obsessiveness paralyzes him in all other respects. Although the Pickwickians themselves are equally rigid—Snodgrass, Tupman, and Winkle will interpret everything in terms respectively of poetry, love, or sport—the satire upon them remains steadily in the realm of light comedy, utterly exempt from moral indictment. They may cause a good deal of mischief, but they are perfectly harmless and very funny.

Intellectual habituation is also a form of rigidity, explaining the narrator's delight in exploding clichés. When at Bob Sawyer's complaints about his landlady's demands for payment of her "little bill" Mr. Ben Allen inquires "How long has it been running?" the narrator comments: " A bill, by the bye, is the most extraordinary locomotive engine that the genius of man ever produced. It would keep on running during the longest lifetime, without ever once stopping of its own accord" (chap. xxxii). The same two are sent off to dinner "with good digestion waiting on appetite, and health on both, and a waiter on all three" (chap. li). The most successful intellectual satire is that of Sam Weller and, to a lesser extent, his father: it is directed against artificial systems, elegant fictions, and careless or willful blindness and is always on the side of an honest grasp of life in full vitality.

Mrs. Weller deserves special attention, for she is the first of a line of characters who exhibit the most striking form of rigidity and repression in the earlier novels, the line of unfeminine or mannish women who repress or pervert the essentially womanly functions in human life. They continue through the later novels, though with significant modification.

Dickens ridiculed the feminist movement of emancipation in his satirical paper "From the Raven in the Happy Family" (*Household Words,* May 11, 1850) with this account by the raven:

> Talking of missions, here's our Proprietor's Wife with a mission now! She has found out that she ought to go and vote at elections; ought to be competent to sit in Parliament; ought to be able to enter the learned professions—the army and navy, too, I believe. She has made the discovery that she has no business to be the comfort of our Proprietor's life, and to have the hold upon him of not being mixed up in all the janglings and wranglings of men, but is quite ill-used in being the solace of his home, and wants to go out speechifying. That's our Proprietor's Wife's new misison. Why, you never heard the Dove go on in that ridiculous way. She knows her true strength better.

This may be simple conservatism or the reactionary assertion of a dominating man, but I think it is more. In his work Dickens reveals a certain consciousness, though never articulated, of a polarity between the male and female that is both physiological and psychological and of this duality of the sexes as a reflection of metaphysical realities. In a just blend of psychology and mysticism, the idea is still available—and quite fascinating—today.[7] Sexually the woman is receiving, passive, and, at the same time, nourishing and creative. Psychologically she is the possessor of intuition or poetic knowledge as opposed to the masculine discursive reason or scientific knowledge. The female is soft and comforting or dark and mysterious, but never hard or aggressive. The human ideal should be a complementary, androgynous harmony between the two aspects of being. Dickens appears to have felt peculiar pain at the specter of unwomanliness and to have seen it more and more as perverse masculinization, as deliberate disregard of feminine values, and finally as the denigration of the feminine by intellectualism and the interests of business and technology. As he came increasingly to conceive this duality of male and female as a matter as much of values as of the traditional distinctions between the sexes, his concern with a particular kind of unpleasant character merged more fully with his broader vision of an unpleasant world.

The entrance of women into politics and business or the "janglings and wranglings of men," therefore, is a symptom of a loss of the peculiarly womanly qualities—comfort, solace, and all that the Dove represents—with a consequent diminishing of human life. The feminine is closely associated with the vital, primarily in the life-giving and life-sustaining roles of maternity

7. In his *The Flight from Woman* (New York, 1965), Karl Stern considers modern civilization's "ghastly spectre of a world impoverished of womanly values." He offers a perspective from Descartes to his own psychiatric patients, with the antirationalist celebrants of the Eternal Feminine as cultural heroes. Much of the terminology of this paragraph is adapted from his. Dickens's female characters—their types and places within the thematic structures of the novels—show a peculiarly Victorian grasp of the crisis of femininity in Western society. Dorothy Sayres's wonderful attack on this mystique (in her introduction to Dante's *Purgatory* [Baltimore, Penguin Books, 1955]) should not be forgotten, although it ultimately only endorses the likelihood of such a conception on Dickens's part.

(hence the importance of food in Dickens) but in the later works in sexual vitality as well. The sense of a power of death in the world is therefore first conveyed in a perception of women no longer womanly and thus of an absence of womanhood from life. Critics have frequently observed the number of incomplete or perverse father-child relationships in Dickens's novels, but equally regular and perhaps even more significant is the deprivation of a mother suffered by such children as Oliver Twist, Madeline Bray, the Marchioness, Little Nell, Hugh, Martin Chuzzlewit, Mary Graham, Paul and Florence Dombey, Walter Gay, David Copperfield, and, in the later novels, Esther Summerson, Sissy Jupe, the Dorrits, Lucy Manette, Pip, Jenny Wren, Lizzie and Charley Hexam, and in fact Caddy Jellyby and Bella Wilfer, whose mothers are worse than none. The vision of an absence of womanly mothers—loving providers of food, warmth, and shelter—is complemented by the power of termagants, false mothers, and nurses actually indifferent to the nourishment of life.

To some degree, Mrs. Bardell of *Pickwick Papers* and her little women's club of supporters are the first of the viragos. But, as we said before, the novel is partial to the bright world of comedy. Although Mrs. Sanders and Mrs. Cluppins may be unredeemed, they are minor figures against whom satiric anger would be wasted; Mrs. Bardell is more a dupe of Dodson and Fogg whose matrimonial desires, despite Mr. Pickwick's panic, are rather kindly and affectionately meant. The unwomanly women in this novel are not cruel, repressive figures but characters who, in a long tradition of comedy, fail in the virtues of solace and comfort. Mrs. Raddle, Bob Sawyer's landlady, is a most persistent henpecker who, abetted by her friends, makes an art of abusing her husband. This is one instance:

> "Lauk, Mary Ann! What's the matter?" said Mrs. Cluppins.
>
> "It's put me all over in such a tremble, Betsy," replied Mrs. Raddle. "Raddle ain't like a man; he leaves everythink to me."
>
> This was scarcely fair upon the unfortunate Mr. Raddle,

> who had been thrust aside by his good lady in the commencement of the dispute, and peremptorily commanded to hold his tongue. He had no opportunity of defending himself, however, for Mrs. Raddle gave unequivocal signs of fainting; which, being perceived from the parlour window, Mrs. Bardell, Mrs. Sanders, the lodger, and the lodger's servant, darted precipitately out, and conveyed her into the house. [chap. xlvi]

The manly duty Mr. Raddle had shirked and Mrs. Raddle usurped was to haggle with a cab driver. She too, however, is a minor figure carrying no deep moral indictment.

More serious treatment is given Mrs. Weller, particularly when she and Mr. Stiggins come under satiric fire for their unchristian, repressive religion. She shows her worst side in maltreatment of her husband. Yet this is consistently comic and cannot be taken very seriously, particularly in light of how well Tony bears up under it. He tries to keep out of the way, but when that fails he still has his own weapons. He recounts his actions at a prayer meeting during which the shepherd had singled him out as an example of vice:

> "Presently he pulls up again, and lookin' wery hard at me, says, 'Where is the sinner; where is the mis'rable sinner?' and all the women groans again, ten times louder than afore. I got rather wild at this, so I takes a step or two for'ard and says, 'My friend,' says I, 'did you apply that 'ere observation to me?' 'Stead of begging my pardon as any gen'l'm'n would ha' done, he got more abusive than ever: called me a wessel, Sammy—a wessel of wrath—and all sorts o' names. So my blood being reg'larly up, I first give him two or three for himself, and then two or three more to hand over to the man with the red nose, and walked off." [chap. xxii]

We are granted the punishment we long to administer; again, tension is fully released. For whatever discomfort she has caused, Mrs. Weller is absolved when on her deathbed she repudiates before her husband the false religion she has followed and the mistakes she has made, especially in relation to him (chap. lii). Satire gives way to the repentance and reconciliation of comedy, and the true anti-woman does not appear until *Oliver Twist.*

Steven Marcus has aptly taken for *Pickwick Papers* the adjective "transcendent"[8]—the transcendence is to comedy in the broad sense of celebration. The Pickwickians, with their Shandean hobbyhorses, are objects of no more than good-humored raillery—for this is a world in which words have a special Pickwickian sense in addition to their common sense; in which one of the leading features of the Pickwickian theory is general benevolence; and in which Mr. Samuel Pickwick, for whom all this is named, bursts from his slumbers like "another sun" (chap. ii). This book more than any of Dickens's later works has much of the joyful, exuberant comedy that makes the Bergsonian type seem negative. One early—and unforgettable—incident will illustrate its celebrative nature. The Pickwickians and their new friend Mr. Jingle leave the Golden Cross together in the coach "Commodore":

> "Heads, heads—take care of your heads!" cried the loquacious stranger, as they came out under the low archway, which in those days formed the entrance to the coach-yard. "Terrible place—dangerous work—other day—five children—mother—tall lady, eating sandwiches—forgot the arch—crash—knock—children look round—mother's head off—sandwich in her hand—no mouth to put it in—head of a family off—shocking, shocking!" [chap ii]

In *Pickwick* this is hilarious. Later, the peculiar dissociation Mr. Jingle displays in this careless narration is comic only in a bitter or ironic way: witness the Hands of Coketown or Mrs. Merdle as a Bosom. This manner of speaking in abrupt explosions of phrases becomes pointed satire when used by the lawyer Mr. Tangle in *Bleak House* as he propounds Jarndyce and Jarndyce before the Lord Chancellor:

> "Have you nearly concluded your argument?"
>
> "Mlud, no—variety of points—feel it my duty tsubmit

8. Marcus, *Pickwick to Dombey*, p. 17.

> —ludship," is the reply that slides out of Mr. Tangle. . . .
> "Begludship's pardon—victim of rash action—brains." [chap. i]

But in *Pickwick* it was still pure comedy.

Oliver Twist, like *Pickwick,* opens with specific satire, but here the satire succeeds because the object of attack participates in the central theme of the novel—offense against life.[9] The workhouse directors, Noah Claypole, and Mrs. Sowerberry are all one in their oppression of youth; by his perversion of it, Fagin joins them. In the vision of a struggle between vitality and rigidity, the child becomes an important symbol of the former; sin against him becomes sin against life. Here Dickens is strikingly close to Blake. In *Oliver Twist* the simple being's desire for life—the living stomach's cry for "more"—is opposed by a board of directors and a man in a white waistcoat whose anonymity itself is inhuman. Oliver's floggings are cruel, sadistic rites of death. The first scene in the poorhouse includes his birth, but it is immediately followed by the death of his mother, and the narrator's last comment suggests that if Oliver has come hither crying, it is for even better reason than he can know. In the next chapter, the narrator plays upon the irony of minimal, even crippling, nourishment with an exploded metaphor: when Oliver is sent out to a baby farm, he remarks that "It cannot be expected that this system of farming would produce any very extraordinary or luxuriant crop" (chap. ii). For the most part, this novel lacks the glorious comedy of *Pickwick;* satiric deflation is still humorous, but the dark undertow is very strong. If the beadle's logic is absurd enough to be funny, it perpetrates too much evil to be dismissed with laughter alone. There is a curious tension in the comedy of observations such as the following, upon the beadle's having sent some medicine to a pauper:

> "But what's the consequence; what's the ungrateful behaviour of these rebels, sir? Why, the husband sends back word that the medicine won't suit his wife's com-

9. Cf. chapter 2 above, p. 30.

> plaint, and so she shan't take it—says she shan't take it, sir! Good, strong, wholesome medicine, as was given with great success to two Irish labourers and a coal-heaver only a week before—sent 'em for nothing, with a blackin'-bottle in,—and he sends back word that she shan't take it, sir!" [chap. v]

Or in this advice to Mrs. Sowerberry:

> "You've overfed him, ma'am. You've raised a artificial soul and spirit in him, ma'am, unbecoming a person of his condition: as the board, Mrs. Sowerberry, who are practical philosophers, will tell you. What have paupers to do with soul or spirit? It's quite enough that we let 'em have live bodies." [chap. vii]

In this novel the anti-woman appears fully. In chapter i Oliver's mother, dying in childbirth, is nursed by a Mrs. Thingummy (her name illustrates the relation of these women to the vision of human reification), who is more intent upon a certain green bottle than upon her patient. Despite her sympathetic statements in the presence of the surgeon, she is eventually revealed to have robbed the dying body of a gold ring that would have assured Oliver's well-being. She reappears on her own deathbed to confess, but what hope there might be in her repentance is ironically undercut by the encircling of her dying figure with three attendant hags (Mrs. Corney and two subordinates), all as coarse toward the waning life before them as she herself once was. In chapter ii she is followed by Mrs. Mann, keeper of the baby farm. Her name too seems deliberately ironic: the woman whose profession is the nurture of babies should represent the ultimate in womanliness; her unfeeling cruelty is a denial of the values of her sex, and the man in female form who results is a monster. Mrs. Corney, matron of the workhouse, is of the same line; when, however, she turns upon her new husband (Mr. Bumble), the victim well deserves the punishment of her aggressive, unfeminine rule. Finally, Charlotte, the Sowerberrys' kitchen maid who elopes with Noah Claypole, is the termagant (she exhibits this nature precociously) who starves Oliver but who is punished by subjection to perhaps the most repulsive character in the book.

If the economic policies that support Bumble, the board, or the Sowerberrys are ugly modern advances in mechanistic cruelty, the philosophy behind them also goes back to dog-eat-dog savagery. This is the principle of Number One that Fagin so lucidly expounds to Noah Claypole in chapter xliii. An early simile for the old man points to its atavistic nature:

> It seemed just the night when it befitted such a being as the Jew to be abroad. As he glided stealthily along, creeping beneath the shelter of the walls and doorways, the hideous old man seemed like some loathsome reptile, engendered in the slime and darkness through which he moved; crawling forth, by night, in search of some rich offal for a meal. [chap. xix]

The image seems almost to anticipate *Bleak House* and the ironically retrogressive activity of its dunces. In an earlier chapter, the narrator's comments when the Dodger and Master Bates join the chase after Oliver for pickpocketing Mr. Brownlow enunciate the parallels between the modern "philosophy" justified by abstract theorizing and primitive self-preservation:

> I need hardly beg the reader to observe, that this action should tend to exalt them in the opinion of all public and patriotic men, in almost as great a degree as this strong proof of their anxiety for their own preservation and safety goes to corroborate and confirm the little code of laws which certain profound and sound-judging philosophers have laid down as the mainsprings of all Nature's deeds and actions: the said philosophers very wisely reducing the good lady's proceedings to matters of maxim and theory: and, by a neat and pretty compliment to her exalted wisdom and understanding, putting entirely out of sight any considerations of heart, or generous impulse and feeling.

In both it is a reduction of the great life of nature to a simple and selfish mechanical principle; the difference is only a matter of style:

> If I wanted any further proof of the strictly philosophical nature of the conduct of these young gentlemen in their very delicate predicament, I should at once find it in the fact (also recorded in the foregoing part of this narrative), of their quitting the pursuit, when the general attention was fixed upon Oliver; and making immediately for their home by the shortest possible cut. Although I do not mean to assert that it is usually the practice of renowned and learned sages, to shorten the road to any great conclusion (their course indeed being rather to lengthen the distance, by various circumlocutions and discursive staggerings, like unto those in which drunken men under the pressure of a too mighty flow of ideas, are prone to indulge); still, I do mean to say, and do say distinctly, that it is the invariable practice of many mighty philosophers, in carrying out their theories, to evince great wisdom and foresight in providing against every possible contingency which can be supposed at all likely to affect themselves. [chap. xii]

In the novel itself, the most striking difference presented between the world of socially respected inhumanity and the criminal underworld is only that one is rendered in satire, the other in melodrama.

The vision of evil, impressive as it is, is balanced—at least in imputed strength—by a brighter world. Though perhaps only with the aid of some very artificial plotting, the bright world is the one that triumphs. Oliver, whose childish goodness is extreme, is trapped in a dark world first by social and then (through Monks and Fagin) by individual abuse, but at the end he is rescued permanently into the light one to which he properly belongs. Only one character is misplaced and never righted: Nancy's death is the epitome of horror in the dark world. The Manichean nature of Dickens's vision is clearly apparent in this novel, as two antithetical worlds vie for power.

Nicholas Nickleby shows a similar division into bright and dark worlds—though there is far less shadow in the dark and more animation in the bright—and a similarly contrived triumph of the bright. Both worlds are defined primarily by the benevolent or criminal individuals who inhabit them. The first object of satiric attack is Squeers, an oppressor, and eventually a murderer, of boys. His deeply rooted viciousness is expressed in the bitter fullness of demonic parody. When he and Mr. Snawley come to claim poor Smike as Mr. Snawley's lost son, the two indulge in a little histrionic support of their imposture:

> "What was it," said Snawley, "that made me take such a strong interest in him, when that worthy instructor of youth brought him to my house? What was it that made me burn all over with a wish to chastise him severely for cutting away from his best friends, his pastors and masters?"
>
> "It was parental instinct, sir," observed Squeers.
>
> "That's what it was, sir," rejoined Snawley; "the elevated feeling, the feeling of the ancient Romans and Grecians, and of the beasts of the field and birds of the air, with the exception of rabbits and tom-cats, which sometimes devour their offspring. My heart yearned towards him. I could have—I don't know what I couldn't have done to him in the anger of a father."
>
> "It only shows what Natur is, sir," said Mr. Squeers. "She's a rum 'un, is Natur."
>
> "She is a holy thing, sir," remarked Snawley.
>
> "I believe you," added Mr. Squeers, with a moral sigh. "I should like to know how we should ever get on without her. Natur," said Mr. Squeers, solemnly, "is more easier conceived than described. Oh what a blessed thing, sir, to be in a state o' natur!" [chap. xlv]

The satire on all that is connected with Dotheboys is again upon the "offense against life" that the characters perpetrate. This is also true to some extent of Ralph Nickleby's manipulation of people as though they were objects to be used by the powerful in the gratification of their own desires—his in particular being social eminence and money—and of Arthur Gride's intent to fasten his hideous, impotent self upon a beautiful young woman. Yet these figures are hardly treated satirically: Kate and

Nicholas are simply too insipid, and Ralph and Gride too much the villains of melodrama. These parts of the plot do not approach the real horror that is embodied, though with a good deal of free-running sentiment, in Smike's story.

Mrs. Squeers is a fuller development of *Oliver Twist*'s Mrs. Mann. Instead of feeding and nurturing the boys in her charge, she ladles into them a foul-tasting appetite-depressant. Her husband tells Mrs. Snawley that to Smike "Mrs. Squeers has been . . . mother, grandmother, aunt—Ah! and I may say uncle too, all in one" (chap. xxxviii); he may say so with more fitness than intended, because in Mrs. Squeers the womanly qualities that would give meaning to the distinctions between the words "aunt" and "uncle" are nonexistent. Her son Wackford Squeers is a hideous, bloated parody of the well-fed child, representing gluttony and robbery (he not only eats what should be given to the other boys but also takes their clothing); her daughter Fanny desires Nicholas in a travesty of feminine love.

This book contains perhaps the highest proportion of blatantly unintegrated satire. The United Metropolitan Improved Hot Muffin and Crumpet Baking and Punctual Delivery Company soon detaches itself from the novel. The parody of a silver-fork novel that Kate Nickleby reads to Mrs. Wittiterly is more successful and perhaps of some service in characterizing that lady, but it is still an obvious interpolation. The parodies of melodrama and the critic Mr. Curdle's discourse upon the unities are of the same order, though the latter especially is so delightful that one is rather glad not to have lost it in the cause of thematic relevance. Much of the satire is based upon rigidity of character. Though the acting troupe remains a charming and lively company, Mr. Crummles himself becomes a satiric butt when he carries his acting too far over into life, fails to recognize and yield to the differences between the two, and poses instead of lives—as when Nicholas and Smike take leave of the company. Similarly, though the Mantalinis are purely comic figures, Miss Knag's jealousy of Kate's youth and beauty and insistence on the superiority of her own aged ugliness is satirized as a refusal to accept life's changes. Mrs. Nickleby's compulsive babbling, constantly trailing off onto tangents of unnecessary detail, is another manifestation of the absence of any true relation to the world. Yet although it is often comically self-revealing, it seems to have little to do with anything else in the book. One might compare the glorious chatter of Flora Finching in *Little Dorrit* and its analogical relation to the dominant theme of that novel.

For all its evil, *Nickleby* still envisions a triumphant bright world. Yorkshire has its John Browdies and London its Cheerybles (excessively bluff and hearty though they may appear to modern tastes), Nicholas wins Madeline Bray, Kate wins Frank Cheeryble, Dotheboys is broken up, and all who deserve it live prosperously ever after. When the evil characters have been caught and punished, their power is vanquished. The novel works as melodrama—despite its own parodies of that genre—rather than as anything one could properly call satire. The vision of Dotheboys is satiric, and there are a number of satiric characters, but the evil of Ralph, Gride, Sir Mulberry Hawk, *et al.* is melodrama; Crummles and company, the Mantalinis, Fanny Squeers, and Miss La Creevy remain in comedy and farce. The pretensions of the Kenwigses are satirized, but their satire, like that upon the Wittiterlys, is not integral to the novel. In regard to these characters, *Nickleby* is picaresque, with both a hero and a heroine moving through a society that is ridiculed and then passed by.

If, with its parodies of melodrama and its simultaneous enactment of a highly melodramatic plot, *Nicholas Nickleby* is something of an anomaly, *The Old Curiosity Shop* is an even stranger amalgam. The pseudo-biblical rhetoric of pathos can be amply illustrated from any of a large number of passages. The following is from chapter xv:

> There was a pool of clear water in the field, in which the child laved her hands and face, and cooled her feet before setting forth to walk again. She would have the old man refresh himself in this way too, and making him sit down upon the grass, cast the water on him with her hands, and dried it with her simple dress.

The child who "laves" rather than washes her hands, whose

"simple" dress needs notation as such, is part of a rhetorical syndrome of the narrator matched only by a cheery enthusiastic voice equally cloying:

> Dear, dear, what a place it looked, that Astley's; with all the paint, gilding, and looking-glass . . . the fiddlers looking carelessly up at them while they tuned their instruments, as if they didn't want the play to begin, and knew it all beforehand! What a glow was that, which burst upon them all, when that long, clear, brilliant row of lights came slowly up; and what the feverish excitement when the little bell rang and the music began in good earnest, with strong parts for the drums, and sweet effects for the triangles! Well might Barbara's mother say to Kit's mother that the gallery was the place to see from, and wonder it wasn't much dearer than the boxes: well might Barbara feel doubtful whether to laugh or cry, in her flutter of delight. [chap. xxxix]

The trouble is partly in the child's point of view. *David Copperfield,* and to an even greater extent *Great Expectations,* show how terrifying the world can be when seen through a child's eyes; and the vitriolic Jenny Wren in *Our Mutual Friend,* herself a satirist in the cursing tradition of ancient bards, is a signal demonstration of the pain and evil of perverted human relationships. With great tact, children can also successfully be pathetic: Paul Dombey is more tolerable than Little Nell in part because we see him more through the eyes of the adult characters than directly. In this novel, however, the juvenile penetration is as thorough as it is ultimately exasperating. What in both earlier and later novels is the subject of satire or humor is here given a melodramatic, pathetic, or apparently "tragic" turn. The law, for instance, is from *Pickwick* through *Our Mutual Friend* one of the most consistent of these subjects—even in *Oliver Twist* the Artful Dodger turns the trial scene into one of delight—but Kit's trial is an exception. The evils of industrialism are treated in *Hard Times* in terse satiric terms as the ugliness and inhumanity of Coketown are revealed with little fustian; this, on the other hand, is its prototype in *The Old Curiosity Shop:*

> But, night-time in this dreadful spot!—night, when the smoke was changed to fire; when every chimney spurted up its flame; and places, that had been dark vaults all day, now shone red-hot, with figures moving to and fro within their blazing jaws, and calling to one another with hoarse cries—night, when the noise of every strange machine was aggravated by the darkness; when the people near them looked wilder and more savage; when bands of unemployed labourers paraded in the roads, or clustered by torch-light round their leaders, who told them, in stern language, of their wrongs, and urged them on to frightful cries and threats; when maddened men, armed with sword and firebrand, spurning the tears and prayers of women who would restrain them, rushed forth on errands of terror and destruction, to work no ruin half so surely as their own—night, when carts came rumbling by, filled with rude coffins (for contagious disease and death had been busy with the living crops); when orphans cried, and distracted women shrieked and followed in their wake—night, when some called for bread, and some for drink to drown their cares, and some with tears, and some with staggering feet, and some with blood-shot eyes, went brooding home—night, which, unlike the night that Heaven sends on earth, brought with it no peace, nor quiet, nor signs of blessed sleep—who shall tell the terrors of the night to the young wandering child! [chap. xlv]

The night itself and what it means are frightening enough, but the effectiveness of the passage is seriously undermined by our finally being asked to consider it, not in relation to those who tramp and work and die and mourn, but to the fears it arouses in "that young child." That is not wherein the full horror lies, and Dickens's attempt so to bias it casts a tone of falsity, of contrivedly lurid lighting, over the whole piece.

Yet the novel is not all like this. It almost seems that the further away we get from Little Nell—and from Kit as well—the closer we come to humor and satire, which are still viable. There is a sort of *danse macabre* in the motley group that Nell and her grandfather encounter on the road: the Punch-show owner, Short Trotters, and his gruff assistant, Mr. Codlin; Mr. Grinder, with his son and daughter on stilts; Jerry and his dancing dogs; Vuffin, owner of a giant and a limbless lady; Sweet William, the card-trick man and conjuror; and Mrs. Jarley of the waxworks and her driver George. Aside from this, the oddly successful part of the novel is that concerning Dick Swiveller and the Brasses. With them the narrator can, as in *Nicholas Nickleby,* deride the conventions of melodrama:

> It may be necessary to observe, lest there should appear any incongruity in the close of this soliloquy, that Mr. Swiveller did not wind up with a cheerful hilarious laugh which would have been undoubtedly at variance with his solemn reflections, but that, being in a theatrical mood, he merely achieved that performance, which is designated in melodramas "laughing like a fiend,"—for it seems that your fiends always laugh in syllables, and always in three syllables, never more or less, which is a remarkable property in such gentry, and one worthy of remembrance. [chap. lvi]

Yet this is in the same book that features Quilp, a Richard III out-Richarded, "with great suavity in his manner, but still more of a quiet malice about his eyes and mouth" (chapter vi). The juxtaposition of modes can be even closer:

> The sun was setting when they reached the wicket-gate at which the path began, and, as the rain falls upon the just and unjust alike, it shed its warm tint even upon the resting-places of the dead, and bade them be of good hope for its rising on the morrow. The church was old and grey, with ivy clinging to the walls, and round the porch. Shunning the tombs, it crept about the mounds, beneath which slept poor humble men: twining for them the first wreaths they had ever won, but wreaths less liable to wither and far more lasting in their kind, than some which were graven deep in stone and marble, and told in pompous terms of virtues meekly hidden for many a year, and only revealed at last to executors and mourning legatees. [chap. xvi]

From out of this Gray's Elegy debased and made maudlin comes a sudden sharp satiric bite. Similarly though in larger blocks, in chapter xxxi the entrance of Miss Monflathers in self-revelatory satire brings the relief of a spirited scene.

Sometimes the jointures are strongly labored. Chapter xxxii ends with Nell's wistful longing at the sight of two loving sisters followed by Mrs. Jarley's warning of impending financial difficulties for the Exhibition. The distance from this world to that of the Brasses is emphasized by the drastic change of tone with which, in order to make the transition, the narrator then opens chapter xxxiii:

> As the course of this tale requires that we should become acquainted, somewhere hereabouts, with a few particulars connected with the domestic economy of Mr. Sampson Brass, and as a more convenient place than the present is not likely to occur for that purpose, the historian takes the friendly reader by the hand, and springing with him into the air, and cleaving the same at a greater rate than ever Don Cleophas Leandro Perez Zambullo and his familiar travelled that pleasant region in company, alights with him upon the pavement of Bevis Marks.

This is not Dickens at his best—rather, it is Dickens attempting to be something between Fielding and Byron, which never quite works—but above all it is Dickens getting as far away as possible from the tone of the previous chapter. In terms of the plot, probably only the machinations of so fantastic a creature as Quilp could bring together two imaginative worlds so differently conceived. The hideous Sally Brass who succeeds Mrs. Squeers and the Dick Swiveller whose beloved Sophy Wackles seems a burlesque of Sophia Western (just as he himself seems somewhat a Victorian perception of Tom Jones) belong to a vision whose values are ultimately positive. Daniel Quilp's guzzling of boiling rum and devouring of unshelled hard eggs are indexes of inhumanity; Dick Swiveller's riotous feasting whenever credit allows is not exactly praiseworthy, but the sin is only venial, and its indulgence is finally a sign of bursting vitality. Sally Brass joins Quilp in a work of melodramatic villainy, but the satire upon her is directed against the antecedent perversion that makes her capable of such action: the subversion of femininity. Like Mrs. Mann's, her name reflects hardness and rigidity. Dickens does not make too much of her spinsterhood, but her suppression and starvation of the Marchioness and the unanswered queries as to the child's origin comprise a sufficient denial of womanliness. The ludicrous appellations ("beauty," "fair charmer") emphasize her masculinity. The depravity, itself an offense against life, is spelled out by the narrator: " 'He, he!' simpered Brass, who, in his deep debasement, really seemed to have changed sexes with his sister, and to have made over to her any spark of manliness he might have possessed" (chap. lxvi). The values are clearly the positive virtues of kindness and life. It is through the humane generosity of bringing the little Marchioness out from her cellar that Dick Swiveller earns the right to be nursed back to life by her, despite all his light-hearted and even madcap self-indulgence. Similarly, her instinctive capabilities as a nurse who nourishes and brings back to life mark the Marchioness unequivocally as the one good to arise out of the Brass establishment.

The world of Little Nell, however, is more ambivalent. Steven Marcus has described this novel as pervaded by "spiritual necrophilia."[10] Certainly the Little Nell plot shows a longing for peace to the point of inertia, with its antithesis, the energy of life gone wild, envisioned as the evil of Quilp. Whether or not this mood grows out of the effect of Mary Hogarth's death upon Dickens, the retreat in this novel is a step beyond the idyllic life finally granted Oliver and Nicholas, to a countryside remarkable and desirable for quiet, peaceful graveyards. The "single gentleman" who is the equivalent of Mr. Brownlow and the Cheeryble brothers this time arrives too late, but Nell's death, though its rendering is lachrymose, is conceived as beatific. The Garlands and Kit Nubbles may find a world that is relatively happy, but Nell, with blessings upon her, escapes it altogether. Her protection by an exhibitor of distressingly humanlike wax figures, her contentment in the empty church, and

10. Marcus, *Pickwick to Dombey*, pp. 143–46.

her acceptance of a cemetery as garden are part of a soothing movement consummated by her death.

If my analysis is so far correct, then there is a distinct duality to the novel: the dominant theme essentially expresses a longing for death perhaps underpinned by an ironic vision of life as a circus or *danse macabre,* while a subtheme or group of characters resist this movement with satiric attacks ranging from the hilarity of Dick Swiveller to the cruelty of Sally Brass. To force these two movements into concurrence would probably be a mistaken overexertion of critical interest, for whatever life there is to the novel arises from the conflict of the two. The psychological reference is in this regard particularly attractive, because with it we can see in the Swiveller-Brass movement the vital Dickens of *Pickwick* struggling with the depressive lethargy consequent upon the death of Mary and figured forth in the Little Nell movement. Certainly the treatment of Little Nell represents a unique mood in Dickens, when the blessings of quietude outweigh the sluggishness and rigidity that are the usual aspects of life approaching death.

To the opposition between rigidity and torpor on the one hand and flexibility and vitality on the other, *Barnaby Rudge* adds a third possibility: violence. The problem is not rendered so clearly as it will be in *A Tale of Two Cities,* where the people rise up against their oppressors in rebellion at least initially justified; judgment upon the nature of the violence that ensues, however, is held in finer suspension. The social malaise causing the people to riot in the name of what is for the vast majority a trumped-up cause of no meaning is never satisfactorily defined, though a few supposedly representative individuals are examined with care. There is no clash between oppressors and oppressed, because the riots are the work of the wronging party and the victims as often the neutral bystanders as those wronged. The one thing clear is that violent disorder is rising out of bigotry, vanity, cruelty, and lust. Once the chaos of the riots has come, however, a certain ambivalence is produced by the evident relish and empathy of description in such scenes as the storming of Newgate. Here, momentarily, the upholder of social order and due process (perhaps already beginning to despair over the effectuality of due process) indulges in the release of violent reaction. The ambiguity is never resolved and remains indeed one of the finer things in the book. Nevertheless, although Dickens was to become increasingly dismayed at evidence of widespread political apathy, this novel already shows that he would not be able to recommend the alternative of violence.

As in its depiction of the Gordon Riots the novel deals with an eruption of violence spread through society, in the Rudge murder it examines the effects of a violent deed when both its enactment and the knowledge of it are rigorously private. The result to all concerned is a life of anguish; to the criminal, hunger, cold, and utter divorce from society as well. Of course, there is never any ambiguity about the criminal nature of murder; the guilt of this private instance does reflect, however, upon the mob's disrespect for individual life.

The coordinate problem of *Barnaby Rudge* is that of sincerity. Sir John Chester represents a way of life that has rejected this value outright and elevated, quite consciously, its antithesis. Barnaby's father is forced by his crime to lead a life of continual concealment and disguise. The worst of the rioters are those who join the mob not out of sincere religious conviction but out of idleness or vanity (both chargeable to Sim Tappertit), for private gain (most notable in Mr. Gashford, Lord Gordon's secretary), or out of sheer bloodlust (which, in Dennis, so strong and so embedded in hypocrisy, renders him the most horrifying of all). Yet Dennis's repeated citations of the British constitution, as they reach a climax in his insistence upon saving those Newgate prisoners condemned to death so that the hangman's office may not go neglected, may have satirical reflection upon the constitution he glorifies as well as condemnatory reference to the man himself. The shallowness of much Protestant support is further exhibited in Miggs and Mrs. Varden and the satiric deflations visited upon them: at one point, for instance, they are described as gaining the locksmith's consent to a proposal he opposes by means of verbal consolations "moral, religious, and miscellaneous" (chap. xix). Geoffrey Haredale, on the other hand, is an unfailing moral standard for honesty and unselfishness, for which his rough, abrupt manner is meant to be direct evidence. And because of the sincerity of his conviction, Lord Gordon is exempt from the attack that glances off instead onto his henchmen.

The novel treats its themes primarily in modes of horror or nightmare. Barnaby's recollection of the whole experience—which for him alone among the characters includes the culminations of both plots—is as of a bad dream:

> Some time elapsed before Barnaby got the better of the shock he had sustained, or regained his old health and gaiety. But he recovered by degrees: and although he could never separate his condemnation and escape from the idea of a terrific dream, he became, in other respects, more rational. [chap. lxxxii]

This "terrific dream" is the essential quality of the more serious parts of the novel: the murder and the riots. What comedy there is comes mainly in conjunction with the equally occasional satire. This satire again turns against those who seek to confine, constrict, or suppress joy and vitality.

Mrs. Varden, whose life is conducted in shrewish opposition to her husband's, turns the joy of religion into the gloom of a Protestant manual, bitter medicine from which she reaps little but bigotry. The true religion—opposed both to this and to the fanaticism of the rioters—is enunciated by the narrator in that pseudo-biblical rhetoric so hard to take:

> Ye men of gloom and austerity, who paint the face of Infinite Benevolence with an eternal frown; read in the Everlasting Book, wide open to your view, the lesson it would teach. Its pictures are not in black and sombre hues, but bright and glowing tints; its music—save when ye drown it—is not in sighs and groans, but songs and cheerful sounds. Listen to the million voices in the summer air, and find one dismal as your own. Remember, if ye can, the sense of hope and pleasure which every glad return of the day awakens in the breast of all your kind who have

> not changed their nature; and learn some wisdom even from the witless, when their hearts are lifted up they know not why, by all the mirth and happiness it brings. [chap. xxv]

Dickens is memorable as a satirist in his role as subversive and deflator, for that is when he brings into play his superb talents for comic conception and manipulation of language. When he comes to enunciate the positive norms, he often seems to find it necessary, particularly in the earlier works but to an uncomfortable extent throughout his writing, to cast himself as prophet and to use an idiom appropriate to that role. Despite the language, however, the standards of vitality, joy, and love are forcefully affirmed.

John Willet is a self-indulgent old man in heavy opposition to all these values, except insofar as they gratify his senses. Like many of Dickens's rigid characters, his use of language is automatized to the repetition of rote phrases. Overwhelmed by the arrival of Lord Gordon's suite, he recovers sufficiently to make some offer of accommodation: "in short, to run over such recommendatory scraps of language as were painted up on various portions of the building, and which in the course of some forty years he had learnt to repeat with tolerable correctness" (chap. xxxv). His basic stupidity is manifest in the boastful self-assertion he shares with other Dickensian thick-headed fools: Mr. Bumble in *Oliver Twist,* Pumblechook in *Great Expectations.* As with these two, Willet's bloated expansion becomes most dominating when it is aimed at putting down a young person. The opposition of age to youth is shown in this novel in Sir John Chester's selfish exploitation of Edward and rejection of Hugh, but it is most repulsive, because accompanied by the most bombast, in Willet's treatment of his son Joe. His attempts to suppress him are a denial of his manhood; after Joe has run away, for example, "in his advertisement Mr. Willet had obstinately persisted, despite the advice and entreaties of his friends, in describing his son as a 'young boy'; and furthermore as being from eighteen inches to a couple of feet shorter than he really was" (chap. xxxiii). We are only glad to know that this assures Joe's freedom.

Sim Tappertit and Miggs, male and female counterparts of one another despite their disagreements, are satirized for their ridiculous pretension and, as shown in the combination of vanity and ugliness in each, self-centeredness absolute to the point of utter blindness. Miggs is not to be pitied in her ugliness, for her spiteful jealousy of Dolly Varden and her selfish idiocy harden this well-deserved accident of nature. (Esther Summerson will be the almost graphic demonstration of how little feminine attractiveness has to do with a pretty face.) Miggs's falseness more than anything else has made her an automaton repulsive even to Sim. Thus she assists her mistress in subjugating the good locksmith:

> "Here's matter, mim," said Miggs. "Oh, what a happiness it is when man and wife come round again! Oh gracious, to think that him and her should ever have a word together!" In the energy of these sentiments, which were uttered as an apostrophe to the Heavens in general, Miss Miggs perched the bonnet on top of her own head [it is Mrs. Varden's newest], and *folding her hands, turned on her tears.*
>
> "I can't help it," cried Miggs. [chap. xix; italics mine]

Sim Tappertit's falsity is effective in deceiving himself more than others. He is to some extent a parodic inversion of the two heroes, Edward Chester and Joe Willet. They are abused by their fathers and deprived of the manhood their true natures warrant; Sim attempts to abuse the gentlest and best of fathers, Gabriel Varden, and believes himself possessed of a virility ludicrously mocked by his diminutive legs. His aspirations toward Dolly in self-conceited rivalry for her hand point up the comparison. Sim lives in a world of ridiculous fantasy—though in the chaos of the riots this too is turned to destructive account.

The objects of satire have in common opposition to or destruction of the beauty, joy, and vitality of life. Even Sim Tappertit turns what should be the happiness of his own youth into an agony of frustration. These characters are set against those who treasure and nourish such values: Mrs. Rudge and

Geoffrey Haredale as parents; Dolly, Emma Haredale, and Gabriel Varden as standards of moral and ethical consideration. But there is another repressive evil behind the visible individuals—society. The personification of society in this novel is barely significant, but it is the beginning of what will become central to the later, more satiric novels. Here that strangely potent "it" enters to support Mr. Chester against his son:

> So it soon got whispered about, that Mr. Chester was very unfortunate in his son, who had occasioned him great grief and sorrow. . . . And when Edward's name was spoken, Society shook its head, and laid its finger on its lip, and sighed, and looked very grave; and those who had sons about his age, waxed wrathful and indignant, and hoped, for Virtue's sake, that he was dead. [chap. xxxii]

Society is an enforcer of philistine convention, and the personified, capitalized concept "Society" represents a disregard for distinguishing individuality, the sign of life.

But the most fearful product of the sin against life in this novel is Hugh, and the treatment of this character is not satiric. He has been denied kinship by his father and nurture by society (a society which hanged his mother for stealing in order to feed her child); the continuance of this criminal process by the repressive John Willet produces instead of a man an animal who finally leads the violent eruption of chaos. Hugh's father, Sir John, who could express natural vitality only in fornication and who denied even that covert expression in the subsequent neglect of his victims, is a figure of intermittent satire. Hugh, however, is rendered in sympathy gradually giving way to fear. As is revealed by his protection of Barnaby, his violence lacks the malignity of Dennis's, and unlike that of the mob it is unquestionably based in a justified sense of wrong. There is something rather exhilarating about Hugh charging through chaos on his enormous horse, as there is about the mob setting fire to Newgate prison. This is not really surprising, for though violence can never be commended, the real evil in Dickens's vision is lethargy, torpor, or any form of death-in-life. And although this novel depicts a strongly predominant dark world despite its relatively happy ending and its occasionally uncontrolled pastoralism, its world is colored by the excitement of violent action.

This understanding of the dark vision in Dickens's early novels may explain one difficult aspect of the bright pictures he holds up in contrast. Women who suppress or pervert their feminine qualities to become aggressive forces of repression are repeatedly contrasted with those who tend to embody the antithetical qualities of passivity and nurture. The excessive femininity of the "golden girls" in the early novels is an illustrative exaggeration toward ideality, the ideal being conceived in direct reaction to masculine hardness and strength. The female is soft, kind, gentle, passive, receptive; Dickens transfers these qualities from the sexual to the whole personality, thus creating the insipid figures who now appear so unreal and, indeed, undesirable: Rose Maylie, Madeline Bray, Kate Nickleby, Dolly Varden, Mary Graham, Ruth Pinch. Less in evidence but of complementary significance to the golden girls are the good motherly figures: Mrs. Maylie, Mrs. Nubbles, Miss La Creevy and Mrs. Jarley in their own eccentric ways, and Mrs. Rudge. Nancy's attempts to help Oliver are a response to the womanly qualities in her that have so long been abused; her loyalty to Bill Sikes is a further index of womanly devotion, and psychologically realistic to boot. In *The Old Curiosity Shop* the small servant is brought out of the cellar in which the termagant Sally Brass had confined her to become the nurse, and eventually the wife, of Dick Swiveller. The benefactor of Oliver Twist, Mr. Brownlow, keeps a housekeeper to fulfill the womanly functions of his home, and the good Mr. Garland of *The Old Curiosity Shop* has a wife. In *Nickleby* the corresponding figures themselves encompass feminine values: the importance of food and nurture explains why the Cheerybles and even their clerk Tim Linkinwater are so emphatically fat, for they embody the comforts of softness, good will, and abundance.

My effort with these novels has been to describe the early

manifestations of rigidity and torpor and to note the occasions of apparently deliberate satire. It is evident that in these works satiric tone and what I define as Dickens's satiric vision frequently do not coincide. Also, as almost everyone notices, Dickens is far more skilled in presenting characters for us to despise than for us to admire. The first difficulty diminishes with the progress of the later novels, as Dickens gradually finds an effective voice to announce the darkness. The second, illustrating incidentally how much more comfortable the satiric mode was for Dickens, is not really defensible in itself; yet it too is less apparent in the later novels, when Dickens has little sunshine to present.

CHAPTER 4

Martin Chuzzlewit

G. K. Chesterton pronounced the American excursion in *Martin Chuzzlewit* "a good satire embedded in an indifferent novel."[1] In many ways the novel harks back to *Nicholas Nickleby* and the earliest works. Its story is virtually the same as that of *Nickleby* and *Oliver Twist:* a young man, through misfortune or misunderstanding deprived of the social position and material comfort rightfully his, undergoes a series of trials that prove his good character, and at the end he is granted his proper reward. There are developments, of course. Martin, unlike Oliver or Nicholas, is not perfect from the start; he has much to learn before he can even be called good. The trials he suffers are consequently not only trouble and pain but an educative process. The benefits denied him are withheld not by a self-seeking enemy (Monks and Fagin or Ralph Nickleby) but by a wiser man who sees that Martin must grow up to become worthy of them. Just as Old Martin is always in ultimate control (it is very soon evident that his weakness is a disguise), the impotence of the opposing character, Pecksniff, is apparent to the reader almost from the beginning. The story thus diminishes whatever tensions there were in the fortunes of Oliver or Nicholas, turning attention more fully to character and the exposition of vice. The brilliance of its characters, Pecksniff and Mrs. Gamp in particular but all the minor satirized figures as well, is the triumph of the novel that, the plot notwithstanding, renders it better than "indifferent." The English part of the book is steeped in satire that soon becomes its central interest, and the American journey forms a continuous development of the same satiric preoccupation. This thematic concern itself gives

1. *Charles Dickens*, ed. Marcus, p. 147.

the novel a new coherence; the consciousness of its application is attested by Forster in his statement that Dickens considered the novel a treatment of selfishness.[2] *Martin Chuzzlewit,* taken as a whole, is Dickens's most thoroughly satirical novel thus far. While the English story is embellished with the romance of Young Martin and Mary Graham, the sentimental pathos of Tom and Ruth Pinch, and the melodrama of murderous Jonas Chuzzlewit, the American segment is as close to pure satire as Dickens ever comes and has indeed always claimed consideration in that genre.

The satire of this book has a vigor new to Dickens's work, especially with respect to the two novels that preceded it. It is signaled in the tone of the opening paragraph:

> As no lady or gentleman, with any claims to polite breeding, can possibly sympathise with the Chuzzlewit Family without being first assured of the extreme antiquity of the race, it is a great satisfaction to know that it undoubtedly descended in a direct line from Adam and Eve; and was, in the earliest times, closely connected with the agricultural interest. If it should ever be urged by grudging and malicious persons, that a Chuzzlewit, in any period of the family history, displayed an overweening amount of family pride, surely the weakness will be considered not only pardonable but laudable, when the immense superiority of the house to the rest of mankind, in respect of this its ancient origin, is taken into account.

The concluding paragraph of this chapter begins:

> This history having, to its own perfect satisfaction, (and, consequently, to the full contentment of all its readers,) proved the Chuzzlewits to have had an origin, and to have been at one time or other of an importance which cannot fail to render them highly improving and acceptable acquaintance to all right-minded individuals, may now proceed in earnest with its task.

2. Forster, *Life of Dickens,* 2:19.

This tone of facetiousness toward the reader, with its distinctly satiric bias, has hardly been heard since *Pickwick Papers.* It recurs throughout *Martin Chuzzlewit,* yet it is not consistently maintained. The free and extremely diverse mixture of all varieties of Dickens's style makes this book, stylistically as it is chronologically, a middle-period novel: the transition from early to late Dickens is evident in a sort of loose suspension of both modes.

From the early Dickens, there are familiar passages of pathos or sentiment. For instance, in a novel in which all the eligible characters are actively seeking marriage, Tom Pinch is accorded a special celibacy. At the close, the narrator discovers him at his organ:

> Ah Tom, dear Tom, old friend!
> Thy head is prematurely grey, though Time has passed between thee and our old association, Tom. But, in those sounds with which it is thy wont to bear the twilight company, the music of thy heart speaks out: the story of thy life relates itself.
>
> Thy life is tranquil, calm, and happy, Tom. In the soft strain which ever and again comes stealing back upon the ear, the memory of thine old love may find a voice perhaps; but it is a pleasant, softened, whispering memory, like that in which we sometimes hold the dead, and does not pain or grieve thee, God be thanked!

This is the narrator as benevolent preacher, in rhetoric associated primarily with the pathos of Oliver Twist or Little Nell. The tone is maintained to the end of the book, as even the last glimpse of Pecksniff comes through Tom's gentle vision. Not that any reconciliation or reform has made the satirist dispensable: Tom has the closing nine short paragraphs, but the rest of the final chapter is spent in a last turn against Charity Pecksniff. The flight of dear Augustus, sending back a note to express "the anguish with which I now subscribe myself—amid the tempestuous howlings of the—sailors, Unalterably, never yours, Augustus," rather than the concluding summary is in keeping with the tone of the novel as a whole; the abrupt juxtaposition of the two moods is typical.

Martin Chuzzlewit differs from the later satirical novels fundamentally in that it is organized around the exposition of a certain vice rather than toward the projection of an entire society (as in *Bleak House* and the novels that follow it). The looser structure allows for startling contrasts of tone; the thematic impulse, however, often gives them significant relation. The part of *Martin Chuzzlewit* that has worn least well is probably the section on the "particulars of the domestic economy" of Tom and Ruth Pinch, beginning:

> Pleasant little Ruth! Cheerful, tidy, bustling, quiet little Ruth! No doll's house ever yielded greater delight to its young mistress, than little Ruth derived from her glorious dominion over the triangular parlour and the two small bedrooms.
>
> To be Tom's housekeeper. What dignity! Housekeeping, upon the commonest terms, associated itself with elevated responsibilities of all sorts and kinds; but housekeeping for Tom implied the utmost complication of grave trusts and mighty charges. Well might she take the keys out of the little chiffonier which held the tea and sugar; and out of the two little damp cupboards down by the fireplace, where the very black beetles got mouldy, and had the shine taken out of their backs by envious mildew; and jingle them upon a ring before Tom's eyes when he came down to breakfast. [chap. xxxix]

This is but the beginning. The fullness of Dickens's enthusiastic style is only reached a number of paragraphs later with the baking of the beefsteak pudding. But before we dismiss it as simply Victorian sentimentality of the hearth, we might compare this passage from the same novel:

> Truly Mr. Pecksniff is blessed in his children. In one of them, at any rate. The prudent Cherry—staff and scrip, and treasure of her doting father—there she sits, at a little table white as driven snow, before the kitchen fire, making

> up accounts! See the neat maiden, as with pen in hand, and calculating look addressed towards the ceiling, and a bunch of keys within a little basket at her side, she checks the housekeeping expenditure! From flat-iron, dish-cover, and warming-pan; from pot and kettle, face of brass footman, and black-leaded stove; bright glances of approbation wink and glow upon her. The very onions dangling from the beam, mantle and shine like cherubs' cheeks. Something of the influence of these vegetables sinks into Mr. Pecksniff's nature. He weeps. [chap. xx]

The two passages are immediately distinguished from one another by style: one could never mistake Dickens's sarcasm. The qualification of the second sentence in the paragraph quoted above; the archaic "see the neat maiden"; the calculating look such as no Ruth Pinch could ever have, with its implications more of stinginess than economy; the absurd onions which alone can make Mr. Pecksniff honestly weep—all these mark the passage as clearly ironic. In a sense it is an anticipatory parody of the sentimentality upon Ruth Pinch, but a parody that does not devalue its object. Rather, the two passages complement each other in their contribution to the thematic argument of the book. Ruth is the standard by which Cherry is satirized; Cherry shows the falsity and evil in the world that justify exuberance about such innocence as Ruth's.

The series of paragraphs in chapter xxxvi marked by recurrent use of "yoho" have a similar function. Tom is aboard a coach bound for London, and the narrative adopts his point of view:

> Yoho, past hedges, gates and trees; past cottages and barns, and people going home from work. Yoho, past donkey-chaises drawn aside into the ditch, and empty carts with rampant horses, whipped up at a bound upon the little watercourse and held by struggling carters close to the five-barred gate until the coach had passed the narrow turning in the road. Yoho, by churches dropped down by themselves in quiet nooks, with rustic burial-grounds about

> them, where the graves are green, and daisies sleep—for it is evening—on the bosoms of the dead. Yoho, past streams in which the cattle cool their feet and where the rushes grow; past paddock-fences, farms and rick-yards; past last year's stacks, cut slice by slice away, and showing in the waning light like ruined gables, old and brown. Yoho, down the pebbly dip, and through the merry watersplash, and up at a canter to the level road again. Yoho! Yoho!

There is a much longer passage to come, and one's first response might be a longing recollection of DeQuincey. I have quoted at length, however, in order to bring out the essential quality of these paragraphs: the detail is extensive even for Dickens, and it is all directed toward human activity in a benign setting. The preceding two chapters have been occupied with getting Martin and Mark out of Eden and back to England. This burst of joy is not merely Tom's exhilaration atop the coach; it is the beatific vision that contrasts the satiric morass of the swamplands. Even the English burial ground is attractive, for in Eden Mark buried his friends' child under a tree in the middle of nowhere.

One must admit, however, that there is still much in this novel that is unrelatable to any thematic or argumentative concern. This is true both for satiric passages (neither the extravaganza on the Chuzzlewit pedigree nor the sneer at emendators in chapter i seem to go anywhere) and enthusiastic outbursts (for instance, the description of nightfall in Salisbury in chap. ii). We may be able to explain or justify the addresses to Tom as "thou" (beginning in chap. v); it is more difficult to enjoy them.

Yet if one mode of biblical rhetoric renders the innocents pathetic, there is also a more invigorated form directed against their oppressors. There are no children—except perhaps Tom —in *Chuzzlewit,* but the blighters never lack victims. Mr. Pecksniff, for instance, upbraids poor Mrs. Todgers for worshipping "the golden calf of Baal for eighteen shillings a week" in accepting her youngest boarder; the narrator explodes:

> Eighteen shillings a week! Just, more just, thy censure,

> upright Pecksniff! Had it been for the sake of a ribbon, star, or garter; sleeves of lawn, a great man's smile, a seat in parliament, a tap upon the shoulder from a courtly sword; a place, a party, or a thriving life, or eighteen thousand pounds, or even eighteen hundred;—but to worship the golden calf for eighteen shillings a week! Oh pitiful, pitiful! [chap. x]

This example has the saving qualities of the best of such attacks: the biblical tone in the use of "thy" and in the structure of the second sentence is tempered by the sarcasm that follows; the rhetoric is in the service not of pathos or sentiment but of satire, which gives it some bite and strength; the passage is short. But like most such apostrophes, the explanation it carries to the reader is an unnecessary and therefore irritating enforcement of points already conveyed dramatically. True to the inconsistency of style, however, the narrator can on other occasions content himself with flat statement; here the effectiveness, unlike that of the exclamatory manner, has not been sapped by time. Dickens concludes a paragraph describing quite tersely the misery of the dupes in Eden: "Such things are much too common to be widely known or cared for. Smart citizens grow rich, and friendless victims smart and die, and are forgotten. That is all" (chap. xxxiii).

One stylistic device that will become a principal weapon in the later novels shows up brilliantly toward the end of this book, when Pecksniff stations himself as overseer to an interview between Martin and his grandfather, who are as yet unreconciled. Whenever it appears to his advantage, he interjects some remark. The narrator explains that "Mr. Pecksniff did not address himself immediately to any person in saying this, but assuming the position of the Chorus in a Greek Tragedy, delivered his opinion as a commentary on the proceedings" (chap. xliii). At his next interruption, the narrator denotes him "Mr. Pecksniff, as Chorus." Then, less than a page later, he comments that "the Chorus put its hand in its waistcoat, and smiled." Similarly, in *Hard Times* young Tom is called "the whelp," not by the narrator's inspiration but by Harthouse's;

and in *Bleak House* the beadle, through his own hopes, becomes "the active and intelligent." This hilarious reduction is part of the main theme of *Little Dorrit,* with Mrs. General the Varnisher and Mrs. Merdle the Bosom; and in *Our Mutual Friend* we have Reginald Wilfer as Cherub, the butler as Analytical Chemist, and Mrs. Veneering as a rocking horse.

Such comic satire informs the more successful parts of *Martin Chuzzlewit* on both continents. The subject is selfishness, and in England the characters who principally embody it are wonderfully hypocritical. This leads to a division of self, seen at its most terrifying in the schizophrenia of Jonas when, hastening home after the murder of Montague Tigg, he begins to feel strange sensations for the dummy he left in his bedroom (chap. xlvii); the division is most hilarious and unsympathetic in Sarah Gamp's creation of Mrs. Harris, the ego who praises the Mrs. Gamp–ego so that the latter can safely affect modesty. Between the two stands Pecksniff, the complete impostor, who achieves a partial (as Jonas suffered a total) separation from his own body. In conversation with Mrs. Lupin, we see him "warming his back (as he had warmed his hands) as if it were a widow's back, or an orphan's back, or an enemy's back, or a back that any less excellent man would have suffered to be cold" (chap. iii). Pecksniff can work this attitude to his own glorification, as Harold Skimpole in *Bleak House* will work it to his own unaccountability, but for Mr. Merdle in *Little Dorrit* it will create extreme discomfort, causing him to take himself into custody by his own wrists. The assortment of later characters who show peculiar relation to their gloves (Vholes in *Bleak House,* Mrs. Sparsit and her mittens in *Hard Times,* Mrs. General in *Little Dorrit,* a variation in Mrs. Joe and her apron in *Great Expectations,* and Mrs. Wilfer in *Our Mutual Friend)* seem to have reached similar dissociation.

On the English side, at least for the Chuzzlewit relations, the gauge of selfishness is greed. In this regard Old Martin serves as the satirist's agent, his gold as the talisman. He explains to Pecksniff:

> "To what man or woman; to what worthy, honest, incorruptible creature; shall I confide such a talisman, either now or when I die. Do you know any such person? *Your* virtues are of course inestimable, but can you tell me of any other living creature who will bear the test of contact with myself?"
>
> "Of contact with yourself, sir?" echoed Mr. Pecksniff.
>
> "Aye," returned the old man, "the test of contact with me—with me. . . . The curse of my existence, and the realisation of my own mad desire, is that by the golden standard which I bear about me, I am doomed to try the metal of all other men, and find it false and hollow." [chap. iii]

Old Martin's cynicism, though an excessive reaction he must outgrow, is unfortunately well founded. Greed is also the primary motivation for Mrs. Gamp and Mr. Mould. And the greed of Montague Tigg, after he has dropped his unprofitable friendship with Chevy Slime, leads him to form the Anglo-Bengalee Disinterested Loan and Life Assurance Company. In the company's interest, three initiating figures—David Crimple, Mrs. Todger's boy Bailey, and Tigg himself—all change their names, acquiring new identities hardly more hollow than their old ones.

Mrs. Gamp shares with Pecksniff the position of chief satiric villain—she may even be, in a sense, his female counterpart. She is also the most fully developed of the masculine anti-women visible in all Dickens's novels. Like Mrs. Thingummy in *Oliver Twist,* Sairey is a nurse with a decided taste for putting a bottle to her lips whenever "so dispoged." Her experience with death has made her as comfortable with it as with life: "Like most persons who have attained to great eminence in their profession, she took to hers very kindly; insomuch that, setting aside her natural predilections as a woman, she went to a lying-in or a laying-out with equal zest and relish" (chap. xix). The only natural predilections that appear, however, are for food, drink, money, and personal praise, and these need not be set aside. The last is amply supplied by the fictitious Mrs. Harris, Sairey's substitute for a friend. Mrs. Gamp is a walking travesty of the Christian virtues, as her garbled religious phrases suggest ("this Piljian's Projiss of a mortal wale"). The consolation she derives from knowledge that "rich folks may ride on camels, but it ain't so easy for 'em to see out of a needle's eye" (chap. xxv) is a triumph of comic confusion. The value of womanhood is the human instinct to give of oneself; Mrs. Gamp, central to this fable of selfishness, takes continually and undiscriminatingly. Her association with Mr. Mould the undertaker is a union of perfect reciprocity, as each, thriving upon mortality, assists the support of the other.

The attitude toward femininity in the novel remains consistent. Mrs. Prig is disturbingly masculine; she "was of the Gamp build, but not so fat, and her voice was deeper and more like a man's. She had also a beard" (chap. xxv). The American ladies at Pawkins's boardinghouse and in Watertoast are scorned for their unwomanly pursuits. Mrs. Lupin, in contrast, is surrounded by the atmosphere of the Blue Dragon's warmth and plenty, and Ruth Pinch reaches her glory with a beefsteak pudding. Ruth's marriage is furiously opposed, the narrator imagines, by a termagant of a laundress named only Fiery-face. And Mrs. Todgers is rescued from the satiric mold in which she flattered and encouraged Mr. Pecksniff by a triumph of feminine nature:

> Commercial gentlemen and gravy had tried Mrs. Todger's temper; the main chance . . . had taken a firm hold on Mrs. Todgers' attention. But in some odd nook in Mrs. Todgers' breast, up a great many steps and in a corner easy to be overlooked, there was a secret door, with "Woman" written on the spring, which at a touch from Mercy's hand, had flown wide open and admitted her for shelter. [chap. xxxvii]

Allied to this is the nonmasculinity of Tom Pinch. As Tom rides to Salisbury, even the "sparkling eyes and snowy breasts" greet him happily: "They were all merry: They all laughed. And some of the wickedest among them even kissed their hands as Tom looked back. For who minded Mr. Pinch? There was no harm in *him*" (chap. v). They are right, and without any criticism of Tom. In a sense, his celibacy is inevitable, but it carries nothing of the distastefulness of asexuality. Tom's femininity is not epicene: it is the feminine as instinctually gentle, kind, and generous, as the obverse of the masculine woman. One might also compare the unpleasant braggadocio that constitutes American virility.

A brief comparison with *American Notes* will point up the extent to which the American part of *Martin Chuzzlewit* is deliberately satiric, determined primarily to anatomize the national follies as no native Juvenal or Swift would dare. *American Notes,* written earlier than *Martin Chuzzlewit* and therefore, one might expect, more likely to reflect the disappointment and exhaustion Dickens felt toward the end of his first visit to the United States, is actually more careful to balance criticism with praise. In the early descriptions of social institutions, much space is devoted to unqualified admiration, and later criticism is frequently tempered with reminders and acknowledgments of what is still good in American character and society. The one question upon which Dickens pours forth unmitigated denunciation is Negro slavery (this was still almost twenty years before the Civil War). As the book is a personal account by an immensely popular author, there are ample opportunities for him to record instances of special kindness and encounters with great men whose worth is acclaimed without reservation; secondary faults such as the habit of spitting can be described with humor. In all these respects, *Martin Chuzzlewit* is more stringent.

The form of the American satire is highly conventional: the traveler from abroad, innocent by his ignorance, learns more and more to the discredit of the land he is visiting. On his first evening in New York, Martin joins in the conversation of some gentlemen who have gathered to dine at Major Pawkins's boardinghouse. The sentence that describes his own contribution has a clearly eighteenth-century tone generally used by Dickens only in formal moments: "Once or twice, when there was a pause, Martin asked such questions as naturally occurred to him, being a stranger, about the national poets, the theatre, literature, and the arts" (chap. xvi). Martin's role in America as the satirist's agent, something like his grandfather's role in England, is here defined. Its aim is made unmistakable a few pages later in the kindly acquaintance's warning (quoted above, p. 3) about the possibilities for acceptable satire in the United States.[3] Dickens may have learned from Swift the advantage of putting his agent into ironic perspective. The separation between America and England assists this double focus: Martin may be a satirical observer in America, but in England he was an object of satire. The faults he exhibits as a satiric butt are the same as those he recognizes in the Americans. When Martin realizes his own selfishness, however, it is because he has learned not from the analogous vices of the Americans but from the selflessness of Mark Tapley, a quality which would have been just as noble in England or on an Arabian desert. The satire and the bildungsroman are not so inevitably welded together.

In the progress of his journey, Martin encounters a variety of people and adventures; the more he learns, the worse things look. The primary emotion for Martin, as it was in real life for Dickens, is disappointment. The United States had been a land of hope and promise, a chance for society to build a better world through the lessons of past mistakes. Freedom from the past did not bring these benefits; rather, it worked only negatively, manifest in the lack of good manners and ceremony which Dickens interpreted as absence of tradition or "civilization." The first shock, that of disregard for privacy, Martin receives even before he has landed. Newsboys hasten on board ship to cry out the names of their papers: the *New York Sewer,* the *New York Stabber,* the *New York Family Spy,* the *New York Private Listener,* the *New York Peeper,* the *New York Plunderer,* the

3. The final irony of the close of his warning, that "where a native writer has ventured on the most harmless and good-humoured illustrations of our vices and defects, it has been found necessary to announce that in a second edition the passage has been expunged, or altered, or explained away, or patched into praise," came in the explanatory and apologetic postscript that in 1868 Dickens asked be added to all future editions of both his American works.

New York Keyhole Reporter, and the *New York Rowdy Journal*. The ludicrously self-betraying expressiveness of these names is an index of the nonrealistic, emblematic nature of the further satiric objects to be presented. The people, the assemblies, the institutions will all be shown in similarly definite perspective. This is not a satirically biased travel book as *American Notes* was; it is moral, and perhaps also social, parable.

The trip to Eden is almost an inverted parody of the perpetual story of a search for an earthly paradise. Its name is an overtly ironic epitome of all America was meant to be. Although the journey from New York is far more to the south than west, there is a vague impression that Martin and Mark are traveling toward the center. The difficulties and discomforts, the passage along a strange river, have overtones—again ironic— of legend. The climax, which completes the subversion, is the discovery of Eden: a garden of primitive swamp where nothing grows and the air is fatally pestilent. Here another mythic line seems to emerge: the final purgation of the Christian hero, of whom Martin is ultimately a sort of middle-class nineteenth-century version. Martin sets out for an external Eden but gains instead an understanding of the paradise within. In his last resolve not even to announce his reformation, "there was not a jot of pride . . . nothing but humility and steadfastness—the best armour he could wear. So low had Eden brought him down. So high had Eden raised him up" (chap. xxxiii).

The trouble with Martin, with the Americans, and with the principal satiric monsters of the English story is basically, as Dickens told Forster, selfishness. Hence the American section is definitely a part of the satiric vision of the whole novel and should be treated as such. The consequence of selfishness is isolation, which undermines all vital relationships. The marriage of Mercy Pecksniff and Jonas, for example, is a mockery of union; Mrs. Gamp's only knowledge of friendship is with a figment of her own narrow brain in whose name she renounces her one real acquaintance, the hardly more admirable Mrs. Prig; the self-absorption of all those around him drives poor Chuffey into the isolation of near imbecility. Isolation on a national scale is insularity, in this novel a dominant trait in the

United States. (In *Little Dorrit,* with the attitude of the inhabitants of Bleeding Heart Yard toward Mr. Baptist, and in *Our Mutual Friend,* in the opinions of Mr. Podsnap on whatever is un-English, Dickens will accuse Britain of the same fault.) From the outside, insularity appears as provincialism, narrow and rigid. One who reads *American Notes* today might be amused at Dickens's own displays of insularity, chiefly in an occasional tendency to measure everything by British standards and then to take a dislike to something mostly because it is unfamiliar. Martin and Mark, however, are kept free from such irony by the narrator; their views of America are offered as perfectly clearsighted.

The perpetual boasting of the Americans arises from their provincial ignorance. The greatest moment comes with the insistence of General Choke and his fellow railway travelers that the Queen of England resides in the Tower of London—Martin and Mark being woefully misinformed upon the matter—and therefore must read the *Watertoast Gazette* regularly, which is sent to her there "per mail" (chap. xxi). What is simultaneously very funny and very appalling is that this, like other such assertions, is not an instance of deceit: Pecksniff, Gamp, and the other English butts are canting liars, but these Americans really believe in their own cant, though they can be hypocrites too. As these characters are seen more as a group than as a variety of individuals, they tend to participate in vices that are national characteristics rather than to possess highly eccentric natures like Pecksniff or Mrs. Gamp. Aside from the outright lies of the swindlers, the hypocrisy of America is on two principal issues: aristocracy and Negro slavery. When the Civil War came, Dickens refused to believe that the North was fighting upon any but economic grounds, and here he shows the Northerners to have no more honest respect for the Negro than the Southerners. Similarly, he depicts their disregard for aristocracy as far more loudly proclaimed than deeply felt.

The great failure of America, however, is self-created constriction. The liberty people constantly boast about simply is not there, for the twin tyrannies of public opinion and anarchy have become absolute. Bound by proprieties and conventions without grace, they have compounded the barbarousness of this lack of tradition with utter material self-enslavement. "All their cares, hopes, joys, affections, virtues, and associations, seemed to be melted down into dollars" (chap. xvi). Life, which should have expanded in the boundless freedom and space of the new world, instead has shrunk. The great American eagle, bird of fantastic soaring flight, has broken down into a menagerie of lesser fowl. Mark Tapley would draw it " 'like a Bat, for its short-sightedness; like a Bantam, for its bragging; like a Magpie, for its honesty; like a Peacock, for its vanity; like a Ostrich, for its putting its head in the mud, and thinking nobody sees it' " (chap. xxxiv). Martin's hope that it might also have the phoenix's power of springing up from the ashes of its vices to soar anew is never realized.

Despite its thematic continuity and high degree of satiric anatomizing, *Martin Chuzzlewit* distinctly lacks the kind of satiric vision that will permeate the later novels. The dramatic and satiric characters exist more in parallel than in conflict. Even as Pecksniff is throwing some blight upon the lives of young Martin and Tom Pinch, we know that old Martin is righting them. Characters like John Westlock and Ruth Pinch are never in any real danger. The novel moves through local intrigues and diversions rather than centering upon one major contest. Furthermore, as I mentioned above—and here I think lies the essential difference—the novel is organized about the anatomizing of one vice rather than the reflection of a world. Hence character, not society or institution, is still paramount. Pecksniff is the central figure of the satire (though not of the melodrama or bildungsroman); this satiric figure will be the relatively minor Rev. Chadband in *Bleak House* and Podsnap in *Our Mutual Friend*. There is little sense of place in the sections on America: the land is its people. We can illustrate this further by noting two descriptions of London in *Martin Chuzzlewit*. The first comes with the arrival there of the Pecksniff family:

> At length they began to jolt and rumble over horribly uneven stones, and Mr. Pecksniff looking out of window said it was tomorrow morning, and they were there.

> Very soon afterwards the coach stopped at the office in the city, and the street in which it was situated was already in a bustle that fully bore out Mr. Pecksniff's words about its being morning, though for any signs of day yet appearing in the sky it might have been midnight. There was a dense fog too, as if it were a city in the clouds which they had been travelling to all night up a magic beanstalk, and there was a thick crust upon the pavement like oilcake, which one of the outsides (mad, no doubt) said to another (his keeper, of course), was snow. [chap. viii]

The picture is comic but ugly; the fairy lore is ironic. The second description is for Tom's arrival:

> Two stages, and the country-roads are almost changed to a continuous street. Yoho, past market-gardens, rows of houses, villas, crescents, terraces, and squares; past waggons, coaches, carts; past early workmen, late stragglers, drunken men, and sober carriers of loads; past brick and mortar in its every shape; and in among the rattling pavements, where a jaunty-seat upon a coach is not so easy to preserve! Yoho, down countless turnings and through countless mazy ways, until an old inn-yard is gained, and Tom Pinch getting down, quite stunned and giddy, is in London! [chap. xxxvi]

London changes to suit the characters who visit it. In *Bleak House* there will be fog and mud, even for Esther, and nothing charming about the maze.

This separation between the novelistic and satiric elements of the book allows the novel to have its happy ending, reward and marriage for those who deserve it and punishment for those who do not, without putting down the principal satiric villains. The criminals lose their lives, but though Pecksniff and Sarah Gamp are exposed and berated, they remain unregenerate. Pecksniff goes on plaguing Tom Pinch into old age, and America is left to maintain its disappointing ways. In this degree the satire is unmitigated—and very good.

CHAPTER 5

Dombey and Son

Dombey and Son contains as little satire, if we speak in terms of tone and treatment, as any of Dickens's novels. In thematic concerns it stands as firmly between the early and the dark novels as does *Martin Chuzzlewit*. One might say that *Chuzzlewit* has the satiric attitudes, *Dombey* the gloom. In *Dombey,* Dickens develops to its fullest the vision of rigidity as the repudiation of womanly values, but he still sees this denaturing as individual sin and not yet as social malaise. *Dombey* is as long as any of the later novels, and indeed much longer than *Hard Times,* but, unlike *Bleak House* or *Little Dorrit* or *Our Mutual Friend,* its space is occupied less with the kinds of mirroring that determine the scope of those later books and more with the comic, Whittingtonian tale of Walter Gay. The novel has no outreaching symbol like Chancery or the Marshalsea, no paradigmatic place like Coketown or the London waterfront. Mr. Dombey is deeply absorbed with his business, but that business really has no world: it resides in the breast of Dombey. The indictment of mercantilism in the novel is only tentative, and that of technology and industrialism even more so. The ambivalence toward the railroad is an index of this hesitancy. The train may be "a type of the triumphant monster, Death," but the very paragraphs that exclaim upon it as such are filled with breathless excitement (chap. xx), and the one victim we see deserves no better fate. It may be an earthquake that has turned Staggs's Gardens into a jumble typical of the chaotic scene of satire (cf. chap. 1 above, pp. 7–9, and chap. vi of the novel), but it also may only be revealing an old and ugly truth:

> Everything around is blackened. There are dark pools of water, muddy lanes, and miserable habitations far below.

> There are jagged walls and falling houses close at hand, and through the battered roofs and broken windows, wretched rooms are seen, where want and fever hide themselves in many wretched shapes, while smoke and crowded gables, and distorted chimneys, and deformity of brick and mortar penning up deformity of mind and body, choke the murky distance. As Mr. Dombey looks out of his carriage window, it is never in his thoughts that the monster who has brought him there has let the light of day in on these things: not made or caused them. [chap. xx]

The implication is that this thought is right, that the railroad itself is not culpable. The blame then is reflected back to Dombey; the railroad has in fact done very well by Mr. Toodle, who is almost its vindication. Thus the novel turns away from the goals and methods of society for its objects and back to isolatable characters and occasional institutions. But these formulations are no longer adequate: they cannot contain the intensity of vision Dickens has to express. The result is a narrative that never quite bears out the ominous sense about it and that is consequently often cumbersome. In the growth of Dickens's satire, however, the fault itself is interesting.

In many aspects, *Dombey and Son* seems to be trying out types and configurations that will be developed more fully in later novels. The relation of the child Florence to her father contains much that will become explicit between Sissy Jupe and Mr. Gradgrind. Dombey's house in London is very like the Dedlock London mansion or the Merdle house; the difference is mainly —and significantly—that the last two are parts of whole streets, whereas the gloom of Dombey's house makes it stand out among its neighbors. Sir Barnett Skettles seems a sketch for elements in both Sir Leicester Dedlock and Mr. Veneering. The amiable Toots's "Silent tomb" is the beginning of Guppy's more extensive and ultimately repulsive jargon *(Bleak House),* Young John's comic pathos *(Little Dorrit),* and Mr. Venus's gruesome lamentations in *Our Mutual Friend.* The proud Edith becomes a woman in her love for Florence much as Lady Dedlock will be touched by Rosa. In the relish of power that marks Carker's confrontation with Edith in chap. xlv, in his whole bearing toward her, Carker seems a less sophisticated version (the serpent imagery is blatant) of Tulkinghorn trapping Lady Dedlock. Finally, Susan Nipper has characteristics that Dickens later uses to make Jenny Wren a satirist: black-eyed, nipping, and with a certain vinegar of her own especially apparent at the beginning, she is a gentle soul of very sharp exterior. At least until the final chapters, Susan's love for Florence never gets maudlin; in fact, she is at first so disciplined that we are not quite sure whether she be ogre or angel. The question is soon resolved by her animosity toward Mrs. Chick and Miss Tox, which will continue in instant hostility toward Mrs. Pipchin and Mrs. MacStinger. The emotion, like satiric anger, demands release:

> There was anything but solitude in the nursery; for there, Mrs. Chick and Miss Tox were enjoying a social evening, so much to the disgust of Miss Susan Nipper that that young lady embraced every opportunity of making wry faces behind the door. Her feelings were so much excited on the occasion that she found it indispensable to afford them this relief, even without having the comfort of any audience or sympathy whatever. As the knight-errants of old relieved their minds by carving their mistress' names in deserts, and wilderness, and other savage places where there was no probability of there ever being anybody to read them, so did Miss Nipper curl her snub nose into drawers and wardrobes, put away winks of disparagement in cupboards, shed derisive squints into stone pitchers, and contradict and call names out in the passage. [chap. v]

Polly enunciates the point a few paragraphs later when she soothes the Nipper: "You're angry because you're a good little thing." It is Susan who is compelled to tell Mr. Dombey the truth, though the consequence be banishment—but the effect of this upon the reader is already mitigated by the process of sentimentalization that at the end will overtake Susan and everyone else in the novel.

Most of *Dombey's* secondary characters are still largely comic even when satirized. Even Major Bagstock, perhaps the ugliest force in the book just because he is more convincing than Carker, seems to be conceived in a sense of comedy that will barely survive in his successor, Silas Wegg. Dickens described his intentions to Hablôt Browne in March 1847: "I want to make the Major, who is the incarnation of selfishness and small revenge, a kind of comic Mephistophelean power in the book" (*Letters,* II, 17). The phrase "comic Mephistophelean" embraces this duality, which Dickens emphasizes again in his instructions for the illustration of Dombey's first meeting with Edith to include the Major's "apoplectico-mephistophelean observation of the scene" (*Letters,* II, 18). The novel itself calls him an "overfed Mephistopheles" (chap. xx).

Other characters, like their predecessors in earlier novels, are satirized in attitudes of rigidity and antivitalism. There is the marvelously automatic Miss Tox, the now familiar termagant Mrs. MacStinger, and the mannequin Mrs. Skewton. Mrs. Skewton abets the novel's tendency to embrace modernity insofar as she expresses Dickens's disgust with any glorification of the "good old times." The good old times were brutal, and Mrs. Skewton exalts them in a gush of "poetic" sensibility to be equalled only by Mr. Skimpole in *Bleak House:*

> "Those darling bygone times, Mr. Carker," said Cleopatra, "with their delicious fortresses, and their dear old dungeons, and their delightful places of torture, and their romantic vengeances, and their picturesque assaults and sieges, and everything that makes life truly charming! How dreadfully we have degenerated!" [chap. xxvii]

Skimpole, though, will be a good deal more convincing. Mrs. Skewton has retained this "Cleopatra" attitude for fifty years (chap. xxi): her rigidity, unlike Miss Tox's, is utterly self-regarding and self-imposed, and so whereas Miss Tox is finally sheltered under the sentimental umbrella, Mrs. Skewton leaves the novel earlier and unforgiven. Her perpetual youth is balanced in the more somber part of the book by Paul's premature old age; it is a persistent enactment of an unconscious but nonetheless savage mockery of life. She anticipates Mrs. Merdle in her Arcadian longings but ends in the perfect metaphor for death-in-life: a paralytic seizure.

Mrs. Skewton's false exterior is meant to appear real; Carker's teeth, by his dissociation of self particularly marked in a deceitful smile, have become an apparently separable item of his body. Nobody knows this better than his unhappy follower, Rob Toodle: " 'Will you hold your tongue, Misses Brown?' interrupted the miserable Grinder, glancing quickly round, as though he expected to see his master's teeth shining at his elbow" (chap. xlvi).

The cant of religion receives passing attention in this novel in the Reverend Melchisedech Howler and the "ranting persuasion" to which, not surprisingly, Mrs. MacStinger adheres loyally. The real exposé is of the cant of education. The name Charitable Grinders alone anticipates the Gradgrind academy in *Hard Times,* and like the later school it produces cowardly criminals. The Blimber establishment fares a bit better, but it is still attacked in what Philip Collins considers naïve anti-intellectualism.[1] Distinctions must be made, however, between Dickens's belief in the value of education on the one hand and his satire upon pedantry (intellectual rigidity) and exclusive intellectualism on the other, and between both these and his satire upon misdirected schools. Collins himself admits that in *David Copperfield* intellectual life is taken seriously and that its educated hero is both happy for it and sympathetic to us. As to the schools, Dickens's satire is a virulent and—as satire must be—exaggerated attack on the Benthamite inclination of educa-

1. Philip Collins, *Dickens and Education* (London, 1963), p. 193: "The anti-scientific and anti-rational tendency of the Romantics, which leads to such rubbish as Blake's attacks on Newton, Wordsworth's picture of the botanist collecting specimens from his mother's grave, and Keats's distress at the prismatic explanation of the rainbow, recurs with a similar naiveté in Dickens. But he is besides a significant figure in the covert alliance between Romantic anti-rationalism and Victorian Philistine anti-intellectualism."

tional authorities of the time.[2] The Benthamite theory enshrined all the tendencies to systemization, uniformity, and mechanization of the individual that Dickens's satire denounced. The hard, debased utilitarianism that became the focus of attack in *Hard Times* symbolized a potent force of antivitalism and thus was allied in the later novels with other forces of necrosis threatening the life of society. The intellectualism that denies the validity of poetic knowledge is like the blind faith in technology that elevates the mechanical above the human. In *Dombey and Son,* the machinery of the Charitable Grinders (epitomized in the outlandish uniforms imposed on the boys), the forcing of the Blimber academy (in the extended image of a hothouse in chapter xi expressly contrasted to natural growth), and the masculine Mrs. Pipchin are aspects of a world in which the concerns of business are driving out the natural human values of love and warmth. The Blimbers are rendered in varying degrees of mockery, from the misguided Doctor, through his daughter, Cornelia—short-haired, spectacled, and digging "like a ghoul" in the graves of dead languages—and the fatuous Mrs. Blimber, to the rather pathetic human barrel organ, Mr. Feeder, B. A. They turn boys into "rigid and absorbed young anchorites" (chap. xiv).

Most important to the concerns of this study, however, are the major characters and the plot that involves them. The

2. In this regard Collins does finally praise Dickens, though still with reservation: "Dickens was wise and useful, then, in protesting against educational schemes which neglected the imagination and which ignored the child's need to develop at a natural pace in an atmosphere of affectionate encouragement and happiness. . . . Perhaps on balance it was better that his strength lay where it did; the educational reformers and administrators were more Benthamite than Coleridgean, and the part of truth which he had to offer was therefore the more valuable, as a corrective" (Ibid., p. 199). Cf. Robert A. Donovan, "Structure and Idea in *Bleak House,*" *English Literary History* 29 (1962): 175–201, who writes that Dickens's "anti-intellectualism, if I may give it a currently fashionable name, is a kind of instinctive response to any attempt to stifle or destroy the irrational part of man's nature, hence Dickens' affectionate regard for the weak-minded and the prominent symbolic role given to the non-rational entertainments of Sleary's Circus in *Hard Times* (the logical culmination of a series, beginning with Mr. Vincent Crummles and Mrs. Jarley)" (p. 176).

theme, clearly, is the flight from woman. The novel opens with a dying mother clutching her disregarded daughter. The father cares only for sons and more for Dombey and Son as a business firm and idea than for Paul Dombey and his son. Polly Toodles, a truly hopeful substitute, is brought in and immediately deprived of dignity, selfhood, and sex by being given the name of Richards. When she nonetheless betrays her womanliness in yielding to the search for Rob, she is expelled from the house. Her replacement is the despondent Mrs. Wickam, who is followed by the absolute termagant Mrs. Pipchin. The introductory description of that lady develops, in a mixed aura of morality and fairy tale, all the salient characteristics of her type:

> This celebrated Mrs. Pipchin was a marvellous ill-favoured, ill-conditioned old lady, of a stooping figure, with a mottled face, like bad marble, a hook nose, and a hard grey eye, that looked as if it might have been hammered at on an anvil without sustaining any injury. Forty years at least had elapsed since the Peruvian mines had been the death of Mr. Pipchin; but his relict still wore black bombazeen, of such a lustreless, deep, dead, sombre shade, that gas itself couldn't light her up after dark, and her presence was a quencher to any number of candles. She was generally spoken of as "a great manager" of children; and the secret of her management was, to give them everything that they didn't like, and nothing that they did—which was found to sweeten their dispositions very much. She was such a bitter old lady, that one was tempted to believe there had been some mistake in the application of the Peruvian machinery, and that all her waters of gladness and milk of human kindness, had been pumped out dry, instead of the mines.
>
> The Castle of this ogress and child-queller was in a steep by-street at Brighton . . . [chap. viii]

In all respects, she is antimaternal. She maintains human relations with no one, even in imagination. After submitting his children to her, Mr. Dombey gives her his wife's place as housekeeper.

Allied to Mr. Dombey's neglect of his daughter is the exploitation of their daughters by Mrs. Skewton and Good Mrs. Brown. Here Dickens explores the cultivation of external womanly qualities for perverted ends. Dickens's novels had presented prostitutes before, but they were all portrayed as simply wayward or misled, never linked in essence with any phenomena of necrosis, even the termagant women. Edith, however, is exactly the kind of woman a man like Mr. Dombey would seek as consolation—a female version of himself—after freezing out the life of his first wife and his only son. Unlike the termagants, Edith and Alice represent a hardening that has nothing masculine about it: the profanation and devitalization of sexuality. With both, ultimate culpability passes to their mothers. This deflection allows us to glimpse in the daughters a repressed but fervent womanhood and so to understand this version of denatured woman not merely as an absence of good—something bad or worthless like Mrs. Pipchin or Mrs. Chick—but as a loss of good—something good willfully made bad. Yet the point remains that, in the frigid world of Dombey or Carker, sex can only be a matter of finance or convenience. It is this contingency, forgotten by Carker, that enables Edith at last to triumph over him. It is also what makes the sight of Florence, no longer a child but a woman, so striking, then so distasteful, and finally so haunting to Mr. Dombey when he comes home from Bath: he has never seen a woman before. The struggle between Dombey and Florence ultimately becomes the center of the novel until, at the end, as Miss Tox remarks, Dombey and Son becomes a daughter after all. The bright picture at the close is of a total feminization brought about through the flexibility of change ranging from Mr. Dombey's radical conversion to Toots's happy adaptation. The minor subplot of Mr. Morfin is parabolic: he realizes the relation of habit and routine to paralysis (chap. xxxiii), acts against it, and at last leaves his bachelorhood for Harriet, a generous, nurturing, loving Carker.

Though the line of termagants will continue, *Dombey and Son*'s association of Edith with sex marks an important beginning. In *Hard Times* the inattention to affection in Louisa's marriage will prove, especially in view of the near-success of

James Harthouse, to have been a fatal disregard of physical passion. Miss Wade in *Little Dorrit* will be a very paradigm of frigidity, almost entrapping the confused Tattycoram in the loneliness of her spiritual amputation and in a suggestion, though necessarily faint, of lesbianism. Finally, in *Great Expectations,* Estella will display the same beauty, pride, and coldness Edith Dombey had, and to this hauteur Miss Havisham will add the perversity of using the attractive powers of sexuality to degrade men. Thus Dickens will render the loss of womanly values as the rejection or perversion of womanhood in sexual as well as in maternal or romantic terms. Correlatively, his best women in the later novels will have true sexuality. The most remarkable of these is Sissy Jupe, as F. R. Leavis's translation of the horse-riding part of *Hard Times* into Laurentian terms indicates.[3] The dark-eyed, dark-haired girl, allied to the circus whose men and women live in comfortable squalor and are brilliantly free in their bodies, possesses a rich vitality of instinct and emotion opposed to the bloodless mechanics of Gradgrind existence. Her sexuality is never explicit, but it is nonetheless strong in her symbolic associations. In *Our Mutual Friend* the same is true of Lizzie Hexam's association with the river, which runs through the book. The river is an agent of death but also of rebirth, and Lizzie—in her easy relation with this powerful natural force and in her finding life (in her rescue of Eugene) where everyone else in the novel can only find death—comes to embody the strength of life, especially in the aspect of regeneration. Finally, with Helena Landless, Dickens seems to be moving toward a concept of womanhood in a sort of female power new to his work, though somewhat anticipated in Sissy Jupe. Helena is dark, daring, exotic—utterly self-reliant yet feminine as well. She combines goodness of an eerie spiritual sort with a distinct, though never articulated, sexuality.

3. F. R. Leavis, "Analytic Note," *The Great Tradition* (London, 1948).

A Note on *David Copperfield*

David Copperfield, only incidentally satiric and a personal rather than social record, contains a complementary development important for the novels to come. My focus is Dora Spenlow. As a child David saw a world in which the beautiful, womanly qualities of his mother were subverted by Mr. Murdstone and replaced by the harsh and repressive Miss Murdstone. In Dora he saw again his mother's feminine gentleness and love. But Dora, as everyone notes, was a revelation: the golden girl turned out to be but a poor wife, and the hitherto idealized passivity at last became somewhat trying. Clara reveals the weakness of the figure, and Dora adds pettishness. After this the golden girl is never quite the same: Ada Clare is lovely, but helpless against Richard's self-destruction; Pet Meagles's innocence only leads her to an unfortunate marriage; Lucy Manette, it must be admitted, seems something of a throwback, but she is soon compensated for in the apparently golden but inwardly frigid Estella and finally in Sophronia Akershem, an utter fraud; Bella Wilfer is quite unlovable so long as she is intent on that golden role. Instead, there emerges a new type who combines the charm of young womanhood with the practical bent that graces the good mothers. It has its beginnings in Florence Dombey, but Florence remains virtually a child through most of the novel. The true type first appears in Agnes Wickfield, young and pretty but also as practical as Betsey Trotwood and as motherly, we are sure, as Peggotty. Esther Summerson, her successor, points up the moral: after the fever has ruined her looks, her deeper beauty shows through all the more clearly; and Esther, with her jingle of housekeeping keys, is almost too practical to bear. When Caddy Jellyby begins to work out her own salvation, it is to make herself neat rather than pretty and to emulate Esther and repudiate her mother with loving attention to those about her and practical management of a family. In *Little Dorrit* the contrast to the beautiful and good but rather useless Pet is of course Amy, and it is marked in Arthur Clennam's relations to both. In the course of the novel, one gathers that Amy too is pretty, but she is so useful and kind that no one ever notices her appearance as other than pathetic. The antithesis is Fanny Dorrit, all charm and no soul, and the possibility of nemesis is the poor, hilarious Flora Finching.

The concept of womanhood in these last three novels will be considered more closely in the following chapters, as it involves in a variety of ways the total visions of those books. In general, what the novels achieve in this respect is a distinction between extreme femininity and essential womanhood, an understanding that the former is neither the necessary external embodiment of the latter nor even its most desirable coordinate. With this comes a perception of womanliness, not as a set of qualities attached to one of the sexes, but rather as a group of human values to be treasured by both. The full realization of this truth is seen in *Great Expectations.* This novel is in many ways a sterner rewriting of *David Copperfield.* The earlier narrator occasionally held his younger self in a mildly ironic light, but he treated him very tenderly and generously allotted justifying circumstances for his mistakes; the light of irony upon Pip is strict and honest. Furthermore, as the mistaken values and misdirected energy this novel reveals are charged not only to Pip but also to the society that encouraged them in him, it has much wider social implication. The greater fluidity in dealing with problems of value emerges also in the final maturation of the concept of womanliness. In *Copperfield* it was a more or less simple matter of contrast between Dora and Agnes, both—along with their reflections in Clara, Betsey Trotwood, and Peggotty—opposed to the mannish Miss Murdstone. Similarly, in *Great Expectations,* Pip sets up a polarity between Mrs. Joe and Estella, failing until much later in life to recognize that the best woman is Biddy, though plain and without acquired elegance or charm. But from the development in the intervening novels, a new vision arises: there is another character who embodies the womanly values of love and nurture yet is thoroughly virile. When Joe comes to nurse Pip through the crisis of fever, he combines the masculine power of Orlick and the womanly gentleness of Biddy in an androgynous harmony of being that is truly a state of grace.[1]

1. Compare Paul Pickrel on Joe's "poetic view of experience"—usually granted only to women—in "Teaching the Novel: *Great Expectations,*" *Essays on the Teaching of English.* ed. Edward J. Gordon and Edward S. Noyes (New York, 1960), pp. 223–24.

PART III

Forms of Satire

CHAPTER 6

Bleak House

In the foregoing chapters, the novels through *David Copperfield* were considered in regard to special themes, and a limitation to specific interests often only tangential to the whole meaning of a novel was obvious. The following readings are also concerned with special aspects, though these aspects—the mood and tone of satire and the themes of devitalization, mechanization, and devaluation of womanhood—are now central. This change renders the specificity of focus less apparent. I do believe that to treat *Bleak House, Hard Times,* and *Little Dorrit* as Dickensian satire is to grasp the main stem of each, but I am equally aware that many branches will be left untouched.

In a letter of October 1855, Dickens described to Forster an art exhibition he had attended in Paris and the English painting represented (naming such artists as Mulready, Leslie, and Stanfield):

> The general absence of ideas is horribly apparent. . . . It is of no use disguising the fact that what we know to be wanting in the men is wanting in their works—character, fire, purpose, and the power of using the vehicle and the model as mere means to an end. There is a horrid respectability about most of the best of them—a little, finite, systematic routine in them, strangely expressive to me of the state of England itself. . . . There is no end of bad pictures among the French, but Lord! the goodness also!— the fearlessness of them; the bold drawing; the dashing conception; the passion and action in them! Don't think it is a part of my despondency about public affairs, and my fear that our national glory is on the decline, when I say that mere form

> and conventionalities usurp, *in English art, as in English government and social relations,* the place of *living* force and truth. [*Letters,* II, 700; italics mine]

In the last sentence, Dickens wishes to make it clear that his interpretation of English painting is not biased by the despondency he feels about all things British, but the form of the denial itself indicates a connection between the usurpations of conventionality both in art and in social matters. As the italicized phrases show, the phenomena of decline in the two areas are related by a common failure: a little, finite, systematic routine.

The letters mark the mid-fifties as the period when Dickens spoke most gloomily of the political and social future of England.[1] In the novels this mood gains ascendancy somewhat earlier: *Bleak House,* begun in November 1851, is the first novel in which the vision of life losing meaning and energy is pervasive, touching the story at all points, and thus the first that is primarily satiric. In Dickens's earlier novels, interest centers mainly on a normal hero's struggle for success in a normal society, although satirized, absurd characters or society may have a significant place in this struggle.[2] In *Oliver Twist, Martin Chuzzlewit,* and *David Copperfield,* for instance, the objects of satire tend to be the elements opposing the hero; though the satiric figures may remain unregenerate, the hero triumphs over them to find a secure place in a comfortable world. An utterly nonsatiric hero and the ongoing normal society render the satire secondary, and the certainty of the hero's success keeps it comic. The later novels concentrate attention upon the absurd society, making satire their principal mode. In *Bleak House, Hard Times,* and *Little Dorrit,* all of society is absurd. The protagonists do not find a place in it because moral integrity forces

1. See, for example, the letter quoted in chapter 2 above (pp. 28–29), and others quoted by Monroe Engel in his article "The Politics of Dickens' Novels," *PMLA* 71 (1956): 945–74.

2. I am using Frye's terms in defining satire as "irony which is structurally close to the comic: the comic struggle of two societies, one normal and the other absurd" *(Anatomy of Criticism,* p. 224).

them rather to retreat. Normal society exists only as an ideal the characters struggle to realize, and the achievement of it finally appears in a withdrawal from the world about them. The prevalence of absurdity and the threat it poses give a sharp edge to the comedy.

In these novels the contest between the normal and absurd worlds, as it focuses upon one or two principal characters, becomes the plot. This is a clear development beyond the relation mentioned above between heroic and satiric figures in the early novels. The major differences are in the scope and power of rigidity and stagnation. Stylistically, it now becomes possible to see central meaning in Dickens's free conjunctions of incongruous modes. I think it best to let the illustration of this argument, as well as its development from novel to novel, emerge as the works are discussed separately.

The vision of *Bleak House* is satiric to the degree that the condition of thwarted and diminishing vitality is pervasive. That condition is no longer a matter of isolated criminal individuals or unnatural, mannish women, for such characters now appear as the agents or products of a larger phenomenon. In *Dombey and Son* the frigidity of the mercantile world was contained in Mr. Dombey; in *Bleak House,* conversely, Vholes, Tulkinghorn, and the Smallweeds are only versions of a wider breed. The chief social institution of the novel is Chancery, but the reflections of its essential nature indicate that it is less a canker upon a healthy organism than an epitome of widespread disorders. Chancery is, in fact, only a metaphor for society and what is happening to it, and this is where it differs from such institutions as the workhouses attacked in earlier books.

The signal qualities of the world perceived by the satire of *Bleak House* and represented in Chancery are futility and disorder to the point of chaos, with death looming behind. The problem of order is therefore central to the satiric concerns of the novel. The principal agent of chaos is Chancery itself, and its nature is revealed in a variety of ways. Its hopeless confusion of paper and red tape, and the confusion of mind that produces this, are repeated in the clutter of Krook's rag and bottle shop, a concise parody of the court. Its predatoriness is manifested in the individuals who adhere to Chancery—Vholes, Tulkinghorn, and the lesser brood of lawyers; its incomprehension of the simple matters of human life—birth, struggle, and death—in the Lord Chancellor. Its victims are presented in the set figures of Miss Flite and Gridley; the workings of destruction in the breakdown of Richard Carstone.

In addition to Chancery and Krook's shop, a third center of disorder is Mrs. Jellyby's house. In this instance the jumble is of household items:

> But such wonderful things came tumbling out of the closets when they were opened—bits of mouldy pie, sour bottles, Mrs. Jellyby's caps, letters, tea, forks, odd boots and shoes of children, firewood, wafers, saucepan-lids, damp sugar in odds and ends of paper bags, footstools, blacklead brushes, bread, Mrs. Jellyby's bonnets, books with butter sticking to the binding, guttered candle-ends put out by being turned upside down in broken candlesticks, nutshells, heads and tails of shrimps, dinner-mats, gloves, coffee-grounds, umbrellas . . . [chap. xxx]

Mrs. Jellyby's house makes it clear that the opposition is not between order and energy but between order and the enervating confusion of total disorder. Chaos is not an excess of energy run riot but the beginning of paralysis. True energy—that which feeds into life—is swamped in objects that through breaking, disuse, or misuse have become virtually formless. Since the objects have no purpose, their shapes are now absurd, and they are as much material debris as Krook's insane collection. Similarly, the manic activity of Mrs. Jellyby is swamped in correspondence.

Mrs. Jellyby's house is a microcosm of the chaotic world in which Jo is the preeminent representative of lost, degraded humanity:

> It must be a strange state to be like Jo! To shuffle through the streets, unfamiliar with the shapes, and in utter darkness as to the meaning, of those mysterious symbols, so abundant over the shops, and at the corners of streets, and on the doors, and in the windows! To see people read, and to see people write, and to see the postmen deliver letters, and not to have the least idea of all that language—to be, to every scrap of it, stone blind and dumb! It must be very puzzling to see the good company going to the churches on Sundays, with their books in their hands, and to think (for perhaps Jo *does* think, at odd times), what does it all mean, and if it means anything to anybody, how comes it that it means nothing to me? To be hustled, and jostled, and moved on; and really to feel that it would appear to be perfectly true that I have no business, here, or there, or anywhere; and yet to be perplexed by the consideration that I *am* here somehow, too, and everybody overlooked me until I became the creature that I am! [chap. xvi]

Reading and writing are here the emblematic activities of civilized society; it is not merely that Jo is illiterate but that he wanders through an incomprehensible world which recognizes his humanity no more than that of horses, dogs, or cattle.

The individuals who can make some order out of the mess, or even find their way through it, are the repositories of hope for salvation. Thus Inspector Bucket becomes heroic: he has the unparalleled talent to find things and people, to look through the haze and distinguish some sort of trail. Hence the relish of emphasis upon the organization of the police, the prompt and silent response to the flash of a lantern, the brief and efficient conferences, the general air of thinking competence.

But if the system of the police is immensely satisfying, system itself is suspect. System in excess of the requirements of simple efficacy, though the opposite extreme from disorder, leads back through rigidity to chaos. Therefore the system of Chancery and the law, which does not clarify or organize but obfuscates and thwarts all motion, is equally subject to satiric attack. By its very nature it produces an unpardonable removal from human immediacy:

> "There again," said Mr. Gridley, with no diminution of his rage. "The system! I am told, on all hands, it's the system. I mustn't look to individuals. It's the system. I mustn't go into Court. . . . My Lord knows nothing of it. He sits there to administer the system. I mustn't go to Mr Tulkinghorn. . . . *He* is not responsible. It's the system. But, if I do no violence to any of them, here—I may! I don't know what may happen if I am carried beyond myself at last!—I will accuse the individual workers of that system against me, face to face, before the great eternal bar!" [chap. xv]

Such universal abdication from responsibility creates a system too remote to be combated. The struggle of the individual against that system, the vital being against the debilitating machine, is the protest of life against living death. Between chaos and the rigidity of inflexible ordering, a mean of workable flexibility must be struck. The mess of Mrs. Jellyby's house is contrasted not to rigid tidiness (though there is a brief instance of that at Greenleaf, the school where Esther finds refuge after Miss Barbary's death) but to an order that in its organic vitality contains a comfortable diversity and plenitude: the crazy structure of Bleak House with its pleasing irregularity of arrangement and furniture. Ada and Esther find in their rooms a variety of objects almost as incongruous as Mrs. Jellyby's furnishings —but held together by "their perfect neatness" (chap. vi). The "mess" of Bleak House diverts but never defeats its inhabitants, as the jingle of housekeeping keys continually reminds us. Opposed to the confusion of Mrs. Jellyby's house and of the world that confronts Jo, opposed to the false order of Chancery, Bleak House represents the true mean. Esther's keys are its symbol, and it is Esther who joins Inspector Bucket at the end in the chase to save Lady Dedlock.

The false order that in society is preeminently exemplified in Chancery is reflected in the individual as rigidity of character.

Thus the satiric representation of rigid characters that has been evident throughout Dickens's earlier work is here part of the novel's main theme. A variety of characters in *Bleak House* belong to this group. For example, Tulkinghorn and Vholes, as suggested above, are very much branches of Chancery. Vholes's inhumanity makes him a cannibal (chap. xxxix) and a vampire (chap. lx); the key to his understanding, an equation of immoral and unlawful, suggests that his care for three daughters and an aged parent in the Vale of Taunton may be a convenient fabrication of piety. Family relations are beyond the sympathies of these isolated characters. When Mr. Tulkinghorn thinks of family, he thinks of a name rather than a group of people; Mrs. Bayham Badger speaks of her former husbands "as if they were parts of a charade" (chap. xvii); and Mrs. Pardiggle's "mechanical way of taking possession of people" (chap. viii) has alienated her children. Mrs. Jellyby, on the other hand, has simply forgotten her husband and children. Mrs. Snagsby, surrounded by "her own dense atmosphere of dust, arising from the ceaseless working of her mill of jealousy" (chap. liv), has perverted her relationship to her husband and become, in a typically Dickensian extension, "bone of his bone, flesh of his flesh, shadow of his shadow" (chap. xxv).

Other characters as well have ceased to feel life in human terms. Mr. Turveydrop, rigid in an outmoded dandyism and as artificial as Mrs. Skewton, obstructs his son's marriage until he realizes that he can make it serve his own comfort. The outrageously ponderous Mr. Chadband addresses Jo as "my human boy" (chap. xxv), as if to imply that he might conceivably be something else. Mr. Guppy rather pathetically tries to construct a relationship of human love, but he is betrayed from the start by his own hilarious banality. He explains to Esther that his "mother, though highly exasperating to the feelings, is actuated by maternal dictates." When he sees how much fever has changed her looks, he revokes his proposal but hopes "it will ever be a retrospect entwined—er—with friendship's bowers" (chap. xxxviii). His language does not change with his heart; he tells Mr. Weevle that

> "circumstances over which I have no control, have made a melancholy alteration in my most cherished plans, and in that unrequited image which I formerly mentioned to you as a friend. That image is shattered, and that idol is laid low."
>
> "I may repeat that the idol is down. I have no purpose to serve now, but burial in oblivion. To that I have pledged myself. I owe it to myself, and I owe it to the shattered image." [chap. xxxix]

The mixture of legal and sentimental, romantic jargon is perfect.[3] Harold Skimpole, on the other hand, is not trapped in artificial constructs but willfully takes refuge in them, finding "poetry" much more pleasant than life. The landscape, for instance, is not a prospect of living earth; it is a picture and thus can be peopled and given poetry by slaves (chap. xviii). In chapter xxxi the point is demonstrated almost graphically. Jo, in fever, has been put to bed in the loft-room of Bleak House, and Mr. Skimpole, who had insisted that they turn him out and who will soon sell him to Mr. Bucket, entertains the company with some ballads

> about a Peasant boy,
> "Thrown on the wide world, doom'd to wander
> and roam,
> Bereft of his parents, bereft of a home,"

3. In his essay "Satire and Symbolism in *Bleak House,*" *Nineteenth-Century Fiction* 12 (December 1957): 284–303, Louis Crompton describes Guppy as "a legal automaton bedeviled by human emotions which only make him look pathetic and ridiculous" (p. 295). The relation of the whole of Mr. Crompton's discussion to mine is somewhat perplexing. He anticipates, at least with reference to this particular novel, my attention to mechanization and emotional deadness in society, and often he selects as illustrations the same quotations I have chosen. His emphasis, however, seems sufficiently different from mine to warrant another treatment: Mr. Crompton keeps his reading in societal terms (rather than seeing the specific social phenomena as both symptoms and emblems of vital, moral decay) and is less concerned with the problems of satire in a novelistic medium. The discussions seem to me congenial supplements to one another.

> —quite exquisitely. It was a song that always made him cry, he told us.

He responds—perhaps quite honestly—to literary situations, but not to life. Skimpole's childhood is not a perpetuation of innocence and joy but a stoppage of understanding and moral responsibility. He reflects on a private scale what in politics has been the achievement of the Boodles and Buffys, "who have found out the perpetual stoppage" (chap. xii) and managed to blindfold themselves against contemporary realities. The narrator solemnly warns:

> there is perhaps more Dandyism at Chesney Wold than the brilliant and distinguished circle will find good for itself in the long run. For it is, even with the stillest and politest circles, as with the circle the necromancer draws around him—very strange appearances may be seen in active motion outside. With this difference; that, being realities and not phantoms, there is the greater danger of their breaking in. [chap. xii]

Rigidity in character is an ally of false order, opposed to creativity and flexibility. Yet although it effects torpor in society, it may maintain itself with great energy—energy as false as the order it upholds. A qualification to the opposition between energy and torpor that has been apparent throughout Dickens's work emerges with special clarity in *Bleak House*. Energy that is vibrant but unprincipled may have an exhilarating, even intoxicating quality (as does the eruptive violence in *Barnaby Rudge*) or a humorous attractiveness (like Dick Swiveller's), but to be ultimately affirmed its moral direction must be positive. The celebration of pure energy for its own sake is amoral, and Dickens never allows this. Thus, whereas the riots in *Barnaby* are finally condemned, Dick Swiveller is redeemed because his whimsicality leads him to the Marchioness. In *Bleak House* the distinction admits no equivocation: though the menace of Chancery is torpor, the manic energy of characters like Mrs. Jellyby, Mrs. Pardiggle, or the Smallweeds is demonic. The moral direction is as crucial to the value of energy as it was to order and system.

Behind disorder, confusion, and rigidity looms death. This is the extreme of rigidity, and the disordered world, for all its random or manic motion, is a dying one. The motif of death is explicit in *Bleak House*. The first chapter opens with the "death of the sun," and the novel continues to associate Chancery with death.[4] A particularly striking instance is the description of Lincoln's Inn as the "perplexed and troublous valley of the shadow of the law" (chap. xxxii), indicting death-in-life by an ironic allusion to natural death in the soothing knowledge of a living God. The fashionable world too is a "deadened" one (chap. ii). Its London residences reflect rigidity of both pride and obsolescence:

> It is a dull street under the best conditions; where the two long rows of houses stare at each other with that severity, that half-a-dozen of its greatest mansions seem to have been slowly stared into stone, rather than originally built in that material. It is a street of such dismal grandeur, so determined not to condescend to liveliness, that the doors and windows hold a gloomy state of their own in black paint and dust, and the echoing mews behind have a dry and massive appearance, as if they were reserved to stable the stone chargers of noble statues. Complicated garnish or iron-work entwines itself over the flights of steps in this awful street; and, from these petrified bowers, extinguishers for obsolete flambeaux gasp at the upstart gas. Here and

4. The narrator introduces the case of Jarndyce and Jarndyce with the explanation that "it has been death to many, but it is a joke in the profession" (chap. i). John Jarndyce tells Esther that the property in London under dispute is on a street of houses of which "every door might be Death's Door" (chap. viii), and later she writes of "the dead sea of the Chancery suit" (chap. xxxvii). The narrator describes Mr. Tulkinghorn as "with countenance as imperturbable as Death" (chap. xxxiv). Mr. Vholes has a "lifeless manner" (chap. xxxvii), but he raps the desk that is "as hollow as a coffin" with a sound "as if ashes were falling on ashes, and dust on dust" (chap. xxxix); he does not shake hands but puts his "dead glove" on the other person's fingers (chap. xlv).

> there a weak little iron hoop, through which bold boys aspire to throw their friends' caps (its only present use), retains its place among the rusty foliage, sacred to the memory of departed oil. [chap. xlviii]

Even Chesney Wold, where the bowers are organic and indeed very beautiful, is a dying world. This is how we last see it:

> With so much of itself abandoned to darkness and vacancy; with so little change under the summer shining or the wintry lowering; so sombre and motionless always—no flag flying now by day, no rows of lights sparkling by night; with no family to come and go, no visitors to be the souls of pale cold shapes of rooms, no stir of life about it;—passion and pride, even to the stranger's eye, have died away from the place in Lincolnshire, and yielded it to dull repose. [chap. lxvi]

It is presided over by Volumnia, one of those "peachy-cheeked charmers with the skeleton throats" who toy "in a ghastly manner with large fans—like charmers reduced to flirting with grim Death, after losing all their other beaux" (chap. lxvi).

The decay of Chesney Wold may be a necessary step in the progress of democracy, but other forms of death are inexcusable atrocities. In Tom-all-Alone's, fever worsens barely endurable conditions so that people are carried out of their houses dead and dying "like sheep with the rot" (chap. xxii). According to what Jo can see, people "dies more than they lives" (chap. xxxi). As for himself, as the narrator ironically remarks, "Jo lives—that is to say, Jo has not yet died—in a ruinous place . . . by the name of Tom-all-Alone's" (chap. xvi). The interpenetration of life and death, always to the degradation of the former, is further marked in the description of the cemetery to which Nemo is brought. With the final clause we realize that Nemo, no man, is the modern Everyman, and the cemetery itself another miniature of England:

> With houses looking on, on every side, save where a reeking little tunnel of a court gives access to the iron gate —with every villainy of *life in action close on death,* and

> every poisonous element of *death in action close on life*—here, they lower our dear brother down a foot or two; here, sow him in corruption, to be raised in corruption: an avenging ghost at many a sick-bedside: a shameful testimony to future ages, how civilisation and barbarism walked this boastful island together. [chap. xi; italics mine]

Sir Leicester Dedlock betrays the irresponsibility of false sensibility when Mr. Tulkinghorn flatly announces that Nemo is dead (Sir Leicester is "not so much shocked by the fact, as by the fact of the fact being mentioned" [chap. xii]). This hypocrisy is yet less culpable than the sort of collusion between Death and the Smallweeds. The grandparents sit by the fire "like a couple of sentinels long forgotten on their post by the Black Serjeant, Death." In their house, on a street "bricked in on all sides like a tomb," dwells this family into which no child is ever born:

> The house of Smallweed, always early to go out and late to marry, has strengthened itself in its practical character, has discarded all amusements, discountenanced all story-books, fairy tales, fictions, and fables, and banished all levities whatsoever. Hence the gratifying fact, that it has had no child born to it, and that the complete little men and women whom it has produced, have been observed to bear a likeness to old monkeys with something depressing on their minds. [chap. xxi]

All the sacred relationships of life are perverted. Mr. Smallweed's father's God was Compound Interest: "He lived for it, married it, died of it" (chap. xxi). And his descendants, as the novel amply shows, keep the faith.

In this world of darkness, Spontaneous Combustion is a particularly appropriate form of death for the Lord Chancellor of the Court that is its microcosm: "It is the same death eternally—inborn, inbred, engendered in the corrupted humours of the vicious body itself, and that only" (chap. xxxii). In the macrocosm, the vicious humors will be found in "law and equity, and . . . that kindred mystery, the street mud, which is made of nobody knows what, and collects about us nobody knows whence or how" (chap. x)—the fog that opens the novel. But if nobody knows how the mud collects, it does appear that somewhere the fault is man's: Lincoln's Inn Fields are "fields, where the sheep are all made into parchment, the goats into wigs, and the pasture into chaff" (chap. xlii); it is misdirected human energy that has turned the word *fields* into mockery. In this environment the birds belong to Miss Flite and are imprisoned and dying, in contrast to Mr. Boythorn's free companion. What Miss Flite sees in the wards in Jarndyce is youth and hope and beauty (chap. iii); in chapter lx, two wards in Jarndyce are added to her collection.

The theme of denatured womanhood, in Dickens's earlier novels a notable expression of the sense of an ossifying world, is particularly important in *Bleak House* in the opposing, positive values suggested through Lady Dedlock and Esther. The satirized women may be examined first. They include the new type attacked earlier by the "Raven in the Happy Family" of *Household Words,* May 1850. The warring feminist Miss Wisk makes a brief appearance at Caddy Jellyby's wedding to denigrate the womanly values of love and nurture represented by the home:

> Mr. Quale, with his hair brushed back as usual, and his knobs of temples shining very much, was also there; not in the character of a disappointed lover, but as the Accepted of a young—at least, an unmarried—lady, a Miss Wisk, who was also there. Miss Wisk's mission . . . was to show the world that woman's mission was man's mission; and that the only genuine mission, of both man and woman, was to be always moving declaratory resolutions about things in general at public meetings. . . .
>
> . . . Such a mean mission as the domestic mission, was the very last thing to be endured among them; indeed, Miss Wisk informed us, with great indignation . . . that the idea of woman's mission lying chiefly in the narrow sphere of Home was an outrageous slander on the part of her Tyrant, Man. [chap. xxx]

In this short description Miss Wisk illustrates the linked progression from female aggressiveness through masculine competition to asexuality and sterility. One must remember that, reactionary though it is, this idea is founded upon the belief that total rejection of the feminine is the necessary condition of adopting masculine roles. Miss Wisk's repudiation of the feminine role is translated into action by Mrs. Jellyby and Mrs. Pardiggle. Mrs. Snagsby, who was mentioned above, destroys her marriage through an obsessive suspicion that her husband somehow has begotten the son she has failed to give him. But she began the process in an early assumption of masculine command:

> Mr. Snagsby refers everything not in the practical mysteries of the business to Mrs. Snagsby. She manages the money, reproaches the Tax-gatherers, appoints the times and places of devotion on Sundays, licenses Mr. Snagsby's entertainments, and acknowledges no responsibility as to what she thinks fit to provide for dinner; insomuch that she is the high standard of comparison among the neighbouring wives. [chap. x]

The obverse is true in the brick-makers' maltreatment of their wives. Yet here there is considerable ambiguity and mitigation to their cruel dominance: these men have been brutalized by the inhuman conditions of their lives, which have driven them to the alcohol that in turn fosters the surly oppressiveness their wives dread. Nonetheless the women stay with their husbands, and their fidelity seems to result not only from womanly loyalty (perhaps assisted by the absence of an alternative) but also from recognition that the world has molded their husbands, not vice versa, so that the men's culpability is limited.

The familiar termagant appears as Miss Barbary: she refuses to marry Boythorn in order to punish her sister by taking away the baby, but she "cares" for it mainly to impress upon the child the misfortune of birth and the misery of life. Esther's birthday lesson is that it would have been better had she never been born; the emphasis in her own account of her childhood is strongly upon the absence of a "mama" (chap. iii). Miss Barbary's denial of human relationships leads to her pretense that she is Esther's godmother rather than her aunt. Her servant Mrs. Rachael (the name perhaps is as ironic here as in *Hard Times* it will be tender) is of the same school and continues the work of repression in her later role as Mrs. Chadband. One might note that the Chadbands' victims are Guster and Jo, both children. Lesser variations upon the anti-woman are Judith Smallweed, Volumnia Dedlock, Mrs. Woodcourt, and Hortense. Guppy's mother is a burlesque.

The standards of womanly goodness are equally clear. In opposition to the termagant stands little Charley, child-mother to her brother and sister, Tom and Emma:

> "Mother died, just after Emma was born," said the child, glancing at the face upon her bosom. "Then father said I was to be as good a mother to her as I could. And so I tried. And so I worked at home, and did the cleaning and nursing and washing, for a long time before I began to go out." [chap. xv]

Mr. Gridley's affectionate relation to these children reveals the kindliness and humanity that Chancery has nearly crushed out of him. Charley also shows up the falseness of Mr. Skimpole's conception of childhood. On one occasion, Ada, Esther, and Mr. Jarndyce visit her after being reminded of "Coavinses" by Mr. Skimpole, who tells them his plans to visit Boythorn: "He proposes to frank me down and back again. I suppose it will cost money? Shillings perhaps? Or pounds? Or something of that sort?" The contrast to Charley could not be more direct; she explains that now, instead of staying home to mind the children, she goes out washing as often as she can, "because of earning sixpences and shillings!" (chap. xv).

The golden girl, Ada, is darling but helpless; the desirable women in this novel are all more practical than pretty. The thematic importance of Esther (see below, p. 127) makes the failure in her presentation particularly regrettable. That it is a failure cannot be denied. Its root is probably in the necessity forced upon her of portraying her entire character herself. The first-person narrative in *David Copperfield* succeeded because of the ironic perspective of the speaker looking back upon his younger self; in *Great Expectations* such irony is the core of the book. Esther, although (as we learn in the final chapter) writing some seven years after the close of events, has no such sense of irony; nor do we see her through anyone else. When the Dickensian narrator spoke of the littleness or delicacy of Nell it was bad; when Esther writes about "my trembling little hand" (chap. iii) it is intolerable. What is worse, Esther is occasionally coy and, especially on the subject of Allan Woodcourt, can become cloying. Finally, she is compelled to tout her own worth and her own modesty simultaneously, so that such disclaimers as that about the "old conspiracy to make me happy" following her repetition of the others' praise of her sound false.[5] One thing that offsets this deficiency of portrayal is the presence of the novel's highly satiric characters. These characters are clearly rhetorical or emblematic, and this quality also helps to free the more novelistic characters from strict realism. Thus Esther can be understood as the positive counterpart of grotesques like Mrs. Jellyby or Mr. Vholes, as an emblematic character dramatically embodying the virtues that are implicitly upheld by the satire. Even so, she is hard to take.

5. Of course I am not the first to have made such a judgment. Cf., for example, Robert A. Donovan, "Structure and Idea in *Bleak House*," *ELH* 29 (1962): 175–201: "As narrator she is faced with the necessity of talking about herself, and her modest disclaimers ring false. . . . Esther the heroine is in a sense betrayed by Esther the narrator into assuming a posture that cannot honestly be maintained" (p. 198); Fred W. Boege, "Point of View in Dickens," *PMLA* 65 (1950): 90–105: "David Copperfield demonstrated that the conventional Victorian hero is not a commanding figure in the center of a novel. Esther Summerson proves that the conventional heroine is worse; for the hero is hardly more than colorless, whereas she has positive bad qualities, such as the simpering affectation of innocence" (p. 94); and, much earlier, John Forster, *Life of Dickens:* "To represent a storyteller as giving the most surprising vividness to manners, motives, and characters of which we are to believe her, at all times, as artlessly unconscious, as she is also entirely ignorant of the good qualities in herself she is naively revealing in the story, was a difficult enterprise, full of hazard in any case, not worth success, and certainly not successful" (Bk. VII, chap. i).

The admirable attempt to defend her by W. J. Harvey in "Chance and Design in *Bleak House*," *Dickens and the Twentieth Century*, ed. John Gross and Gabriel Pearson (London, 1962), 145–57, I do not find ultimately convincing.

The significance of Esther's loss of beauty has been discussed above (chap. 3). Its coordinate is the jingle of her housekeeping keys, for she is the ordering spirit of this self-created family. She is, in fact, as busy as Mrs. Jellyby ("Well! I was full of business, examining tradesmen's books, adding up columns, paying money, filing receipts, and I dare say making a great bustle about it" [chap. ix]), but the purpose and effect of her bustling are diametrically opposite. Complementing this efficiency are her natural appeal to children (Peepy Jellyby) and her display of motherly tenderness early in the novel (chap. viii) when, with Ada, she soothes the tiny baby of the brick-maker's wife. Esther is preeminently the "little woman" whose life is consumed in care for others, and that is the epithet Mr. Jarndyce repeatedly uses to describe her. In hilarious inversion, Dickens also has Mr. Snagsby use it for his most unhelpful mate. Positive reflections of the "little woman" character are Caddy Jellyby, whose marriage is a deliberate attempt to turn from her mother to Esther as model, and Mrs. Bagnet, summed up in her apparently continuous occupation of washing greens. Mr. Bagnet's habit of calling her the "old girl" appears when they are first introduced to the novel in a visit from Mr. George (chap. xxvii); as this directly follows Mr. George's visit to the Smallweeds, Mr. Bagnet's phrase ironically points the contrast between his wife and that family. It is with reference to Mr. Bagnet that the narrator suggests the radical essence of such peculiarly womanly qualities:

> Some men rarely revert to their father, but seem, in the bank-books of their remembrance, to have transferred all the stock of filial affection into their mother's name. Mr. Bagnet is one of these. Perhaps his exalted appreciation of the merits of the old girl, causes him usually to make the noun-substantive, Goodness, of the feminine gender. [chap. xlix]

It may be observed that Mrs. Bagnet regulates her household affairs as much as Mrs. Snagsby controls hers. As with energy, however, spirit is the crucial determinant. Mrs. Bagnet even rode army wagons without diminishing her essential womanliness, and, subscribing to the fiction that "discipline must be maintained," she conducts her present life without diminution of her own motherliness and wifeliness or of her husband's virility.

Mrs. Rouncewell is forgiven her rigidity as loyal housekeeper to an aristocratic family through her overriding warmth as a mother. The triumph of the latter instinct propels her frantic petition to Lady Dedlock, which is all explained in terms of maternal love. In the scheme of the novel, her reunion with her long-lost George contrasts with the continued frigidity imposed upon Esther and Lady Dedlock. Yet womanliness redeems Lady Dedlock too. She is as passionate as Hortense, but what seethes inside her is the instinct and desire of motherhood, and through it she escapes the anonymous inhumanity of the fashionable world. Her pride, we soon learn, is the mask forced upon her by social circumstance. Her deeper nature first shows itself in kindness to Rosa: "Is this Lady Dedlock standing beside the village beauty, smoothing her dark hair with that motherly touch, and watching her with eyes so full of musing interest? Aye, indeed it is!" (chap. xxviii). Her immediate love for Esther, though nonrealistic and unlikely, is schematically right. Critics who love to exult over Dickens's Victorian prudery tend to cite the punishment visited upon Lady Dedlock for her sin, severer even than little Em'ly's. What matters here, however, is not what happens to Lady Dedlock in the story but the reader's attitude toward her that the story engenders; by the end of the book it is one of complete sympathy. Sir Leicester takes the lead in his moving scrawl for "full forgiveness" (chap. lvi). Whatever wrong she may have committed in loving Captain Hawdon is submerged in her devotion to him and to her child and in the suffering she undergoes because of it. The antithesis—sterile propriety—is all too evident in Volumnia.

The endearment of Lady Dedlock to the reader is made possible in large part by the stronger emphasis in this novel than in any of its predecessors upon the social nature of evil and abuse. As these phenomena are conceived in relation to institutions (in the sense that the fashionable world is also an institution as opposed to a group of discrete individuals), individual characters can become either more frightening or less culpable. An instance of the former development is Vholes, whose reptilian loathsomeness is all the more horrible for the professional backing that supports him. Lady Dedlock is of the latter type. She begins as a satirical image of fashionable boredom, but, as Tulkinghorn unravels her mystery, her manner becomes understandable. She escapes the trap of monotonous uniformity that makes it possible to talk about society as a single body—and she escapes satire, to become a sympathetic, dramatic character. Even more striking is the change in Sir Leicester. At the opening he is a figure of satire characterized principally by pompous verbosity. His ridiculousness is underscored as he creates a specter of social destruction that is a burlesque of the novel's vision of disintegration. Sir Leicester's reactionary conservatism lives in continual fear of radical social upheaval:

> From the village school of Chesney Wold, intact as it is this minute, to the whole framework of society; from the whole framework of society, to the aforesaid framework receiving tremendous cracks in consequence of people (ironmasters, lead-mistresses, and who not) not minding their catechism, and getting out of the station unto which they are called—necessarily and for ever, according to Sir Leicester's rapid logic, the first station in which they happen to find themselves; and from that, to their educating other people out of *their* stations, and so obliterating the landmarks, and opening the floodgates, and all the rest of it. [chap. xxviii]

His next step is usually a reference to Wat Tyler. The rigidity of this belief, comically reflected in the fixed terms in which it is always rendered, sums up all that Sir Leicester represents as an object of satire. This never changes. Nor does the stroke he suffers at the crisis precipitated by Mr. Tulkinghorn change him; what it does change is his relationship to the reader. The emphasis shifts to reveal fuller dimensions of his character. Sir Leicester's devotion to his lady has been mentioned but until now it has been only an amiable sidelight upon a ridiculous figure. With the fullness of love expressed by his forgiving anxiety, that sidelight becomes central, and under it Sir Leicester escapes the satiric mold to become a figure of admirable pride and of pity. Once he has been confronted with Mr. Bucket's results, the Smallweed-Chadband blackmailing, and Mlle. Hortense, the floodgates are really opened—but Sir Leicester says nothing and is reduced to "inarticulate sounds" that can pronounce only "her name" (chap. liv). The irony that now "what he whispers sounds like what it is—mere jumble and jargon" (chap. lvi) is somehow more sad than cutting. The narrator does not leave the change in nuance:

> His formal array of words might have at any other time, as it has often had, something ludicrous in it; but at this time it is serious and affecting. His noble earnestness, his fidelity, his gallant shielding of her, his generous conquest of his own wrong and his own pride for her sake, are simply honourable, manly, and true. Nothing less worthy can be seen through the lustre of such qualities in the commonest mechanic, nothing less worthy can be seen in the best-born gentleman. [chap. lviii]

To appreciate the advance in technique applied to Sir Leicester, one might compare him to Mr. Dombey, who also changes from a dehumanized object of satire to a sympathetic figure. With Dombey the change is a reformation of character, and its violence, emphasized in his nervous breakdown, is unacceptable by any standard of credibility. Even when read emblematically rather than psychologically, it is a reversal that jars with the harsher analysis and truer understanding of the rest of the novel. The plot is suddenly jerked round to bear out the moral, and the character with it. In *Bleak House,* on the other hand, Dickens has learned to change not the character himself but his relation to the narrator and consequently the reader. Sir Leicester no doubt retains his fear of the obliterated landmarks and opened floodgates, but we are no longer concerned with that; and the depth of love that does concern us has been developed from the beginning. His movement from a rhetorical counter to a dramatic character is the triumph of a novelistic impulse; it becomes possible when the satire turns from the characters to institutions or other larger forces.

The Dedlock story moves from the static form of pure satire to one of novelistic development and sympathy. The Chancery plot contains both of these from the beginning. The satiric attack upon Chancery appears in the narrator's denunciations; in Krook, its parodic counterpart; and in the fixed characters of victims like Miss Flite and Gridley and of predators like Vholes. It is also intensified by the spectacle of Richard Carstone's neurotic deterioration. His story casts satiric reflection upon Chancery, but it is presented in itself with understanding and compassion. Thus a dramatic character serves a rhetorical purpose.

Richard demonstrates Dickens's effective conjunction of satire and novelistic interest in this novel. The satire uses static portraiture and, characteristically, lacks a conventional plot. The dramatic characters—those of novelistic interest—struggle against this satiric stasis; their efforts generate an overabundance of plot activity, ranging from the lonely meditations of Esther to the melodramatic pursuit of Lady Dedlock. The apparent incongruity of modes in the novel is not merely resolvable or acceptable; it is essential, because the structural and thematic patterns of *Bleak House* are one. Satiric and novelistic worlds oppose each other, and the contest between them is the plot. The threats to the novelistic world are part of the satiric argument, and the efforts of that world to resist constitute the satiric standard. Richard tries to force Chancery into action, but instead Chancery manages to make him as rigid as Miss Flite and Gridley and finally to destroy him. The dark vision of the victorious satiric world is offset by Esther, who searches for self-definition and eventually finds the values of womanhood. Lady Dedlock becomes more novelistic as she struggles against the rigid society she had dominated. In the minor third area of satire, misguided philanthropy, Caddy Jellyby resists the absurd world of her mother and escapes into marriage, though her scar manifests itself in her prematurely old baby. The characters in *Bleak House* who engage our sympathy are those who fight against becoming inhuman and rigid like the satiric figures. They may still be highly emblematic, but they participate in dramatic action and in a comprehensible world of humane values. The alien world of this novel is rendered in satire; the struggle for something better, with its varying degrees of success, is generally novelistic. The counterpoint is understood by the use of two narrative tenses: the continuous present, with which the impersonal narrator describes the satiric stasis, and the simple past, which itself implies movement in time and which Esther uses to recount the struggle against this stasis.

The division, of course, is highly fluid; otherwise the novel would be hopelessly schematic. Esther, naturally quite innocent, often becomes the voice of the *faux-naif*. Mr. Turveydrop and Harold Skimpole, for instance, though seen only through her eyes, are clearly satiric characters. So is Mrs. Jellyby, though she is given overt satiric treatment by the first narrator as well:

> Jo is brought in. He is not one of Mrs. Pardiggle's Tockahoopo Indians; he is not one of Mrs. Jellyby's lambs, being wholly unconnected with Borrioboola-Gha; he is not softened by distance and unfamiliarity; he is not a genuine foreign-grown savage; he is the ordinary homemade article. [chap. xlvii]

Also, the tone of the following passage, in which Esther is recounting the sorts of soliciting letters Mr. Jarndyce received, should be noted:

> They wanted wearing apparel, they wanted linen rags, they wanted money, they wanted coals, they wanted soup, they wanted interest, they wanted autographs, they wanted flannel, they wanted whatever Mr. Jarndyce had—or had not. Their objects were as various as their demands. They were going to raise new buildings, they were going to pay off debts on old buildings, they were going to establish in a picturesque building (engraving of proposed West Elevation attached) the Sisterhood of Medieval Marys; they were going to give a testimonial to Mrs. Jellyby; they were going to have their Secretary's portrait painted, and presented to

> his mother-in-law, whose deep devotion to him was well known; they were going to get up everything, I really believe, from five hundred thousand tracts to an annuity, and from a marble monument to a silver teapot. [chap. viii]

The extravagant flourish, especially regarding the mother-in-law of the secretary, cannot be Esther's: it is the Dickensian satiric voice intruding. This flaw occurs more than once in the narrative, and it reveals that the static, satiric world itself calls up the tone of irony.

A mixed range of characters is needed to represent both the satiric, undesirable world and the normal world. Characters from these different world are not kept apart like the complementary portraits in Pope, but they meet and interact continually. What happens when they are brought into confrontation and how the grotesques and humorous characters, who have unimpeachable validity in satire, mesh with the natural or novelistic characters can be seen in the initial meeting between the wards in Jarndyce and Miss Flite. As Esther narrates:

> We looked at one another, half laughing at our being like the children in the wood, when a curious little old woman in a squeezed bonnet, and carrying a reticule, came curtseying and smiling up to us, with an air of great ceremony.
>
> "O!" said she. "The wards in Jarndyce! Ve-ry happy, I am sure, to have the honour! It is a good omen for youth, and hope, and beauty, when they find themselves in this place, and don't know what's to come of it."
>
> "Mad!" whispered Richard, not thinking she could hear him.
>
> "Right! Mad, young gentleman," she returned so quickly that he was quite abashed. "I was a ward myself. I was not mad at that time," curtseying low, and smiling between every little sentence. "I had youth and hope. I believe, beauty. It matters very little now. Neither of the three served, or saved me. I have the honour to attend Court regularly. With my documents. I expect a judgment. Shortly. On the Day of Judgment. I have discovered that the sixth

> seal mentioned in the Revelations is the Great Seal. It has been open a long time! Pray accept my blessing."
>
> As Ada was a little frightened, I said, to humour the poor old lady, that we were much obliged to her.
>
> "Ye-es!" she said mincingly. "I imagine so. And here is Conversation Kenge. With *his* documents! How does your honourable worship do?"
>
> "Quite well, quite well! Now don't be troublesome, that's a good soul!" said Mr. Kenge, leading the way back.
>
> "By no means," said the poor old lady, keeping up with Ada and me. "Anything but troublesome. I shall confer estates on both,—which is not being troublesome, I trust? I expect a judgment. Shortly. On the Day of Judgment. This is a good omen for you. Accept my blessing!"
>
> She stopped at the bottom of the steep, broad flight of stairs; but we looked back as we went up, and she was still there, saying, still with a curtsey and a smile between every little sentence, "Youth. And hope. And beauty. And Chancery. And Conversation Kenge! Ha! Pray accept my blessing!" [chap. iii]

The reference to children in the wood gives a slight suggestion of fairy tale to the atmosphere of Miss Flite's entrance. At this point in the novel, it is not absolutely established whether she will be the good fairy she almost appears or an old hag with false smiles. She seems kindly, but her predictions are ominous. Her last words distill the irony of the book: youth and hope and beauty, but then Chancery, and between them the amiable Conversation Kenge, pernicious in the very degree that he is amiable and un-Vholesian, delighting in verbal flow. Richard immediately protects himself from the old lady with the judgment "Mad!" She retaliates by relating the similarities of her own origin and that of the young, "sane" people. Ada has reason to be frightened. While Esther is trying to placate Miss Flite, Mr. Kenge arrives. His naturalness has already been established in the novel, but Miss Flite, much as she has pointed out similarities between herself and the wards in Jarndyce, undermines his reality: "And here is Conversation Kenge. With *his* documents!" The syntactical echo of her self-description ("With my documents") reflects the dubious light cast upon them by the Day of Judgment, Revelations, and the Great Seal upon Kenge's documents too (if indeed he is carrying anything), and so upon the man himself. Kenge's "Now don't be troublesome" is also an attempt to protect himself from her. The nervousness of these characters in the presence of Miss Flite is partly an inevitable fear of even the most harmlessly insane, but in the context of the novel it has still more specific significance. In Dickens's earlier novels the satiric, static characters generally presented physical or material threats to the protagonists. In the later novels their threat is more psychological or spiritual: the satiric characters confront the dramatic characters with images of what they might become if they lose their humanity. Dickens illustrates the moral peril of Richard's hopes through Miss Flite's madness and Conversation Kenge's placid acceptance of the system that dehumanizes everyone it touches.

When the dramatic characters are healthy, their metaphysical incongruity with the satiric characters produces a certain uneasiness when the two groups meet. Esther and the cousins do finally befriend Miss Flite, and her madness puts her outside satiric attack, though she has satiric unreality. But the estranged relationship is evident with other satirized characters. Mr. George, for instance, can hardly tolerate the Smallweeds. Esther has difficulty taking Guppy seriously—although, of course, she remains polite and considerate to him—and feels an instant revulsion from Vholes. Struck by Vholes's "lifeless manner" (she mentions it twice in close sequence in chap. xxxvii) and feeling as if "there were something of the Vampire in him" (chap. lx), she can never accept that he is human. Her sense of a crucial if undefinable distance between herself and Vholes is an index of her human vitality. With Richard, conversely, a fearful symptom of the extent of his sickness is his failure to react to Vholes in this way. Richard feels no disjunction of reality between himself and Vholes, and this tells us that there is something very wrong with Richard.

Thus, through different metaphysical planes, Dickens distinguishes and emphasizes the opposing states that create the thematic tension of the novel. To the degree that Sir Leicester Dedlock is like Boodle, Coodle, or Doodle, he is satiric and static. The measure of the humanity he attains at the climax of the Dedlock plot is the distance Sir Leicester puts between himself and those nameless characters.

We can return to Richard for a further look at the meshing of satire and novel. The one time Richard appears in the impersonal narrative is in chapter xxxix, "Attorney and Client." At that time, we learn for certain that Richard is wholly in the shadow of the satiric world and can be released only on his deathbed. (There is similar significance in Lady Dedlock's shift from the satirist's to Esther's narrative.) Richard enters as the client who "throws his hat and gloves upon the ground—tosses them anywhere, without looking after them or caring where they go; flings himself into a chair, half sighing and half groaning. Rests his aching head upon his hand, and looks *the portrait of Young Despair*" (italics mine). The last phrase has a distinct ring of mockery. Richard is rigid—like a portrait. He takes up satiric gestures. Mr. Vholes tells him, " 'This desk is your rock, sir!' " and "gives it a rap, and it sounds hollow as a coffin." Soon Mr. Vholes raps "the hollow desk" again and repeats, " 'Yes, sir . . . a rock.' " Shortly thereafter we see Richard: " 'Are, or are not, our interests conflicting? Tell—me—that?' says Richard, accompanying his last three words with three raps on his rock of trust." He becomes an indistinguishable type:

> On many such loungers have the speckled shadows of [the Lincoln's Inn] trees often fallen; on the like bent head, the bitten nail, the lowering eye, the lingering step, the purposeless and dreamy air, the good consuming and consumed, the life turned sour. This lounger is not shabby yet, but that may come. Chancery, which knows no wisdom but in Precedent, is very rich in such Precedents; and why should one be different from ten thousand?

And Mr. Weevle marks Richard for Spontaneous Combustion. Later we hear him picking up Vholes's language (" 'Vholes has his shoulder to the wheel' " [chap. xlv]), but by this time he is back in Esther's narrative—Chancery's victim, but only temporarily a part of its world.

The double plot of Chancery and the Dedlocks in *Bleak House* is particularly significant in the advancement of Dickens's satiric technique because the relationship of the two parts is more complex than one of simple analogy. They are opposite sides of the one bad coin that life has become, each the corollary of the other. The key to this conjunction is Esther. Confronted with the grotesque world of Chancery, she is caught up in its chaos but is finally able to escape it. Esther is also at the center of the problem of the Dedlock story, which is that of the absent or lost mother. In addition, she is a chief witness to the neglect of Jo and to the mistaken charity of the Jellyby-Pardiggle breed. It is in Esther that the various strands of the book come together in a single statement of interdependent cause and effect: the moribund world of neglect and disorder in society and of charity (the principal source of hope) misdirected to the point of inhumanity is also the world in which the womanly values transmitted through motherhood (love, solace, nourishment) have been cut off. In the two main branches of the plot, we see Esther seeking salvation from both aspects of this denatured world of decay and loss of human value. Minor figures—villains or victims such as the Bagnets, Rouncewells, and others discussed above—present further variations of this central situation. For instance, on the villainous side, all the termagants bear reference to the loss of love and solace in a Wiglomerated land, and Krook's motiveless distrust and acquisitiveness are a kind of irrational distillation of the qualities that have taken control instead. Of the victims, a number struggle against the grotesquerie for a normal, happier life, but the achievement of salvation is mainly Esther's. Caddy's is a secondary reflection; John Jarndyce has had his key from the beginning.

The nature of salvation is a principal concern of the novelistic or nonsatiric parts of the novel. Sir Leicester and Lady Dedlock achieve personal absolution, but nothing that will serve the continuance of life. For this, escape from the enveloping fog (reform is impossible) must be to a clearer world outside it.

Herein lies the relevance of the strong pastoral motif that runs through the book. The achievement of salvation is contained in the movement from Bleak House in Saint Albans to the new Bleak House in Yorkshire.

Yet the larger satiric landscape of the novel is more than pastoralism; Chesney Wold and Saint Albans show that the mere extra-urban situation does not constitute a green world. Mr. George offers what simple pastoralism there is at breakfast with Phil Squod: " 'There's not a bird's note that I don't know,' says Mr. George. 'Not many an English leaf or berry that I couldn't name. Not many a tree that I couldn't climb yet, if I was put to it. I was a real country boy, once. My good mother lived in the country' " (chap. xxvi). But this idyllic world belongs to a past to which he can never return, except to squire the shattered Sir Leicester. Phil has never seen the country, but he dreams of it, knowing it by the grass and swans. The actual idyllic is first approached in Boythorn's estate, close enough to Chesney Wold to demonstrate the extent of human responsibility. Saint Albans is mutilated, starved country, and Chesney Wold is sterile, but it is the people that make them so. At Chesney Wold the people are in conflict with the rich surroundings; on Boythorn's property, natural abundance combines with human effort and enjoyment (chap. xviii). The novel as a whole pays greater tribute to the human qualities: the iron country of the north has been rendered productive by the energy and ingenuity of Mr. Rouncewell, and the new Bleak House in Yorkshire will become a haven of domestic peace through the virtues of Esther and Allan Woodcourt. The last dreams of the broken but repentant Richard make it evident that the hope of a new world lies in this home:

> "I was thinking, sir," resumed Richard, that there is nothing on earth I should so much like to see as their house—Dame Durden's and Woodcourt's house. If I could be removed there when I begin to recover my strength, I feel as if I should get well there, sooner than anywhere."
>
> "When shall I go from this place, to that pleasant country where the old times are, where I shall have strength

> to tell what Ada has been to me, where I shall be able to recall my faults and blindnesses." [chap. lxv]

The giveaway, of course, is in "the old times," for at heart even Richard realizes they are necessarily past.

To all this Mr. Vholes offers a demonic parody. Esther relates:

> To keep up the conversation, I asked Mr. Vholes if he would like to live altogether in the country?
>
> "There, miss," said he, "you touch me on a tender string. My health is not good (my digestion being much impaired), and if I had only myself to consider, I should take refuge in rural habits; especially as the cares of business have prevented me from ever coming much into contact with general society, and particularly with ladies' society, which I have most wished to mix in. But with my three daughters, Emma, Jane, and Caroline—and my aged father—I cannot afford to be selfish." [chap. xxxvii]

Vholes's debased version does not, however, devaluate either Richard's dreams or Esther's achievement. Neither does Skimpole's, an equally false and far more elaborate poeticism that results in such solaces as this one offered to Esther:

> "In old times, the woods and solitudes were made joyous to the shepherds by the imaginary piping and dancing of Pan and the Nymphs. This present shepherd, our pastoral Richard, brightens the dull Inns of Court by making Fortune and her train sport through them to the melodious notes of a judgment from the bench." [chap. xxxvii]

Nor does the narrator's grotesque metaphor for Volumnia:

> Then, indeed, does the tuckered sylph come out in fairy form. . . . Then, indeed, does she captivate all hearts by her condescension, by her girlish vivacity, and by her skipping about. . . . Then does she twirl and twine, a pastoral nymph of good family, through the mazes of the dance. Then do the swains appear with tea, with lemonade, with sandwiches, with homage." [chap. lxvi]

The full demonic parody is also the narrator's: it consists in the motif of Chancery and the Inns of Court as inverted countryside, in allusions like the metaphor for Lincoln's Inn Fields quoted above (p. 110) and in such references as the following:

> In these fields of Mr. Tulkinghorn's inhabiting, where the shepherds play on Chancery pipes that have no stop, and keep their sheep in the fold by hook and by crook until they have shorn them exceeding close, every noise is merged, this moonlight night, into a distant ringing hum, as if the city were a vast glass, vibrating. [chap. xlviii][6]

The sinister burlesque by the corrupt city ultimately becomes positive reinforcement of the pastoral theme, its horrors of inversion crying out for a return to the true bucolic. A return, however, in a figurative sense only, for it is to spirit but not to place. That the old cannot be repaired and that a new abode must be built instead is signified in the construction of another Bleak House. Esther leaves both London and her old home behind to their inevitable decay under the shadow of Chancery in order to create the new, free order in an untouched home that she hopes will be beyond its reach. The possibility of renewal that the novel offers is thus not in reformation of the old but in total recreation.

As the satiric vision is extended to the whole of society, the thrust of *Bleak House* is in the reverse direction from Dickens's earlier novels. In those novels society is primarily normal with absurd or undesirable elements subject to satire; the hero must overcome or drive out those elements and assimilate himself with the normal society. In *Bleak House* all of society is absurd, and the hero must escape it and create a new, normal society outside its confines.

Because everything is seen in the same light—that of an

6. For a related analysis of the use of pastoral in *Bleak House,* see Louis Crompton, "Satire and Symbolism in *Bleak House.*" He treats in greater detail the themes of pastoral and antipastoral, fertility and sterility, but not the critical relation of modern man to nature and Dickens's consequent complication of the traditional polarity between city and country.

incoherent, crumbling world—*Bleak House* is Dickens's first novel with full thematic control. The theme is not a thesis but a pervasive vision of a world which ultimately, despite the few individuals who strive to hold something together, remains unregenerate: Chadband is still preaching Terewth, Skimpole is still a child, Chesney Wold is as dead as it was always hollow, and the last we hear of Chancery is the laughter of its lawyers. The number of satiric characters who go wholly unpunished (aside from Sir Leicester and Lady Dedlock, only Mr. Guppy and Mrs. Snagsby are made to suffer reality) is an index of the tension Dickens now refuses to release. The institutions, of course, remain untouched. The one hope is in individual escape (this is the Jarndyce solution, which Esther finally adopts), for even the industry of the north appears less as an area of society than as a reflection of Mr. Rouncewell's positive, individual energy. That it can serve equally as a metaphor for rigid, oppressive system will be demonstrated in the next novel.

CHAPTER 7

Hard Times

In *Bleak House* Esther travels through a satiric world, seeing many aspects of it, recognizing it often only intuitively, but never in danger of becoming part of it. A secondary character, Lady Dedlock, and a minor character, Sir Leicester, begin well within this world and escape dramatically but also fatally. Richard, however, is sucked helplessly into the satiric world, and that is the novel's most forceful statement. *Hard Times* shows the same basic configuration of opposing worlds pitted against each other, but the movement is all in the apparently more hopeful direction out of satiric stasis and into humanity. Furthermore, the human world in this novel no longer resides only within the breasts of blessed individuals but is given a symbol, a habitation and a name: Sleary's Horse-Riding. Nonetheless, *Hard Times* offers no vision of social amelioration: it is, if not the most moving, certainly the baldest statement of Dickens's satiric vision. It tends to be the favorite novel of people who don't really like Dickens, but even for the most ardent Dickensian its relative bareness has particular value in laying open many aspects of technique less readily apparent in the profusion of the longer novels.

Hard Times has suffered a good deal in recent criticism for Dickens's failure to offer any practical cure for the ills he attacks. It is argued that he opposed not only the status quo but all the forces attempting to change it, suggesting no workable alternative himself. This criticism has arisen largely in rebuttal to F. R. Leavis's interpretation of the novel as moral fable combining satire and pathos against Utilitarian oppression, and to some degree Leavis invites it.[1] It is certainly true that

1. Leavis, "*Hard Times:* An Analytic Note," *The Great Tradition*. The opposition takes its evidence largely from Humphry House's *The Dickens*

if we use the term *society* in its ordinary signification of a specific political and economic structure, and if we see *Hard Times* as a critique of such society, the novel rests upon very insecure bases. *Hard Times,* however, is not social criticism: it is moral satire. Like all Dickens's fiction, it is concerned essentially with the moral dilemmas of opposition between mechanical rigidity and vital fluidity, scientific learning and intuitive knowledge, self-propelling masculine aggressiveness and nurturing, feminine receptivity. Dickens polarizes these values in the various characters and institutions of the novel. As social and political history, therefore, the presentations of character and institution are necessarily incomplete and quite possibly biased; each embodies a certain moral quality or its absence and is not treated realistically or pragmatically. *Hard Times* is barely mimetic; it is polemical and satiric. As always in satire, its characters are not fully realized individuals but ciphers of a particular attitude or aspect of being that the satirist wishes to condemn or uphold. The institutions or social phenomena they represent naturally reflect this restriction.

The pragmatic treatment comes in Dickens's journalistic work, specifically in the articles in *Household Words.* Opponents of Leavis's claim that the novel contains significant social criticism have been quick to point to Dickens's encomia upon Victorian manufacture and especially to his report of the Preston strike in 1854. This inconsistency alone should indicate that Dickens's novels are not extensions of his journalistic campaigns. That his social concern with labor problems in *Household Words* coincides with his thematic use of those difficulties in a novel does not prove that the novel's purpose is the same as that of the journal. It is only natural for Dickens to order his increasingly satiric vision in terms of certain social problems at a time when those problems were present to him as daily concerns. It is also quite possible that Dickens's view of

---

World (London, 1941) and Raymond Williams's *Culture and Society* (London, 1958). Important discussions are found in John Holloway, "*Hard Times,* a History and Criticism," *Dickens and the Twentieth Century;* David Hirsch, "*Hard Times* and F. R. Leavis," *Criticism* (1964): 1–16; and, in particular, David Lodge, *The Language of Fiction* (London, 1966).

these matters as it appears in his journalism is less defensible than the aesthetically and rhetorically directed reduction in *Hard Times,* but the political acumen of Dickens as citizen is outside the scope of this study.

The vision of heightening rigidity in *Hard Times* is basically the same as that rendered in the individual characters and occasional institutions of the earlier novels and fully developed in *Bleak House* through the metaphor of Chancery and its various cognates. In this book it is expressed chiefly through two phenomena—industrialism and utilitarianism—which are in turn further narrowed. Industrialism is confined to the machinery and uniformity that are its least attractive contingencies (its productive aspects, of great interest in the journalism, are firmly ignored in the novel), and utilitarian philosophy to the most limited sense of unyielding rationalism and exclusive acceptance of material fact. Bounderby and Gradgrind represent the systematic reduction of human beings to machines or numbers: Bounderby sees the men alternatively as Hands or unreasonable demanders of turtle soup and venison fed from a gold spoon; Gradgrind knows them only in statistical form. Louisa's understanding is the joint product of these attitudes:

> For the first time in her life Louisa had come into one of the dwellings of the Coketown Hands. . . . Something to be worked so much and paid so much, and there ended; something to be infallibly settled by laws of supply and demand; something that blundered against these laws, and floundered into difficulty; something that was a little pinched when wheat was dear, and over-ate itself when wheat was cheap; something that increased at such a rate of percentage, and yielded such another percentage of crime, and such another percentage of pauperism; something wholesale, of which vast fortunes were made; something that occasionally rose like a sea, and did some harm and waste (chiefly to itself), and fell again; this she knew the Coketown Hands to be. But, she scarcely thought more of separating them into units, than of separating the sea itself into its component drops. [Bk. II, chap. vi]

That Dickens could write essays and speeches eulogizing the wonders of industry at the same time as he was writing *Hard Times,* and that in the foregoing novel, *Bleak House,* he had made the industrial north a land of hope, almost prove the emblematic nature of the Coketown factories in this novel. The disparity between the opinions expressed in life and those apparently embodied in art should also recall the probability that satiric anger is not simply an overflow of emotional attitude from the man to the satirist but rather a tone created by the satirist with deliberate craft. The anger is therefore not incompatible, as uncontrolled emotionality would be, with the simultaneous necessity for satiric distance.

The deficiencies of both Bounderby and Gradgrind are as significant in their personal relations as in their public functions. This too should indicate that it is not primarily the social and philosophical systems that are at issue but certain more general phenomena in life for which these systems are partial metaphors. These phenomena—rigidity, uniformity, confinement, hardness—are thus equally apparent in the private and public characters of the villains. The conjunction in Bounderby of aggressive, brutal capitalism and personal repulsiveness as a braggart and liar is not the rough but slightly confused justice Raymond Williams finds it to be;[2] it is a deliberate thematic device. Bounderby and Gradgrind exhibit in all respects the defects Dickens's satire attacks. As they treat people like machines, they themselves become robots and their human relations mere forms or utter impossibilities. To Gradgrind love is incomprehensible; when Louisa brings it up in their discussion of her forthcoming marriage, he can only stammer blankly. The marriage itself is a sacrilege against both God and nature, for it is made without love or physical passion and is obviously doomed to sterility. Mrs. Sparsit, as she knows all along, is a far more appropriate mate for Josiah Bounderby of Coketown. Bounderby's incapacity for human relationships is manifest in his repeating that he has married "Tom Gradgrind's daughter" and, above all, in his denial of his mother.

2. Raymond Williams, *Culture and Society* (New York, Doubleday, Anchor Books, 1959), pp. 100–01.

Victimized children throughout Dickens's writings (in this novel, Sissy) suffer from the absence of a mother; Bounderby creates his own myth of such deprivation and revels in it. It is perfectly appropriate for Stephen Blackpool to learn from Bounderby that the love between himself and Rachael must always remain suppressed.

Through Gradgrind, the mechanical rigidity and inhumanity of industrialism are linked with their correlatives in the realm of knowledge. The essence of Gradgrind's intellectual system, as of the factory system, is a removal from life. The trouble with Bitzer's definition of a horse is not simply its excessive pseudo-scientific mathematical terminology but that it still leaves him without a real sense of horsiness. Sissy's knowledge, on the other hand, is immediate and total—like Dürer's of the rabbit. The chapter on M'Choakumchild's school (Bk. I, chap. ii) is called "Murdering the Innocents" because the educational system conducts a continuing campaign against the immediacy of life. In the Gradgrind home, too—the perfect M'Choakumchild school—life is strangled in utter rigidity; at Stone Lodge it "went on monotonously round like a piece of machinery which discouraged human interference" (Bk. I, chap. ix). The word *machinery* is a link to the oppressions of industry. The divorce from life is such that Gradgrind believes he can even prevent the mental changes a maturing organism naturally undergoes. With pride he tells Louisa that " 'it has always been my object so to educate you, as that you might, while still in your early youth, be (if I may so express myself) almost any age' " (Bk. I, chap. xv). His wife, under his tuition, has been utterly desiccated:

> Mrs. Gradgrind, a little, thin, white, pink-eyed bundle of shawls, of surpassing feebleness, mental and bodily; who was always taking physic without any effect, and who, whenever she showed a symptom of coming to life, was invariably stunned by some weighty piece of fact tumbling on her. . . .
>
> Mrs. Gradgrind, weakly smiling, and giving no other sign of vitality, looked (as she always did) like an indiffer-

> ently executed transparency of a small female figure, without enough light behind it. [Bk. I, chap. iv]

This is the alienation of womanhood—though not nearly so marked as Bounderby's repudiation of his mother—against which Louisa finally rebels. Mrs. Gradgrind, especially in her last groping for something forgotten, something "not an Ology at all" (Bk. III, chap. ix), is a pathetic wisp of enervated humanity; on the other hand, the Bounderby female, Mrs. Sparsit, has energy enough for both of them, though energy that moves only from selfishness to demonism. Her prim snobbery is rigid and sexless, but it does not protect her from vicious jealousy of Louisa's marriage. Her insistence on continuing to call Louisa "Miss Gradgrind" is a willful act of rigidity. She envisions Louisa's downfall as suicide and rejoices at the funeral: "Though her teeth chattered in her head from wet and cold, Mrs. Sparsit exulted hugely. The figure had plunged down the precipice, and she felt herself, as it were, attending on the body. Could she, who had been so active in the getting up of the funeral triumph, do less than exult?" (Bk. II, chap. xi).

The negative qualities of hardness, rigidity, and the uniformity that can only exist apart from life, embodied in the antipathetic characters, are further reflected in the physical world they have created around them. The descriptions of Coketown take an ironic twist from the consistent use of organic metaphors. Coketown is a jungle:

> It was a town of red brick, or of brick that would have been red if the smoke and ashes had allowed it; but as matters stood it was a town of unnatural red and black like the painted face of a savage. It was a town of machinery and tall chimneys, out of which interminable serpents of smoke trailed themselves for ever and ever, and never got uncoiled. It had a black canal in it, and a river that ran purple with ill-smelling dye, and vast piles of building full of windows where there was a rattling and a trembling all day long, and where the piston of a steam-engine worked monotonously up and down like the head of an elephant in a state of melancholy madness. It contained

> several large streets all very like one another and many small streets still more like one another, inhabited by people equally like one another, who all went in and out at the same hours, with the same sound upon the same pavements, to do the same work, and to whom every day was the same as yesterday and tomorrow, and every year the counterpart of the last and the next. [Bk. I, chap. v]

The fog of *Bleak House* threatened regression to primal chaos, like the Universal Darkness that looms at the close of the *Dunciad*. The menace in *Hard Times* is closer to that which the later nineteenth- and twentieth-century anti-utopias will envision: not a loss of form but a meaningless multiplication of form, an order that stamps out the diversity of life. The jungle of Coketown lacks the salient quality of teeming life. The serpents do not writhe but are fixed in an endless coil; they are not flesh but smoke. Instead of lush earth, the landscape is hard brick. There is a river, but it is fixed in a canal and dyed an unnatural purple. The elephant is utterly mechanical, and the people, like the streets, have the regularity of processed goods. The fact that the people and the streets are conveniently described in the same sentence itself is telling. Whereas the swift passage and change of time is cause for regret in the pastoral and romantic traditions or for wistful reminiscence, in the world of Coketown it provides the only relief:

> Time went on in Coketown like its own machinery: so much material wrought up, so much fuel consumed, so many powers worn out, so much money made. But, less inexorable than iron, steel, and brass, it brought its varying seasons even into that wilderness of smoke and brick, and made the only stand that ever *was* made in the place against its direful uniformity. [Bk. I, chap. xiv]

In this unrelenting aridity, vegetation is only a shadow—and not even of the real thing, but of a mechanical mockery:

> The atmosphere . . . was like the breath of the simoon: and [the] inhabitants, wasting with heat, toiled languidly in

> the desert. But no temperature made the melancholy mad elephants more mad or more sane. . . . The measured motion of their shadows on the walls, was the substitute Coketown had to show for the shadows of rustling woods; while, for the summer hum of insects, it could offer all the year round, from the dawn of Monday to the night of Saturday, the whirr of shafts and wheels. [Bk. II, chap. i]

The rigidity paralleled in the machines of the factories and the compartments of Gradgrindian thought is further reflected in the local architecture. In Coketown, "the jail might have been the infirmary, the infirmary might have been the jail, the town-hall might have been either, or both, or anything else" (Bk. I, chap. v). The particular buildings so apparently interchangeable are significant: the jail, a place of punishment, isolation, and enforced rigidity; the infirmary, where life should be carefully nurtured; and the town hall, the supposed center of civilized law and order. The Gradgrind home, Stone Lodge, displays the unimaginative regularity of its owner's creativity (Bk. I, chap. iii), well suited to his ridiculously square appearance (Bk. I, chap. i). In contrast, its description is immediately followed by the discovery of Mr. Sleary "in an ecclesiastical niche of early Gothic architecture." Finally, the campaign against fancy and the triumph of industrialism together contribute to the irony of the metaphor of the factories as Fairy Palaces (Bk. I, chap. x).

The gods of Bounderby and Gradgrind are the physical and conceptual correlatives of one another. Gradgrind insists upon nothing but facts, while Bounderby delights in the factory smoke: " 'First of all, you see our smoke. That's meat and drink to us. It's the healthiest thing in the world in all respects, and particularly for the lungs' " (Bk. II, chap. ii). The horror this projects is death-in-life. Even the sun, the source of life and a traditional symbol for renewal, in Coketown is malign: "But the sun itself, however beneficent, generally, was less kind to Coketown than hard frost, and rarely looked intently into any of its closer regions without engendering more death than life" (Bk. II, chap. i). To the people of Coketown it is a sun "eternally in eclipse" (Bk. II, chap. vi). In Mr. Gradgrind's observatory there is a "deadly statistical clock . . . which measured every second with a beat like a rap upon a coffin-lid" (Bk. I, chap. xv). Death, Stephen Blackpool explains, is all that lies ahead for the workers: " 'and look how the mills is awlus a goin', and how they never works us no nigher to onny dis'ant object—ceptin awlus, Death' " (Bk. II, chap. v). At the crisis, Louisa describes her own life as a "state of conscious death" (Bk. II, chap. xii).

Slackbridge as well as Bounderby and Gradgrind must be considered in the light of wider thematic concerns. The novel's conception of the trade unions may well be a "stock Victorian reaction,"[3] but it is also particularly suited to the thematic function of the unions in the satire. An important key to the novel's dismissal of them may be found in House's description of the "Combinations" of the thirties and forties: "They were revolutionary in the sense that they did not accept the doctrine of the natural identity of interests between Capital and Labour, and were in their political activities more or less conscious of class-struggle."[4] The indictment of Bounderby and Gradgrind is based upon their failure to recognize the common bonds of humanity; the unions threaten to be no better. The solidarity of society is essential, for its antithesis corresponds on a class scale to the selfishness that isolates and finally alienates an individual from the world about him. Stephen explains the hopelessness of separation: " 'Nor yet lettin alone will never do 't. Let thousands upon thousands alone, aw leading the like lives and aw faw'en into the like muddle, and they will be as one, and yo will be a anoother, wi' a black unpassable world betwixt yo, just as long or short a time as sitch-like misery can last' " (Bk. II, chap. v). The union puts one part of society in opposition to the rest. Within the novel this divisiveness is less manifest on the level of class-struggle than within the group itself: its index is the ostracizing of Stephen. Again, the fact that Dickens praised what he saw of the behavior of

3. Williams, *Culture and Society* (1959), p. 103.

4. House, *The Dickens World*, 2nd ed. (London, 1952), p. 209.

the men during the Preston strike in his account in *Household Words* (February 11, 1854) but then gave a very different picture in his novel supports one's belief that the latter must be directed by the thematic impulse of satire rather than by history's fidelity to the actual. In the article, however, Dickens also showed himself clearly averse to the hypothesis of opposition between men and masters, at the end recommending arbitration in preference to both strikes and lockouts.[5] A second key to the deficiency of the unions is the nature of Slackbridge's rhetoric, clearly the secular counterpart to the rant of the canting preachers Dickens repeatedly pilloried. Like theirs, its effect is to make men hate, not love, one another; its goal is discrimination and division instead of union. Still this does not mean that Dickens rejected in the novel the workers' right to collective bargaining—just as the portrait of M'Choakumchild does not imply a rejection of schools for children. Finally, since the same man, Stephen Blackpool, both rejects the union and warns Mr. Bounderby of the dangers of laissez-faire and above all of treating human beings "as if they was figures in a soom, or machines" (Bk. II, chap. v), the plot points to the likeness of the two evils. Slackbridge conceives of people like atoms of a large package, exactly as the Gradgrindian bluebooks do. That Dickens gave Stephen's refusal to join the union only the vague reason of an undefined promise to Rachael has irritated most of the novel's critics; the vagueness, however, may have relation to the ineffability of the values that Rachael represents (see below, p. 145). At any rate, Stephen's retreat from this highly aggressive, divisive body is made with clear reference to an embodiment of ideal womanliness.

The essential point of this argument has been that Coke-

5. Cf. Engel, "Politics of Dickens' Novels," on the development of Dickens's ideas on class struggle. Only after 1854 does a final breakdown in relations between classes seem imminent. Before that, although Dickens had recognized social differences, he did not believe there was any difference of interests. Not until 1855 did his personal letters reveal a growing fear of violence and revolution.

town and its villains are emblems of the denial of certain values seen by Dickens as indispensable to meaningful human life:

> Surely, none of us in our sober senses and acquainted with figures, are to be told at this time of day, that one of the foremost elements in the existence of the Coketown working-people had been for scores of years deliberately set at nought? That there was any Fancy in them demanding to be brought into healthy existence instead of struggling on in convulsions? That exactly in the ratio as they worked long and monotonously, the craving grew within them for some physical relief—some relaxation, encouraging good humour and good spirits, and giving them a vent—some recognized holiday, though it were but for an honest dance to a stirring band of music—some occasional light pie in which even M'Choakumchild had no finger—which craving must and would inevitably go wrong, until the laws of creation were repealed? [Bk. I, chap. v]

On the basis of this paragraph, Dickens's Fancy has been criticized as merely a temporary escape which shows up as "bread and circuses" beside the Romantic assertion of man's need for poetry.[6] This judgment unfairly limits the concept of Fancy in *Hard Times,* where Fancy means not simply the horse-riding or other entertainments but all the values embodied in Sissy Jupe, not only wonder and fairy tales but charity and love. Defined in this way, we can see that it is both a faculty of perception and a mode of action, allied to the redemption of the Ancient Mariner when he blesses the water snakes and of Prometheus when he learns to forgive.

Sleary's itself represents more than the diversion of entertainment from relentless Gradgrindery. It is the principal antithesis to the whole world of mechanized, confined, antagonistic nonhumanity—a vital mixture of animals, people, and imagination that embodies the fluidity of life itself. Its symbol—which opposes both the Bounderby self-interest and the divisiveness

6. Lodge, *Language of Fiction,* p. 159.

of the trade union—is a human pyramid: "The father of one of the families was in the habit of balancing the father of another of the families on the top of a great pole; the father of a third family often made a pyramid of both those fathers, with Master Kidderminster for the apex, and himself for the base" (Bk. I, chap. vi). The loyalty is even reflected in the dog Merrylegs. It grows out of a reciprocal interdependence that ultimately becomes, as Mr. Sleary sticks by the man who once helped Sissy, the only means through which the crushed world of Gradgrind can achieve even a modicum of happiness. The circus is an emblem not only of fluidity but of ease with people and situations founded upon a broad humanity of sympathy, joy, and all the feminine values associated with Sissy. The circus is not, however, the novel's offer of an alternative social order to the utilitarian system. To object that the rescue of Tom from Bitzer is unlawful is to miss the point,[7] because what the horse-riders represent is not a system (or anarchy) of laws but a set of metaphysical, moral qualities of being. Saving Tom may disregard a code, but it obeys the humane impulse of generosity in a situation where there are extenuating circumstances that the code's rigidity would not recognize. The illegality of Tom's rescue, in fact, has the same relation to Bitzer's code that the circus has to Coketown: the formal code is so inconsiderate of individual exceptions that the impulse of human forgiveness and charity can only be realized outside it; Coketown has no room for Sleary's, so the values of the latter can be embodied only in a gypsy-like group barely on the fringes of society. When Sissy, representative of the circus, is brought into the M'Choakumchild school, she is immediately rejected. The human loyalty that spares Tom and the fancy that sparks the circus both can find expression only outside the morally dead social world. They must be brought together, joining the circus values to the town life and incorporating both the nomadic ring and the orderly square blocks. Or, as Dickens wrote to Henry Cole:

> I often say to Mr. Gradgrind that there is reason and good intention in much that he does—in fact, in all that he does

7. Lodge, *Language of Fiction,* p. 162.

> —but that he overdoes it. Perhaps by dint of his going his way and my going mine, we shall meet at last at some half-way house where there are flowers on the carpet, and a little standing-room for Queen Mab's Chariot among the Steam Engines.[8]

Sissy Jupe represents the clearest linking in Dickens's work of the womanly with the poetic. Intuitive knowledge and free imagination unite in her against severe rationalism and factualism. She is utterly unable to think in statistical terms, but she knows, in real life, what a horse it. As a motherless child, she combines an overflow of love with a deep sense of beauty and joy; as a woman, in the glimpse into the future that closes the novel, she retains the childlike graces in a full embodiment of femininity:

> But, happy Sissy's happy children loving her; all children loving her; she, grown learned in childish lore; thinking no innocent and pretty fancy ever to be despised; trying hard to know her humbler fellow-creatures, and to beautify their lives of machinery and reality with those imaginative graces and delights, without which the heart of infancy will wither up, the sturdiest physical manhood will be morally stark death, and the plainest national prosperity figures can show, will be the Writing on the Wall. [Bk. III, chap. ix]

This enunciation of the satiric norm concludes the novel.

Fancy should not supplant but supplement the basis of fact entailed by life in the world. A balance is what is sought—union between the masculine and feminine, fact and fancy, business and charity, science and poetry.[9] But just as Matthew Arnold,

8. Dickens to Henry Cole, 17 June 1854, Pierpont Morgan Library. Quoted in K. J. Fielding, "Dickens and the Department of Practical Art," *MLR* 48 (1953): 270–77; and in P. A. W. Collins, "Queen Mab's Chariot Among the Steam Engines: Dickens and 'Fancy,'" *English Studies* 42 (1961): 78–90.

9. I have not taken up the discussion of the aesthetic standards implied by the satire upon the "third gentleman" at M'Choakumchild's school (Bk. I, chap. ii) and his remarks on wallpaper and carpets that was begun by K.

preaching in *Culture and Anarchy* the need for a balance of Hellenism and Hebraism, felt that the present preponderance of Hebraism required him to attempt a balance through an equal overemphasis upon Hellenism, so Dickens in his argument on Fact and Fancy stresses the need for the neglected aspect more than the ultimately desirable harmony of the two.

A fully mature version of Sissy's femininity is offered in Rachael, whose womanly instincts and generosity, in obvious antithesis to Mrs. Sparsit's ridiculous jealousy of Louisa, lead her to nurse the demented rival who obstructs the very deep and mutual love between herself and Stephen (Bk. I, chap. xiii). The frustration of this love reflects the inhumanity of the law that Bounderby finds perfectly fair. With reference to Stephen, it is the complement to his ostracism by his fellow workers. Stephen's position in the novel—despite his opposition to the unions—is not of a moral standard but of a victim whose life has been a span of weary agony.

Like the characters and the setting, the plot of *Hard Times* is entirely continuous with its satiric argument: every line leads directly into the central fable. What Bounderby in fact and Gradgrind in theory believe to be the ultimate achievement of

---

J. Fielding and continued by John Holloway (in the essay cited above), because I believe their argument that the satire is a mistaken attack upon the standards by which Henry Cole and his colleagues were trying to control the monstrosities of mid-Victorian realism has been fully answered by Philip Collins in his *Dickens and Education*. Collins points out that, since the injustice to Cole's department was not recognized until a century later, any specific reference was probably at most a private joke; in addition, the idea of the passage fits the theme of the book: "emotional and aesthetic barrenness of the industrial town and of the 'utilitarian' ideas used to justify such an environment and outlook" (p. 158).

For an analysis of Dickens's general use of the term *fancy*, supporting this interpretation of its place in *Hard Times*, see Collins, "Queen Mab's Chariot." Especially apposite is the quotation from the announcement in *Household Words*, May 28, 1859, of the approaching publication of *All the Year Round*: "That *fusion* of the graces of the imagination with the realities of life, which is vital to the welfare of any community . . . will continue to be striven for" (italics mine).

order, Stephen Blackpool sees as a muddle; and this muddle proves the order specious. Stephen and Rachael in relation to Bounderby and industrialism, Tom and Louisa in relation to their father and philistinism—all expose the false order as lacking the values embodied in the horse-riders and especially in Sissy. With *Bleak House,* consideration of the novel in thematic, satiric terms showed every facet to be contributory; in *Hard Times* every development is essential. The breakdown of Mr. Gradgrind is a prime example. The change in Mr. Dombey was a wrenching of character that completed the argument of the book at the expense of the character itself; in Sir Leicester, it was a shift to novelistic emphasis that moved away from the satiric argument. With Mr. Gradgrind, Dickens virtually manages to have it both ways, for Gradgrind's breakdown and rejection of his system is both the final step of thematic demonstration and the escape of the character himself from the satiric mold to novelistic sympathy. While the satire attacks Gradgrindian philosophy for its rigid inhumanity toward society at large, the index of deficiency lies in the system's pernicious constriction of even its own proponent. Tom and Louisa must go wrong in their respective spheres of business and home to demonstrate the inadequacy of strictly utilitarian training, but only Mr. Gradgrind's realization of failure, his gradual perception of Sissy's values, and his consequent rejection of his own system can fully demonstrate that system's poverty. At the same time, however, that he is used as a satiric counter to make this point, in his struggle to assert the human values he has learned he achieves the novelistic state of a sympathetic character. As he stammers to explain to Bounderby the "enlightenment [that] has been painfully forced upon" him (Bk. III, chap iii), the acute discomfort of a man as yet without words to express his new emotions combines with the unabated bluster of Bounderby to make Gradgrind wholly deserving of compassion and Bounderby the sole satiric villain.

The tricky escape of Tom, almost a practical joke, is the kind of action that the earlier novels would have relished for its own sake. In *Hard Times* its details have meaning, though there is still a degree of simple, spiteful, glorious exhilaration in seeing Bitzer defeated. That only the scorned circus can save Tom—the ultimate product of Mr. Gradgrind's system—has the general import suggested above. It also seems significant that the rescue is effected not by the men alone but by the animals: one horse and one dog. Bitzer could define a Gradgrindian horse, but he is outwitted by a Sleary horse. Through Merrylegs, Sissy has been associated with dogs from the start. The animals seem to represent the absolutely natural: they are reasonable enough to work with natural people but remain untouched by the hard-fact aspect of man that in Gradgrindery swallows the whole. Tom is rescued by the animals, and Louisa grows to true maturity by becoming "learned in childish lore" (the sanctity of childhood in a dehumanizing world reaches back to Oliver Twist and Paul Dombey); Sissy was always the child of horseback riding.

Expansions of incidents that in earlier novels might have been purely sentimental contribute to the ironic emphasis in *Hard Times*. Stephen Blackpool dies, raised aloft and carried in the direction of " 'the star as guided to Our Saviour's home' " (Bk. III, chap. vii), and Dickens closes this chapter with a good cry:

> They carried him very gently along the fields, and down the lanes, and over the wide landscape; Rachael always holding the hand in hers. Very few whispers broke the mournful silence. It was soon a funeral procession. The star had shown him where to find the God of the poor; and through humility, and sorrow, and forgiveness, he had gone to his Redeemer's rest.

The sober reaction that one might have after the indulgence of emotion—this is simply maudlin—is offset by consideration of what Dickens is really doing with the martyrdom of Stephen. A significant detail of the rescue is its organization:

> There being now people enough present to impede the work, the sobered man put himself at the head of the rest, or was put there by the general consent, and made a large

> ring around the Old Hell Shaft, and appointed men to keep it. Besides such volunteers as were accepted to work, only Sissy and Rachael were at first permitted within this ring; but later in the day, when the message brought an express from Coketown, Mr. Gradgrind and Louisa, and Mr. Bounderby, and the whelp, were also there. [Bk. III, chap. vi]

The leader is a drinker, quite unrespectable by Gradgrindian or Bounderby standards. He elects himself and is chosen by the group simultaneously and spontaneously. The group is formed into a ring, a circle, symbolizing wholeness and solidarity, like the ring of the horse-riding. Throughout the description that follows, the group is repeatedly referred to as "the ring" or "the circle." Surprising as it may seem at first, Bounderby and Tom stand within the ring. The truth which is to be revealed through this event includes the fact that even Bounderby and Tom are, in spite of themselves, part of society. Tom, however, is also revealed as a part that must be cast out, and before the ring is broken he takes Sissy's advice to disappear. Yet Dickens postpones telling us of this until the following chapter, so that in chapter vi itself the emphasis remains upon the group's instinctive union around the figure of the erstwhile ostracized Stephen.

But all this is finally ironic. The narrator surrounds Stephen with sacrificial, Christian associations, but in Coketown his death produces no effect either for his fellow sufferers or upon their oppressors. Stephen does not become a hero of any cause: he is forgotten, and the muddle continues. His name may be exonerated by the repentant Mr. Gradgrind, but there is no indication that the next Stephen will not be equally bullied by the next Bounderby and the next Slackbridge. Stephen's death is lachrymose, but it is also bitter.

Harthouse's capitulation to Sissy has all the makings of the stock Victorian conversion of the villain. Like the martyrdom of Stephen, however, it can only be understood ironically. Harthouse yields to Sissy not because the power of her virtue transforms him even temporarily, but because his commitment to Louisa is not strong enough to resist any impediment. It is his nature never to counter any resistance but rather to turn aside and go in for something else that does not present difficulties. Earlier he transferred his affections to Louisa without effort, and now he moves away from her with little more; events have not changed him at all. Dickens points this out clearly:

> The moral sort of fellows might suppose that Mr. James Harthouse derived some comfortable reflections afterwards from this prompt retreat, as one of his few actions that made any amends for anything, and as a token to himself that he had escaped the climax of a very bad business. But it was not so at all. A secret sense of having failed and been ridiculous—a dread of what other fellows who went in for similar sorts of things would say at his expense if they knew it—so oppressed him, that what was about the very best passage in his life was the one of all others he would not have owned to on any account, and the only one that made him ashamed of himself. [Bk. III, chap. iii]

Harthouse does not convert, because there is not enough moral fiber in him for conversion. With similar truth, Dickens does not allow Bounderby to be seriously hampered by his exposure. The nature of Bounderby's death is a satiric punishment, but first he has five more years of undiminished balderdash. The same persistence of satiric view controls the final treatment of Louisa. Here Dickens achieves special force by playing against the expectations of his reader. The "final retrospect," often with a glance into the future, had become the standard ending to Dickens's novels. It is offered self-consciously and formally, though in varying degrees, in the first five novels. In *Martin Chuzzlewit* it is modified as a meditative address to Tom; in *David Copperfield* and *Dombey and Son* it is limited to the present and more smoothly joined to the novel; in *Bleak House* Esther has an additional seven years' perspective beyond the events of the narrative, for which she gives a similar summary. The conclusion to *Hard Times* is formal and highly rhetorical, possibly coy and perhaps even cloying. The narrator speaks through the vision of three different characters. The third is Louisa, and with her the pathos becomes heavier and the rhetoric more strident. First she sees, in "the Present," her father's public confessions. "But how much of the Future?" There is the stoic dignity of Rachael: "Did Louisa see this? Such a thing was to be." Then the misery and repentance of Tom: "Did Louisa see these things? Such things were to be." Finally there is Louisa herself, enshrined as goddess of the hearth, just as the cynic would expect Dickens to place her:

> Herself again a wife—a mother—lovingly watchful of her children, ever careful that they should have a childhood of the mind no less than a childhood of the body, as knowing it to be even a more beautiful thing, and a possession, any hoarded scrap of which is a blessing and happiness to the wisest?

But the satire will not allow it: "Did Louisa see this? Such a thing was never to be." After the sentimental indulgence of the paragraphs immediately preceding, the about-face strikes most effectively as ironic truth. From it Dickens moves to the relatively soft ending he does allow, with Sissy, who was the only true child, granted children of her own, and with Louisa enjoying these blessings through her. The closing note is again stern. In the last paragraph the didactic basis of satire becomes articulate, and the fiction reaches out to the audience: "Dear reader! It rests with you and me, whether, in our two fields of action, similar things shall be or not. Let them be! We shall sit with lighter bosoms on the hearth, to see the ashes of our fires turn grey and cold." Instead of giving us a comfortable vision, the satirist burdens us with responsibility.

The economical plot is perhaps to be expected in a novel so short by Dickens's standards. Equally striking and less referable to the restricted weekly format is the extensive use of satiric counters. The term *counter* includes those devices variously referred to as images, metaphors, or symbols; I choose it in preference to any of the others because attention to the obviousness, univalence, or heavy application of something called a counter will not prejudice its value. Poetry uses symbols; satire—or at least Dickensian satire—uses counters. The technique embraces not only recurrent similes and metaphors but also devices such as tag lines and characterizing mannerisms. The common element of these devices is their evolution into immediately recognizable emblems that become increasingly meaningful. The melancholy elephants and serpents of smoke have already been noticed as inhabitants of the mechanical jungle, ironically contrasted by the agricultural, seasonal metaphors of the book titles "Sowing," "Reaping," and "Garnering." The metaphor of Fairy Palaces is recurrent, too, and a good example of the incremental effect of such counters. Its first appearance is marked only by an ironic scepticism: "The lights in the great factories, which looked, when they were illuminated, like Fairy Palaces—or the travellers by express-train said so—were all extinguished" (Bk. I, chap. x). Inside the palaces we find a "forest of looms." Two chapters later, when Mr. Bounderby's still unrecognized mother leaves Coketown, "the express whirled in full sight of the Fairy Palace of the arches near." But an alternative image in the next paragraph adds a further layer of irony: "The bell again; the glare of light and heat dispelled; the factories, looming heavy in the black wet night—their tall chimneys rising up into the air like competing Towers of Babel" (Bk. I, chap. xii). The irony is complete when Mrs. Sparsit becomes the Bank Fairy (Bk. II, chap. i).[10]

The transformation of a simile (factories like Fairy Palaces) into the vehicle alone (Fairy Palaces) is similar to the progress by which Pecksniff became a Chorus or Chadband a vessel. With those, however, a simultaneous reduction from persons to things constituted further satiric indictment. The growth of the beadle in *Bleak House* into "the active and intelligent" is a closer analogy to the purely ironic expansion of the factories into Fairy Palaces, as in both the image is utterly inappropriate. Mr. Bounderby's windiness shows a merging of the two devices.

10. For an examination of the use of fairy lore throughout the novel, see Lodge, *Language of Fiction*, pp. 159–62. Mr. Lodge finds this technique successful particularly where it is ironic. He also notices the use of "key-words" such as *brazen* or *brass*, for Mr. Bounderby, *Fact* for Gradgrind, and the *whelp* (which he dislikes) for Tom (pp. 152–54).

Though we learn of it early (Mr. Bounderby's hair is always in disorder "from being constantly blown about by his windy boastfulness" [Bk. I, chap. iv]), it is not really developed until his interview with Stephen Blackpool:

> "Well, Stephen," said Bounderby, in his windy manner.
> Mr. Bounderby, who was always more or less like a Wind, finding something in his way here, began to blow at it directly.
> The wind began to get boisterous.
> Wind springing up very fast . . .
> (Gusty weather with deceitful calms. One now prevailing.)
> Mr. Bounderby, now blowing a gale . . .
> Mr. Bounderby, by this time blowing a hurricane . . . [Bk. III, chap. v]

Only with the three unreferenced meteorological asides does it sound as though Mr. Bounderby has, from being like the wind, become a wind or storm himself. With the last two references the image is again clearly a metaphor, and when it recurs once more later on it is a simile ("Bounderby . . . his hair like a hayfield wherein his windy anger was boisterous" [Bk. III, chap. iii]). The brief expansion to the whole personality, however, retains its effect upon the weight of the image.

These counters—"plain Fact," "a muddle," Mrs. Sparsit's Coriolanian eyebrows and Roman nose, "fed on turtle soup and venison with a gold spoon," melancholy mad elephants, the Staircase, "I am Josiah Bounderby of Coketown"—ring through the novel in a structure primarily rhetorical, built up by the narrator to enforce the judgment that is always at the root of satire. They act like basic chords, underpinning such flourishes as the following overflow upon Bounderby:

> Strangers, modest enough elsewhere, started up at dinners in Coketown, and boasted, in quite a rampant way, of Bounderby. They made him out to be the Royal Arms, the Union-Jack, Magna Charta, John Bull, Habeas Corpus, the Bill of Rights, An Englishman's house is his castle,

> Church and State, and God save the Queen, all put together. [Bk. I, chap. vii]

They bind together such contrasts of voice as this prophetic tone of apostrophe:

> Utilitarian economists, skeletons of schoolmasters, Commissioners of Fact, genteel and used-up infidels, gabblers of many little dog's-eared creeds, the poor you will always have with you. Cultivate in them, while there is yet time, the utmost graces of the fancies and affections, to adorn their lives so much in need of ornament; or, in the day of your triumph, when romance is utterly driven out of their souls, and they and a bare existence stand face to face, Reality will take a wolfish turn, and make an end of you. [Bk. II, chap. vi]

and this comic shift in point of view:

> In such condition, Mrs. Sparsit stood hidden in the density of the shrubbery, considering what next.
>
> Lo, Louisa coming out of the house! Hastily cloaked and muffled, and stealing away. She elopes! She falls from the lowermost stair, and is swallowed up in the gulf. [Bk. II, chap. xi]

Nothing else could have equally capped Mrs. Sparsit's absurdity at this point: the creaturely creation of a staircase has fulfilled itself. The early developments in Harthouse's seduction of Louisa determine the story's seriousness; the implications and consequences maintain it to the end. The climactic events, however, are rendered through Mrs. Sparsit's eager eyes in melodramatic *chiaroscuro*. Dickens repeatedly parodied melodrama; here, by making it Mrs. Sparsit's peculiar mode of perceiving what our wider perspective sees as deeply significant, he reveals its ridiculous declination from reality. The switch to a limited point of view is not only comic; it demonstrates that whereas the narrator's satiric distortions serve the clarification of moral issues, the simplifications of melodrama arising from the moral confinement of a Sparsitian intelligence disregard them. As Mrs. Sparsit is laughed away, so must they be.

The illustrations above show Dickens's verbal and imaginative outbursts to be as exuberant as ever, but in *Hard Times* it is particularly evident that they are under the strong thematic control of a clear satiric purpose. This novel brings together the main lines of Dickens's satiric vision into the most succinct and diagrammatic form it will take. *Hard Times* seems to marshal to the expression of that vision the full variety of literary devices—comic, satiric, sentimental, and melodramatic—that Dickens developed in his earlier works.

CHAPTER 8

Little Dorrit

Menacing the world of *Bleak House* is chaos, disorder such as can paralyze all positive forces of human value. Its metaphor is Chancery, the vast social machine run by manic subhumans on the blood of bewildered innocents. The menace in *Hard Times* is almost the inverse: sterility induced by a narrowly conceived and rigorously applied order. Here the metaphor is utilitarianism in political economy and philosophy, endorsing suppression of spontaneous life in all forms. In *Little Dorrit* the menace is stagnation, denial of change; its metaphor is imprisonment. The problem of order in this third novel, in contrast to the first two, is only minor. A more significant difference in *Little Dorrit* is that the menace is no longer something impinging from the outside but something within every individual, always latent and frequently dominant. *Bleak House* exploits the metaphor of disease, but *Little Dorrit* sees the phenomenon of moral death arising from self-induced sickness without the extenuation of criminal neglect or aggression. Chancery was a foggy blight reaching out its tentacles toward accursed victims; the Circumlocution Office, in contrast, " 'is not a wicked Giant to be charged at full tilt; but only a windmill showing you, as it grinds immense quantities of chaff, which way the country wind blows' " (Bk. II, chap. xxviii). This explanation is no less valid coming from Ferdinand Barnacle, because, whatever his actions, Ferdinand speaks truth and ought to know. Chancery was an agent; the Circumlocution Office is a symptom.

The suffering in *Bleak House* is primarily physical—hence the metaphor of disease. People are struck, they sicken, and they die. The fever is not only symbolic, as it links the supposedly separate strata of society; it is actual, bodily misery as well. Jo dies, Gridley dies, Lady Dedlock dies, Richard dies. Allan Woodcourt, the most passive and absent of heroes, is a healer of the sick. Womanly solacing repeatedly takes the form of nursing: Esther and Ada caressing the sick baby of the brickmaker's wife; Esther tending Jo and Charley; Charley caring for Esther; Mr. George virtually hospitalizing Jo and Gridley; Ada serving Richard almost more as nurse than as wife. The consequences of disorder, neglect, and ignorance are the immediate pangs of physical suffering. In *Hard Times,* emphasis is more upon the mind. There is no concern with what the Coketown workers or the Gradgrind children eat, whether they are warm enough, or if they have a place to sleep (except in Bounderby's parodic version). Stephen Blackpool's lodging is humble but reflects his simple nature, just as Bounderby's brass fittings are indexes of his brazen character and Gradgrind's symmetrical square house befits his penchant for arithmetic. Stephen's death is the sheer accident of a perverse fatality worthy of Hardy; Mrs. Gradgrind's has some closer connection to the rigorous world of hard fact, but certainly not the direct relation of the deaths in *Bleak House* to the enveloping fog. Whereas the mental obsessions of *Bleak House* are a sort of disease at some point willfully contracted by the victims and perhaps thereafter impossible of cure, in *Hard Times*—though Bounderby is stupid and perverse and Gradgrind, until the crisis, unenlightened—the victims are simply deprived and helpless. In *Bleak House* the anguish of Richard Carstone and Lady Dedlock, though mental, soon affects their bodily health; *Hard Times,* on the other hand, concentrates almost exclusively upon intellectual starvation and breakdown. With rough justice, then, we can say that from *Bleak House* to *Hard Times* the focus shifts from the body to the mind; with *Little Dorrit* it moves once more—to the soul.

The metaphoric nature of the Marshalsea has been spared the misunderstanding that beleaguers *Hard Times* by the good fortune—and perhaps better judgment—that led Dickens to choose for this novel's guiding metaphor an institution already abolished. No one would discuss *Little Dorrit* as a tract upon prison reform. In fact, a number of Dickens's other novels (*Pickwick Papers, Barnaby Rudge, David Copperfield,* and *Great Expectations*) are far better quarry for his ideas on this subject. Interest in the prison in *Little Dorrit* is confined almost wholly to its reflections of and upon the prisoner's mind; the main theme of Book II is the psychological nature of its bars. Like its many variations in Mrs. Clennam's religion, Miss Wade's perversity, Flora Finching's romantic sentimentality, and the Merdles' Society, the imprisonment the Marshalsea represents is a metaphysical and moral category of being.

No one, of course, has failed to notice this metaphor of imprisonment. Perhaps less remarked upon is the proportion of inmates to whom such punishment is due. The book is rife with frauds of all sorts—from Rigaud and Mr. Merdle, through Casby, Mrs. Clennam, Henry Gowan, and Mrs. Gowan, to William Dorrit, when he tries to obliterate his past. For cheats and imposters, prison is in a sense deserved. (I say this with full recollection of Dickens's advanced views on penology: the deserved prisons in *Little Dorrit* are the metaphorical or self-imposed ones only.) Thus we can understand the omnipresence of prisons as an index of widespread criminality; that is, as many hospitals would suggest a sickly population, many prisons indicate a criminal one. "The name of Merdle is the name of the age" (Bk. II, chap. v). Such interpretation seems to me both valid and secondary. Primarily—in this novel—imprisonment is enforced rigidity. The essence of life is organic change; whatever seeks to obstruct such change seeks to hinder life. Imprisonment is stagnation, imposed by society or by the self.

When a man is imprisoned by society, however, his soul may yet remain free. The opening chapter of *Little Dorrit* dramatizes this relation between the physical prison and the soul of the prisoner. Rigaud, self-proclaimed gentleman and "citizen of the world" (and as such an obvious avatar of Satan, older than creation itself), carries with him through the novel the atmosphere of the jail in which we first see him. Cavalletto—John Baptist, herald of the new gospel of life—is able almost to ignore the prison, and when finally left alone he sleeps in easy innocence; later he remembers it only in association with Rigaud.

From this cell in Marseilles the novel expands to its broad landscape, marked by the recurrent prison. Arthur Clennam's return to his childhood home in chapter iii establishes the metaphoric sense of imprisonment as stagnation. His immediate reaction upon seeing the house is "Nothing changed," and that remark contains the essence of Mrs. Clennam's world: "With her cold grey eyes and her cold grey hair, and her immovable face, as stiff as the folds of her stony head-dress,—her being beyond the reach of the seasons, seemed but a fit sequence to her being beyond the reach of all changing emotions" (Bk. I, chap. iii). Arthur will find Mr. Casby the same: "This was old Christopher Casby—recognisable at a glance—as unchanged in twenty years and upward, as his own solid furniture—as little touched by the influence of the varying seasons, as the old rose-leaves and old lavender in his porcelain jars" (Bk. I, chap. xiii). Casby's speech mannerism is repetition of phrases: he anticipates the broken phonograph record, going around and around in the same groove. Mrs. Clennam and Mr. Casby have both deliberately suppressed life's natural changes. Flora, on the other hand, is a victim of her own girlish empty-headedness; her refusal to change is not evil but simply foolish. Certainly the worst of the shock Arthur experiences in meeting her again is seeing not how she has changed but how she has refused to change:

> Flora, always tall, had grown to be very broad too, and short of breath; but that was not much. Flora, whom he had left a lily, had become a peony; but that was not much. Flora, who had seemed enchanting in all she said and thought, was diffuse and silly. That was much. Flora, who had been spoiled and artless long ago, was determined to be spoiled and artless now. That was a fatal blow. [Bk. I, chap. xiii]

Mr. F.'s Aunt, finally, is "a staring wooden doll too cheap for expression"; she obviously has never changed and never will.[1]

A sense of imminent stagnation is especially strong in the introductory history of the Dorrit family (Bk. I, chaps. vi, vii). When William Dorrit first enters the Marshalsea he is a young man, nervous and excitable but confident that he will soon rejoin the stream of life. He has a young wife and two children; soon come a pregnancy, a birth, a death. But afterward life seems to settle into a routine virtually unchanging, its repetitiveness supported by the Father's love of ritual. Prison is enforcement of constriction by society, but William Dorrit soon makes his own prison, one that he can escape only through death.

The Dorrits and Mrs. Clennam take the foreground in this vision of imprisonment. Secondary figures range from serious to comic. For these, *entrapment* is probably a better word than *imprisonment,* though the rigidity and stagnation involved are still the same. Mr. Chivery the elder, for instance, is a prototype of a character in whom the profession has overtaken the man, the manner outdone the matter, but his indictment is certainly light:

> What Mr. Chivery thought of these things, or how much or how little he knew about them, was never gathered from himself. It has been remarked that he was a man of few words; and it may be here observed that he had imbibed a professional habit of locking everything up. He locked himself up as carefully as he locked up the Marshalsea debtors. Even his custom of bolting his meals may have been a part of an uniform whole; but there is no question, that, as to all other purposes, he kept his mouth as he kept the Marshalsea door. He never opened it without occasion. When it was necessary to let anything out, he opened it a little way, held it open just as long as sufficed for the purpose, and locked it again. Even as he would be sparing of his trouble at the Marshalsea door, and would keep a

1. The relation of Mr. F.'s Aunt to the novel as a whole is discussed in an excellent article by Alan Wilde, "Mr. F.'s Aunt and the Analogical Structure of *Little Dorrit,*" *Nineteenth-Century Fiction* 19 (1964): 33–44.

> visitor who wanted to go out, waiting for a few moments if he saw another visitor coming down the yard, so that one turn of the key should suffice for both, similarly he would often reserve a remark if he perceived another on its way to his lips, and would deliver himself of the two together. [Bk. I, chap. xxv]

The protracted elaboration adds a bit of typically Dickensian comedy to a somber work. Mr. Chivery's son Young John, trapped in his own sentimentality, is even more ridiculous. His mother is caught up in a middle-class turn of mind that makes his own devotion almost noble by contrast:

> Mrs. Chivery, a prudent woman, had desired her husband to take notice that their John's prospects of the Lock would certainly be strengthened by an alliance with Miss Dorrit, who had herself a kind of claim upon the College, and was much respected there. Mrs. Chivery had desired her husband to take notice that if, on the one hand, their John had means and a post of trust, on the other hand, Miss Dorrit had family; and that her (Mrs. Chivery's) sentiment was, that two halves made a whole. [Bk. I, chap. xviii]

Yet this reasoning reflects less upon Mrs. Chivery—herself of little importance in the novel—than upon the marriages among the major characters motivated by desire for place or money. It comments upon them by parody much as *The Beggar's Opera* satirizes the middle and upper classes who never even appear.

Fanny Dorrit's marriage is exactly what Mrs. Chivery advocates: a matching of money with position (though Mr. Sparkler does not lack money). Fanny is led into this marriage of spite through her entrapment in the petty jealousies of an impoverished dancing-girl. When the inheritance has added money and manner to her natural beauty, she can still only continue to work out the rivalry and hate that her poverty had begun. Pet Meagles's marriage, on the other hand, results not from her own but from her parents' entrapment. Their failure to bring her out of childhood into full maturity makes her incapable of a wise choice, and their taint of Circumlocution makes them just shy enough with the Gowans for the latter to triumph. This limitation allows the Meagleses, kind-hearted as they are, to treat. Tattycoram so that her complaints have a modicum of justice. Yet she in turn is trapped in the impatient temper and streak of egotism that for Miss Wade have become prison bars.

Rigidity in character thus varies in this novel from the harmless speech mannerisms of Mrs. Plornish ("not to deceive you") through the still highly comic babblings of Flora and the disconcerting Mr. F.'s Aunt at her side and the Barnacle Junior, utterly helpless with his eyeglass, to the real suffering of Miss Wade. None of these can be considered the victim of a social machine like Chancery or Gradgrindery. Still, the machine makers have not failed in the support of stagnation and rigidity. Stagnation is enshrined in the Circumlocution Office, whose triumphs of How Not To Do It ensure the perpetual stoppage of the "disorder of the Barnacles and Stiltstalkings" (Bk. I, chap. xvi). Its enemies are Doyce, as an inventor the agent of progress, the essence of which is change, and Clennam, who both in Doyce's and in the Dorrits' causes demands to know why change is being thwarted. For the political and economic sides of life, Society has its Circumlocution Office; on the social side, rigidity is maintained by the Chief Butler, Mrs. Merdle, Mrs. Gowan, and Mrs. General. In their different spheres they work to uphold a social order that has long been obsolescent and to uphold not the positive values it may once have had but the rigid formalities of stifling decorum. Mrs. General, "considered as a piece of machinery," is perfect (Bk. II, chap. i).

The character who bridges the two aspects of society—being both of the Circumlocution lobby and of Society—is Mr. Merdle. His position in the novel, however, is peculiarly ambivalent: he is undoubtedly a swindler, but he is also the victim of the Chief Butler. His efforts to propitiate the Society of which this Chief Butler is a self-appointed bulwark have been limitless. Instead of taking a wife for himself, he bought a Bosom for Society. When Mr. Dorrit remarks upon its beauty, he accepts the compliment with the reply: " 'Mrs. Merdle . . . is generally considered a very attractive woman. And she is, no doubt. I am sensible of her being so' " (Bk. II, chap. xvi). He always regards first the belief of Society, then the observable truth, and finally his own feelings. He has bound himself over entirely to Society, and only in the face of disgrace in its eyes does he find the doubtful courage to enact the death he suffered spiritually long since.

Mr. Merdle's denatured spirit makes him feel physically dismembered too. He is the extreme development of the comic type identified by Bergson, a person embarrassed by his body. Bergson suggests the general law: "Any incident is comic that calls our attention to the physical in a person, when it is the moral side that is concerned."[2] He cites as an example our laughter at the public speaker who sneezes at the most pathetic moment of his speech. Merdle's physical automatism, however, is only momentarily funny, for the comic has too much serious implication. His hands, apparently of their own accord, retreat into his sleeves so that when introduced he has only a cuff to present; he attempts to counteract this tendency by taking himself into custody by the wrists. Such dissociation extends to other parts of his body:

> Mr. Merdle turned his tongue in his closed mouth—it seemed rather a stiff and unmanageable tongue.
>
> Mr. Merdle, suddenly getting up, as if he had been waiting in the interval for his legs, and they had just come.
>
> Mr. Dorrit . . . offered his hand. Mr. Merdle looked at the hand for a little while, took it on his for a moment as if his were a yellow salver or fish-slice, and then returned it to Mr. Dorrit. [Bk. II, chap. xvi]

The last excerpt quoted shows this peculiar dissociation extended to other people as well. It is thus analogous to Mrs. General's jingle "Papa, potatoes, poultry, prunes, and prism," in which the sound makes nonsense of the words so that Amy,

2. *Laughter,* p. 95.

for whom people still have special meaning, absolutely must continue to address Mr. Dorrit as father.

The satire of *Little Dorrit* envisions a world in which people have been so reduced to ciphers that names such as Bar or Bishop are perfectly adequate. Form and meaning are inextricable from one another: it is typical of satire to give its characters professions instead of proper names, but it is also part of the message of satire that people have petrified their individuality in the restrictions of professionalism. Dickens then sets Mr. Merdle next to Bar and Bishop, but does not call him Financier. Merdle's degree of pathos in being victimized by the Chief Butler and the Bosom is assisted by this juxtaposition of pure ciphers, allowing him almost to surface from satiric rigidity to novelistic humanity.

It is also typical of satire to present its characters more illustratively than realistically, as with Mrs. General in this speech:

> "If Miss Amy Dorrit will direct her own attention to, and will accept of my poor assistance in, the formation of a surface, Mr. Dorrit will have no further cause of anxiety. May I take this opportunity of remarking, as an instance in point, that it is scarcely delicate to look at vagrants with the attention which I have seen bestowed upon them by a very dear young friend of mine? They should not be looked at. Nothing disagreeable should ever be looked at. Apart from such a habit standing in the way of that graceful equanimity of surface which is so expressive of good breeding, it hardly seems compatible with refinement of mind. A truly refined mind will seem to be ignorant of the existence of anything that is not perfectly proper, placid, and pleasant." [Bk. II, chap. v]

But it is again part of the statement of the novel that Mrs. General has indeed become the inhuman manual of decorum she appears. She would not wish even a change of facial expression. As the "eminent varnisher," she is a microcosm of the society of brittle surfaces that opposes the fluidity of life.

The fluid is whole; the brittle is fragmented. "Fragmentary" is the adjective the narrator uses to describe Mr. Dorrit's manner of speech, and the sentence-paragraph is worded in such a way as to make it equally—and truly—applicable to the whole man: "Mr. Dorrit was even a little more fragmentary than usual; being excited on the subject, and anxious to make himself particularly emphatic" (Bk. II, chap. v). When the unidentified travelers arrive at the convent, we immediately recognize the head of the larger party by this mannerism: " 'New to—ha—to mountains,' said the Chief" (Bk. II, chap. i). He looks different enough from the William Dorrit we knew in Book I, but his speech, which comes from inside, is unchanged: the tag-mannerism has meaning.

Mr. Dorrit's relation to the reader is even more complex than Merdle's. The conditions are quite simple: when he is arrogant and foolish, we dislike him heartily and he is an object of satire; when the pretension is shown to us as the coordinate of pathetic insecurity and an overwhelming desire to be "right" with the world as his weak understanding conceives it, we pity him. The sense of complexity arises mainly from Dickens's rapid and continuous alternation of these feelings. At moments satire and a sort of novelistic sympathy are virtually simultaneous. Chapter xvi of Book II offers one of them. I summarize the chapter to bring out the remarkably ziggurat-like shape that emphasizes its rhetorical nature.

The mood of satire has already been set in the previous chapter, with the last two paragraphs turning from the pathos of Little Dorrit alone in Rome to Mrs. General "scratching up the driest little bones of antiquity, and bolting them whole without any human visitings—like a Ghoule in gloves." The first event is the arrival of Mr. and Mrs. Sparkler in the domain of the Chief Butler. Mr. Merdle takes himself into custody, and Fanny settles into Mrs. Merdle's rooms. Then Merdle goes off to meet Mr. Dorrit at his hotel in Brook Street. Crowds applaud Merdle as he rides through the streets, and the glory of his ascent up the hotel staircase is set off in satirical rhetoric turned upon biblical allusions ("The rich man, who had in a manner revised the New Testament, and already entered into the kingdom of Heaven. . . . As he went up the stairs, people were already posted on the lower stairs, that his shadow might fall upon them when he came down. So were the sick brought and laid in the track of the Apostle"). In the meeting that ensues, Dickens places much emphasis on Merdle's discomfort (not Mr. Dorrit's). At the apex of the ziggurat, Mr. Dorrit gives his estate into Merdle's hands. Then they go downstairs together in a descent, like Merdle's ascent, couched in religious reference ("the general bowing and crouching before this wonderful mortal the like of which prostration of spirit was not to be seen—no, by high Heaven, no! It may be worth thinking of by Fawners of all denominations—in Westminster Abbey and Saint Paul's Cathedral put together, on any Sunday in the year"). There follows a short paragraph on their coach ride, matching Merdle's previous solo ride. Then Mr. Dorrit arrives at the Merdle mansion, with Fanny again mentioned and the Chief Butler once more presiding. If it is all a "rapturous dream" for Mr. Dorrit at the end it is also a nightmare: "for, let him think what he would, the Chief Butler had him in his supercilious eye, even when that eye was on the plate and other table-garniture; and he never let him out of it." Mr. Dorrit has joined Mr. Merdle in the "confinement" of the Chief Butler's eye. The Chief Butler, though both supercilious and ludicrous, can see through gentleman-frauds. Mr. Dorrit's wealth is legitimate, but his character, like Merdle's, is false. Like Merdle, too, he is contemptible, harmful, and pitiful—only all in greater degree. (Merdle's crash affects more people, but harm in the book's terms must be measured as the pain impressed upon the reader; in these terms Mr. Dorrit's sins against his child and brother are well ahead.) The satire manages a novelistic confusion of our feelings.

The ultimate form of stagnation and rigidity is death, and that, accordingly, is the keynote of the novel's opening scene. Forms of "to die" recur frequently in chapter i of Book I and are further emphasized by phrases like "arid," "tomb," and "swim for life" and much talk on such subjects as the guillotine and assassination. This toll of death and the weight of torpor it represents build up to the chapter's closing image, in which even the tremendous motion of the sea is stilled, and the hope of resurrection—return of life—is barely heard: "and so deep a hush was on the sea, that it scarcely whispered of the time when it shall give up its dead." The keynote of death comes back in chapter iii, when Arthur reaches London:

> In every thoroughfare, up almost every alley, and down almost every turning, some doleful bell was throbbing, jerking, tolling, as if the Plague were in the city and the dead-carts were going round. . . .
>
> Mr. Arthur Clennam sat in the window of the coffee-house on Ludgate Hill, counting one of the neighbouring bells . . . and wondering how many sick people it might be the death of in the course of the year. . . . At the quarter, it went off into a condition of deadly-lively importunity.

In his own home he will find a "bier-like sofa," a staircase paneled into spaces "like so many mourning tablets," "a maimed table, a crippled wardrobe, a lean set of fire-irons like the skeleton of a set deceased." The objects reflect the spiritual death that surrounds them. Later we find the carpenters at the theatre joking that Frederick Dorrit is "dead without being aware of it" (Bk. I, chap. xx). When Clennam goes to seek Miss Wade in Calais, he finds:

> A dead sort of house, with a dead wall over the way and a dead gateway at the side, where a pendant bell-handle produced two dead tinkles, and a knocker produced a dead, flat, surface-tapping, that seemed not to have depth enough in it to penetrate even the cracked door. However, the door jarred open on a dead sort of spring; and he closed it behind him as he entered a dull yard, soon brought to a close by the back of another dead wall, where an attempt had been made to train some creeping shrubs, which were dead; and to make a little fountain into a grotto, which was dry; and to decorate that with a little statue, which was gone. [Bk. II, chap. xx]

Though this is far from Dickens's best rhetoric, it is typical in its strategy of reflecting character in place: as Clennam penetrates further into the house he will find the person he seeks, and she too will be, figuratively, dead. Finally, with perfect aptness, Rigaud's favourite oath is "Death."

Chapter i of Book II is in careful correspondence with chapter i of Book I. In diametric contrast, the cold of the Alps is set against the heat of Marseilles, Darkness and Night against the burning glare of the sun. But the parallels are even more important: for aridity there is now "barrenness and desolation," it is again autumn, and the general sterility is once more offset by the rich ferment of grapes. The novel's move from Marseilles to the Alps, only to find the same barrenness, reflects what has happened in the lives of the Dorrits: the circumstantial change has yet left the essence, imprisonment, intact. In a typically satiric configuration of plot, a great deal of change and bustle has brought them back to the original status quo.[3] Change is still not organic but only outward. Then, as the chapter progresses and the visitors to the convent of the Great Saint Bernard approach their destination, the narrative pauses to elaborate a discomforting image:

> While all this noise and hurry were rife among the living travellers, there, too, silently assembled in a grated house, half-a-dozen paces removed, with the same cloud enfolding them, and the same snow-flakes drifting in upon them, were the dead travellers found upon the mountain. The mother, storm-belated many winters ago, still standing in the corner with her baby at her breast; the man who had frozen with his arm raised to his mouth in fear or hunger, still pressing it with his dry lips after years and years. An awful company, mysteriously come together! A wild destiny for that mother to have foreseen, "Surrounded by so many and such companions upon whom I have never looked, and never shall look, I and my child will dwell together inseparable, on the Great Saint Bernard, outlasting generations who will come to see us, and will never know our name, or one word of our story but the end."

3. Cf. Kernan, *Plot of Satire,* pp. 98–100.

> The living travellers thought little or nothing of the dead just then.

The frozen travelers present the outward form of the spiritual state of the living travelers; the commonage of the living and the dead is more than the cloud and snowflakes. Dickens compounds the irony of this juxtaposition by setting a mother at the center of the frozen group, for that is the one significant figure missing from the party of visitors.

Two characters stand outside the scheme of stagnation and change outlined thus far. Both are wholly illustrative, each of an extreme. One, Rigaud, changes with chameleon-like ease. He changes his name from Rigaud to Lagnier to Blandois or back again as it becomes convenient; he changes country, occupation, professions, friends, manners. Only two things do not change: his insistence upon being a "gentleman," and his peculiar smile in which his moustache goes up under his nose and his nose comes down over his moustache. These are marks of the pure evil that Rigaud embodies: the devil comes in many forms, but his smile is always sinister. His insistence upon gentility makes us even more doubtful of the social standard that underlies Henry Gowan's sense of wrong and that Mr. Dorrit espouses so desperately. The second figure, Little Dorrit, is the very antithesis: pure goodness. Born in the Marshalsea, she is ironically the only major character free from imprisonment. She recoils from Blandois with a repugnance the narrator calls "a natural antipathy" (Bk. II, chap. vii); her confrontation with Mrs. Clennam at the end is an obvious setting of the New Testament against the Old (Bk. II, chap. xxxi). She is preeminently the nurturer of life: the financial and moral support of her indigent family, "mother" to the crazed Maggy, the sole link between Frederick Dorrit and life, the last comfort to her father, nurse to Pet Meagles, nurse and finally wife to Arthur. Yet it is Little Dorrit who at the end of Book I is unable to change with the family fortunes, refusing to change her old dress, and throughout the following year writing to Arthur of former days. But Little Dorrit transcends this world of ceaseless, necessary, organic change. She is the unchanging that is the eternal;

she is the hope that Arthur embraces when he realizes that he is still young enough to marry.

Stasis, then, is the menace to life presented by the novel. The use of static types rather than of growing, human characters, common to satire, thus becomes particularly appropriate here. The evil is not only that these people are proud or foolish or wicked but that, in addition, they are somehow trapped in these states—they are static. The character who would grow and change, whose attitudes would be complex and varying, would not be treated satirically. There is one such character in *Little Dorrit*—Arthur Clennam—and about him Dickens writes novelistically. The novel and the satire in *Little Dorrit* join as they share characters, situations, and plot, but above all as they focus upon a common theme. In the course of the book Arthur travels to the state in which the satirized characters begin. The result is almost a textbook illustration of one simple difference between satire and the mimetic novel. Because we follow Arthur through the events that finally deplete the life within him, because we see the depletion in graduated stages, we understand the process and perhaps even sympathize with the character. Understanding and sympathy both drive out satire.

Arthur begins with one blight upon him, not of his own making: the lack of will that he can hardly explain to Mr. Meagles. Mr. Meagles, bursting with will and force, chafes at being a "jail-bird" in quarantine (Bk. I, chap. ii); Arthur is calm, perhaps as much from passivity as from common sense. He emerges from this aimlessness in the partnership with Doyce, but only after the blight has prepared a new cause and a new form for itself. Uncertainty of self disabled Arthur from competing with Henry Gowan, and now the loss of Pet leads him to a second passivity. Arthur fixes upon himself a premature middle age that prevents his grasping the nature of Little Dorrit's attachment to him. His manner of thinking about her constitutes a withdrawal from the activities of life. After the family's rise to fortune

> he thought of her otherwise in the old way. She was his innocent friend, his delicate child, his dear Little Dorrit.

> This very change of circumstances fitted curiously in with the habit, begun on the night when the roses floated away, of considering himself as a much older man than his years really made him. He regarded her from a point of view which in its remoteness, tender as it was, he little thought would have been unspeakable agony to her. He speculated about her future destiny, and about the husband she might have. [Bk. II, chap. viii]

Despite these last speculations, he really considers her a "delicate child," as Dickens frequently points out. He feels suitable only to be the spouse of Pet's dead twin-sister. When the firm of Doyce and Clennam proves to have been prey to the corruptions of Circumlocution and Merdleism through his own fault, Arthur renounces his work too. Without the two associations of life that would define his manhood, he is now truly bankrupt—and therefore ready for the Marshalsea. Spiritual insolvency is described in the introduction to the College (just after the birth of Amy):

> "That a child would be born to you in a place like this?" said the doctor. "Bah, bah, sir what does it signify? A little more elbow-room is all we want here. We are quiet here; we don't get badgered here; there's no knocker here, sir, to be hammered at by creditors and bring a man's heart into his mouth. Nobody comes here to ask if a man's at home, and to say he'll stand on the door mat till he is. Nobody writes threatening letters about money to this place. It's freedom, sir, it's freedom! I have had to-day's practice at home and abroad, on a march, and aboard ship, and I'll tell you this: I don't know that I have ever pursued it under such quiet circumstances as here this day. Elsewhere, people are restless, worried, hurried about, anxious respecting one thing, anxious respecting another. Nothing of the kind here, sir. We have done all that—we know the worst of it; we have got to the bottom, we can't fall, and what have we found? Peace. That's the word for it. Peace. . . ."
>
> Now, the debtor was a very different man from the doctor, but he had already begun to travel, by his opposite

> segment of the circle, to the same point. Crushed at first by his imprisonment, he had soon found a dull relief in it. He was under lock and key; but the lock and key that kept him in, kept numbers of his troubles out. It he had been a man with strength of purpose to face those troubles and fight them, he might have broken the net that held him, or broken his heart; but being what he was, he languidly slipped into this smooth descent, and never more took one step upward. [Bk. I, chap. vi]

The truth and pathos of this attitude are kept submerged under the distant, accusatory tone. The doctor is a buffoon who after this last speech returns "to his associate and chum in hoarseness, puffiness, red-facedness, all-fours, tobacco, dirt, and brandy"; the debtor (Mr. Dorrit) is foolish, weak, and soon to be self-deceiving in the extreme. Clennam of course is very different from these two, but when he enters the Marshalsea he begins a descent certainly analogous. The first step he takes is exactly parallel:

> In the unnatural peace of having gone through the dreaded arrest, and got there,—the first change of feeling which the prison most commonly induced, and from which dangerous resting-place so many men had slipped down to the depths of degradation and disgrace by so many ways,—he could think of some passages in his life. [Bk. II, chap. xxvii]

Arthur is roused for a time by the terrific purpose that drives him to attempt to rescue his mother despite herself. When the discovery of Rigaud ends in disaster, however, he lapses into the deathlike lethargy signified by fever:

> For a burning restlessness set in, an agonized impatience of the prison, and a conviction that he was going to break his heart and die there, which caused him indescribable suffering. His dread and hatred of the place became so intense that he felt it a labour to draw his breath in it. The sensation of being stifled sometimes so overpowered him, that he would stand at the window holding his throat

and gasping. At the same time a longing for other air, and a yearning to be beyond the blind blank wall, made him feel as if he must go mad with the ardour of desire.

Many other prisoners had had experience of this condition before him, and its violence and continuity had worn themselves out in their cases, as they did in his. Two nights and a day exhausted it. It came back by fits, but those grew fainter and returned at lengthening intervals. A desolate calm succeeded; and the middle of the week found him settled down in the despondency of low, slow fever. [Bk. II, chap. xxix]

Only a literary critic would put together these passages from opposite ends of the book to see their similarity. The undesigning reader comes upon the later descriptions as something quite different, for now he is witnessing human experience instead of identifying a type. The different tone itself, sympathetic to the prisoner, turns most of the culpability upon the prison. Despite the likeness between the stasis Arthur suffers and that which afflicts so many of the characters in the book, he is always protected from satire. Arthur is a novelistic character, aware of imprisonment and struggling against it. Up to this point he has been continually in quest of the meaning or values that would lead to victory. Even now, because he is to be saved for the one ray of hope that closes the book (that ray necessarily a novelistic possibility in this otherwise satiric world), he must continue free from satiric focus. Yet there is also a satiric point to be made, and Arthur's condition is part of it. Dickens's solution to this problem shows his mixed mode at its best. In chapter xxvii of Book II, Arthur is mourning the love his blindness has lost him:

Little Dorrit, Little Dorrit. Again, for hours. Always Little Dorrit!

Happily, if it ever had been so, it was over, and better over. Granted, that she had loved him, and he had known it and had suffered himself to love her, what a road to have led her away upon—the road that would have brought her

> back to this miserable place! He ought to be much comforted by the reflection that she was quit of it for ever; that she was, or would soon be, married (vague rumours of her father's projects in that direction had reached Bleeding Heart Yard, with the news of her sister's marriage); and that the Marshalsea gate had shut for ever on all those perplexed possibilities, of a time that was gone.
>
> Dear Little Dorrit.
>
> Looking back upon his own poor story, she was its vanishing-point. Every thing in its perspective led to her innocent figure. He had travelled thousands of miles towards it; previous unquiet hopes and doubts had worked themselves out before it; it was the centre of the interest of his life; it was the termination of everything that was good and pleasant in it; beyond there was nothing but mere waste and darkened sky.

The passage is serious, straightforward, verbally restrained, and admirably successful in its lump-in-the-throat emotion. But here is the paragraph immediately following:

> As ill at ease as on the first night of his [Arthur's] lying down to sleep within those dreary walls, he wore the night out with such thoughts. What time Young John lay wrapt in peaceful slumber, after composing and arranging the following monumental inscription on his pillow:—
>
> STRANGER!
> respect the tomb of
> JOHN CHIVERY, Junior
> who died at an advanced age
> not necessary to mention.
> He encountered his rival in a distressed state,
> and felt inclined
> TO HAVE A ROUND WITH HIM;
> but, for the sake of the loved one,
> conquered those feelings of bitterness, and became
> MAGNANIMOUS.

The first sentence continues the original mood. Then suddenly comes the Dickensian signal of comedy in the archaic phrasing "what time" (compare, for instance, the Veneering crest "in gold and eke in silver" [*Our Mutual Friend,* Bk. I, chap. i]), and we enter into the chronic melancholia of Young John Chivery. At this point in the novel, however, his lugubriousness is virtually a burlesque of Clennam's depression. It does not have a derogatory effect upon the latter: though the emotional tension built up through Arthur's meditation is released in comedy of which the basis is ultimately satiric, the validity of Arthur's emotion remains unaltered. Yet the satirically biased comedy of Young John does have moral relevance to Arthur's situation: the bathos is a comic version of the self-regarding abdication from action and responsibility that Arthur verges upon. By diverting the satiric emphasis of Arthur's apathy onto Young John's dolefulness, Dickens manages to keep Arthur a sympathetic hero even while using him as one illustration of the book's satiric argument.

It takes the business capacities of Mr. Meagles, Pancks, and Doyce to get Arthur technically out of the Marshalsea, but of course it is Little Dorrit who rescues him from spiritual torpor. When he realizes that she is a woman and not a child, he also suddenly knows that he is a man, and through the action he takes upon this knowledge comes their salvation. After the final purgation (fever) comes release—release, however, into something as separate from the world about them as Amy always was. This is inevitable. Arthur is in some degree an early version of the alienated man recurrent in literature since the nineteenth century. He is placed in a society of ciphers called Bar and Bishop, institutions like the Circumlocution Office, and frauds like Merdle, confronting some of them and becoming indirectly involved with others. To become a compliant part of this world would be to move into satire, as Richard Carstone does, rather than away from it. Arthur, consequently, finds work among that society's outcast and neglected: he enters into partnership with the British "criminal" Doyce in an office in Bleeding Heart Yard, employs the foreigner Cavalletto, and befriends the bewildered Plornishes. Similarly, he finds spiritual fulfillment in turning away from the society's restless stagnation to the unchanging truth that is Amy. The peace that Arthur and Amy win at the end is something transcendental; its apartness from this world of endless motion is the burden of the novel's last sentence: "They went quietly down into the roaring streets, inseparable and blessed; and as they passed along in sunshine and shade, the noisy and the eager and the arrogant and the froward and the vain, fretted, and chafed, and made their usual uproar."

Thus form supports meaning: across the satiric, static picture of a rigid, stagnating society moves the novelistically developing figure of Arthur, the man who learns continually that life is growth. Dickens combines satire and novel to set against the darkened vision the standard that also points to the direction of hope. In this way he clarifies the satire; at the same time, the satire provides an emblematic frame for the novel. As Arthur struggles through enervating doubt to the full, though qualified, participation in life signified in his marriage to Amy and his renewed partnership with Doyce, Dickens dramatizes the dangers that threaten him in the novel's grotesques whom Arthur himself encounters: his mother, Jeremiah Flintwinch, Henry Gowan, and Flora Finching. Only Gowan shows apathy akin to Arthur's disenchantment; the others rather display a fierce or manic energy, but they are all dehumanized as Arthur may become—rigid in a single pose.

The formal union of novel and satire is not so abrupt as the extremes alone might make it: there is a median range. It is signaled in the names of the characters, from the wholly illustrative denotations of Bar and Bishop through a group representing a cross between associative meaning and possible reality —Barnacle, Stiltstalking, Merdle, and Mrs. General, for instance —to the entirely realistic proper name of Arthur Clennam. The divisions are not rigid, however; the highly satirized Mrs. Gowan has a quite normal name. In the mixing of static and kinetic characters there is a similar median: a character who changes so markedly that the change is more a positive illustration of the satiric argument than a novelistic development of character. The rebellion of Pancks is a break from stagnation, and in fact its abrupt explosiveness suits him. I find it difficult to determine whether "Pancks the grubber" is ever real or is ironically assumed from the start, but even if the figure is wholly a mask, it develops sufficiently in action to count for evil. Pancks first presents himself to Arthur as a minor version of Mr. Casby. Like his employer, he is impervious to season: " 'As a stranger you feel the climate more than I do, I dare say. Indeed I haven't got time to feel it' " (Bk. chap. xiii). Clennam senses something odd in his manner, but neither he nor we are quite certain what it is. His self-assumed title "Pancks the gypsy" is the first sure mark of separation from the economic Casby-society with its "Whole Duty of Man" to "keep at it." Later, his success in bringing about the Dorrits' change of fortune buoys him up to the final break. He accosts Mr. Casby to force the change those silver locks had denied and to declare his aversion to the heartless extortion he has abetted. Whether from rigid mask or rigid reality, Pancks's escape is the novel's moral.

Mrs. Clennam's flight from Rigaud to Little Dorrit, on the other hand, is barely an escape from rigidity and not at all one from satire. It provides a highly dramatic climax to her part of the story, brings about the defeat of Rigaud, and even offers the circumstances for Tattycoram's return, but it tells little—and nothing novelistic—of Mrs. Clennam's character. When Mr. Gradgrind broke down, he became human and pathetic; Mrs. Clennam remains a stark figuring of Old Testament morality. She has not changed; she comes to this turn only because she is driven into a corner and sees no other way out. Almost as if to emphasize this point, Dickens has her stricken again with paralysis—this time total—as soon as the plot and satiric argument have derived what they need from her action.

Another escape, of hardly less drama and equally emblematic, occurs just before Mrs. Clennam's. Throughout the novel the primary symbol of disregarded womanhood is of course Amy, and it is typical of Dickens's typology that she is, if not a child, certainly childlike. There is also, however, a fully adult complement: Affery. As an instance of femininity suppressed and enslaved in an utterly masculine world, she is both more conspicuous and more emphatic than Mrs. Gradgrind, her predecessor in this role. Affery's wedding, wholly the wish of her master and mistress, could equally have been a "smothering" (Bk. I, chap. iii). In the course of the novel she moves from a degraded but instinctively true human being to a witless bundle of fears. In this condition, with her apron over her head, she almost represents the ghostlike no-thing that Mrs. Clennam has made of the woman inside herself. The reality Affery nonetheless witnesses can only be allowed in the form of "dreams." The chapters on her dreams prepare us for their use at the climax of the Flintwinch-Clennam story. Mr. Pancks opens this scene with the command "Affery, tell your dreams!" (Bk. II, chap. xxx). The mechanics of the scene, however, have no need for Affery. There is nothing she has to tell that cannot (and does not) come out some other way; she corroborates some of Rigaud's assumptions and betrays enough to force Jeremiah to his confession, but in neither of these functions is she really essential. Dickens keeps turning to her throughout the scene for symbolic embellishment: this scene is the forcible overthrow of the devouring masculine, and the hopelessly crippled feminine shouts its release in a frenzy of power (" 'I'll wake the dead! Stop where you are, or I'll make shrieks enough to wake the dead!' " [Bk. II, chap. xxx]).

A number of other characters make attempts at or gestures toward escape from stagnation. The sincerest attempt is Doyce's, and it is successful. The misfortune is that success comes at the painful price of exile. Doyce achieves the opportunity to grow that his intellect and spirit demand only by emigrating to an unidentified foreign land. He returns to England to help Clennam, but there is no sign in the novel that anyone except Clennam, the man who finally escapes happily, recognizes his worth. Henry Gowan, in contrast, maintains a pretense of alienation for which his pose as an artist is well suited. His continual sniping at the society he cannot conquer creates an appearance of desire to escape it altogether, as does his emigration to Italy, but actually this sniping is his best means of keeping as close to society as he can. He derides the upholders of stagnation only because he cannot lead them. In his work and in his relation to the society about him, he is the diametric antithesis to Doyce.

One possible avenue of escape that the novel considers is the pastoral. *Little Dorrit* offers three variations of pastoral aspiration. The most endearing is that of the Plornishes, manifest first in Old Nandy's bucolic songs and then in the fantastic decor of their refurbished house. The pastoral longings are primarily Mrs. Plornish's, and if they do not yield her material escape from Bleeding Heart Yard, they do lead her to bring a degree of happiness to the lives of her father, her husband, and herself. Allied to this are Bob the turnkey's Sunday excursions with little Amy to "meadows" and "green lanes" (Bk. I, chap. vii). The pathetic sincerity of the Plornishes points up by contrast the affectation of Mrs. Merdle's expressions of similar longings. She tells Fanny and Amy Dorrit that " 'a more primitive state of society would be delicious to me. There used to be a poem when I learnt lessons, something about Lo the poor Indian whose something mind! If a few thousand persons moving in Society, could only go and be Indians, I would put my name down directly' " (Bk. I, chap. xx). But her parrot knows better: Mrs. Merdle is as trapped in her cushions as he is in his cage. The third version of the pastoral in this novel is the Meagleses' home, presented as a place of retreat:

> It was a charming place (none the worse for being a little eccentric), on the road by the river, and just what the residence of the Meagles family ought to be. It stood in a garden, no doubt as fresh and beautiful in the May of the Year, as Pet now was in the May of her life; and it was defended by a goodly show of handsome trees and spreading evergreens, as Pet was by Mr. and Mrs. Meagles. [Bk. I, chap. xvi]

To some extent this passage is ironic: across the river comes Henry Gowan, and the taint that allows the Meagleses to lose Pet to him is the taint that belies the purity of this pastoral world. Mr. and Mrs. Meagles have built it with much labor and love, but their hearts have allowed some "microscopic portion of that mustard-seed that had sprung up into the great tree of the Circumlocution Office" (Bk. I, chap. xvi) to creep into this garden. Their escape is therefore not complete, but Mr. and Mrs. Meagles are at least true enough to know and regret this failure, even if they never quite understand it. *Bleak House* ended with two possibilities for salvation. The lesser of these, the industry of the north, became in *Hard Times* the center of an earthly hell. The greater hope—the happy combination of pastoral spirit and place in Esther and Allan in Yorkshire—appears inadequate in *Little Dorrit*. The avenues out of *Bleak House* are closed.

The satiric vision of *Little Dorrit* also gives an ironic perspective to Dickens's early works. First there is the figure of the rich, wise, and benevolent older man, seen by critics who confuse the social reformer with the satirist as the only constructive social and political solution Dickens has to offer. From the later Pickwick and Mr. Brownlow to Old Martin Chuzzlewit and even John Jarndyce, one cannot deny that the figure is disturbingly facile. In *Little Dorrit* it is ironically inverted by the complementary persons who divide the role: Casby, the Father of the Marshalsea, who in reality has nothing to give and only demeaning deference to inspire, and Mr. Merdle, the affluent man who turns out to be a fraud. Merdle is also a bitter commentary upon the type of self-made worker that the Victorian ethic so exalted (a commentary first presented with Josiah Bounderby). The true worker, Daniel Doyce, is thwarted in his efforts and treated condescendingly even by those who support him.

Second, and more important, is the popular device in Victorian novels for rescuing a perplexed hero: the unexpected inheritance. Dickens employs it directly in *Oliver Twist, Nicholas Nickleby,* and *Martin Chuzzlewit.* The convention receives its first twist in *Dombey and Son,* where the problem ironically is not for the heir to find a fortune but for the fortune to find an heir. In *Bleak House* the hero finds his inheritance, but it turns out to be an illusion. Finally, in *Little Dorrit,* the circumstances again follow the basic pattern of *Oliver Twist:* there is a real fortune and an unhappy indigent who, with little enough probability, is discovered to be its heir. Only the result is drastically different: the inheritance is seen to be not a sign of deserving nobility on the part of the heir, but something quite external to him which consequently brings no essential change. In fact, it brings pleasure only as a disguise for further unhappiness and trouble. *Great Expectations* will have this irony for its center; a major theme of *Our Mutual Friend* will be the cleansing of the fortune.

PART IV

Uses of Satire

CHAPTER 9

A Tale of Two Cities and *Great Expectations*

Although there is some satire in *A Tale of Two Cities* and more in *Great Expectations,* in both it is ancillary to other concerns. These novels are relatively short for Dickens, and even for their length they have relatively few characters. The same economy is apparent in other aspects of structure. The following chapter concentrates almost exclusively upon the functions of satire within these structures. Though the satire is ancillary, it is a very effective servant.

From the early fifties Dickens had warned repeatedly, in private letters and in public pronouncements, of the violence that would erupt if human conditions were not soon bettered (this meant, in part, if the import of his satires went unheeded; see, for instance, the 1850 preface to *Oliver Twist).* At the close of the decade, in 1859, Dickens dramatized this point in the most effective medium he had: he chose as subject for his next novel the most obvious historical parallel to the chaos he foresaw.

A Tale of Two Cities impresses its meaning upon the reader largely through adjustment of his sympathy. At first, emphasis is so strongly upon the careless cruelty of the oppressors that revenge (as well as relief) for the oppressed seems fitting; we delight to share in the secret of its preparation. Soon after this alignment has been established, however, we are made to change sides. When power renders the mob itself just as inhuman as the aristocrats had been, sympathy turns away from them—not back to the aristocracy, since Darnay is always clearly an exception to his class, but to the innocent victims of rampant bloodthirstiness. There is none of the exuberance that made judgment upon the violence in *Barnaby Rudge* ambivalent: the mobs of Paris are simply terrifying, the women who knit placidly by the guillotine utterly appalling. Dickens effects this transfer of sympathy largely by using two different modes, satire and melodrama.

Roughly, the satire is confined to the earlier part of the novel and directed against the oppressive establishment; the melodrama—not of the false, sentimental sort Dickens often ridiculed, but of deep and justified terror—presents the violent outcome of an intolerable state of affairs prolonged beyond the limit of human endurance. The emotion engendered by the display of oppression at the beginning is channeled more into satiric anger at the oppressors than into sympathetic involvement with the oppressed. When the Marquis's chariot runs over a peasant child, we are more occupied with the inhumanity of the aristocrat than with the suffering of the child or its parents. The people, in fact, except for Mm. Defarge, are never very attractive; pity for them is aroused only indirectly, as an adjunct of the satiric anger at their lords, rather than directly, through identification with them. The reader stands by the side of the satirical narrator, apart from and in a sense above both parties.

The character whom the reader later does become concerned with as an individual is Darnay, a victim of the mob's implacability. This part of the story is rendered in melodrama. As the novel's satire yields to melodrama, our anger and indignation give way to true sympathy—but for Darnay and those he loves. Our identification with his goals, aided by our distance from the Jacquerie, allows a response of horrified revulsion to the bloodshed that ensues. Any pity for the oppressed that survives even as they oppress is principally intellectual; that is, it survives as recollection of the just causes of their uprising. The satire that aroused it, however, is now in abeyance, and the melodrama that arouses direct, immediate emotion turns our feelings against the mob. No precise moment can be defined when our sympathies change, but as the satire gradually diminishes and the melodrama rises, the novel makes its sequential statement through the different responses the two modes arouse. If conditions that produce satire continue unrelieved, what must follow is too terrible for anything but horror.

From this structural importance in a generally grave novel, the satire derives a number of distinguishing qualities. First, it is much more angry than comic. Secondly, and possibly in consequence of the first condition, it is carried more in the narrator's rhetoric than in the characters. The two eccentrics who resemble the earlier Dickensian satirical types seem almost misplaced in this novel: Jerry Cruncher, with his hair standing on end, married to a termagant whom he terrorizes for her "flopping," seems an unsuccessful attempt to return to the comic dialogue of the early novels; Miss Pross's part in the novel is tenuous, and her victorious battle with Mme. Defarge appeals on essentially chauvinistic bases that are morally at odds with the primary impulses of the novel. Finally, although only the French suffer the violent results of their blindness, the satire is directed equally (except in the Defarge-Pross battle) against both the French and the English, so that the warning by analogy is unmistakable.

After somewhat heavy sarcasm on the state of France in the opening chapter, attention turns to the state of England. In Book II Dickens launches the attack on Philistine self-satisfaction that will reach its peak in the Podsnaps of *Our Mutual Friend:*

> Tellson's Bank by Temple Bar was an old-fashioned place, even in the year one thousand seven hundred and eighty. It was very small, very dark, very ugly, very incommodious. It was an old-fashioned place, moreover, in the moral attribute that the partners in the House were proud of its smallness, proud of its darkness, proud of its ugliness, proud of its incommodiousness. They were even boastful of its eminence in those particulars, and were fired by an express conviction that, if it were less objectionable, it would be less respectable. . . . Tellson's (they said) wanted no elbow-room, Telson's wanted no light, Telson's wanted no embellishment. Noakes and Co.'s might, or Snooks Brothers' might; but Tellson's, thank Heaven!—
>
> Any one of these partners would have disinherited his son on the question of rebuilding Tellson's. In this respect the House was much on a par with the Country; which

> did very often disinherit its sons for suggesting improvements in laws and customs that had long been highly objectionable, but were only the more respectable. [Bk. II, chap. i]

Self-satisfaction and pomposity are manifest in England especially in its legal process, which is a sort of national institution. The great irony of the system is that its bloody cruelty is quite ineffective, yet there is no attempt at improvement: "Altogether, the Old Bailey, at that date, was a choice illustration of the precept, that 'Whatever is is right'; an aphorism that would be as final as it is lazy, did it not include the troublesome consequence, that nothing that ever was, was wrong" (Bk. II, chap. ii). In the same chapter Dickens combines legal jargon and patriotic cant for the kind of exuberant spoof his satire repeatedly turned to:

> Silence in the court! Charles Darnay had yesterday pleaded Not Guilty to an indictment denouncing him (with infinite jingle and jangle) for that he was a false traitor to our serene, illustrious, excellent, and so forth, prince, our Lord the King, by reason of his having, on divers occasions, and by divers means and ways, assisted Lewis, the French King, in his wars against our said serene, illustrious, excellent, and so forth; that was to say, by coming and going, between the dominions of our said serene, illustrious, excellent, and so forth, and those of the said French Lewis, and wickedly, falsely, traitorously, and otherwise evil-adverbiously, revealing to the said French Lewis what forces our said serene, illustrious, excellent, and so forth, had in preparation to send to Canada and North America. [Bk. II, chap. ii]

This chapter and the next form a continuous satiric attack on the inhumanity of "justice." The mob fares no better under satiric treatment than do the scribal verbalizers. For them Dickens uses a reductive strategy familiar from his earlier work. Their unsympathetic, noisy responses are first described in simile: " When the Attorney-General ceased, a buzz arose in the court as if a cloud of great blue-flies were swarming about the prisoner, in anticipation of what he was soon to become" (Bk. II, chap. iii). With the next reference, and in those that follow, the vehicle and tenor are one:

> The blue-flies buzzed again.
> The buzz of the great flies was loud again.
> Buzzing from the blue-flies . . .
> And now, the jury turned to consider, and the great flies swarmed again.

Only when it finally disperses at the end of the chapter does the crowd again become human and merely suggestive of flies: "The crowd came pouring out with a vehemence that nearly took him [Jerry] off his legs, and a loud buzz swept into the street as if the baffled blue-flies were dispersing in search of other carrion." As in Pope, the metaphor of men as insects is a physical image of moral pettiness.

The world is also turning men into machines. Mr. Lorry is this novel's member of what appears to be a series of characters beginning with the mechanized Pancks in *Little Dorrit*. Pancks insisted he was an automatic engine of "keep at it" because it was the only way of life he could see in the society about him. In submission to Tellson's, Mr. Lorry makes similar and far more elaborate professions:

> "Miss Manette, I am a man of business. I have a business charge to acquit myself of. In your reception of it, don't heed me any more than if I was a speaking machine—truly, I am not much else. . . .
>
> "These are mere business relations, miss; there is no friendship in them, no particular interest, nothing like sentiment. I have passed from one to another, in the course of my business life, just as I pass from one of our customers to another in the course of my business day; in short, I have no feelings; I am a mere machine. . . .
>
> "Feelings! I have no time for them, no chance of them.

I pass my whole life, miss, in turning an immense pecuniary Mangle." [Bk. I, chap. iv]

The automata of Dickens's earlier novels became such through the rigidity of their own unconscious natures; in the later novels an even more disturbing type appears, the man whose instincts are toward life and feeling but who deliberately adopts an attitude of rigidity as the only means of survival in the world around him. The motivation of Pancks is unclear but appears to be simply economic. Mr. Lorry, on the other hand, is obviously afraid of emotional involvement, afraid that to free his natural flow of emotions in the business world will be to destroy himself. His successor in the next novel, *Great Expectations,* will reach a compromise with life: Wemmick is a post-office figure of impassivity for his employer Jaggers but, on the other side of his moat, an indulgent son to the Aged Parent and a persistent suitor to Miss Skiffins. Jaggers himself is a machine in that he cuts off—or, rather, regularly washes off—human involvement, but he is redeemed from satire by the attractiveness of his superb ability and the final indication of human understanding in his defense of having given Estella to Miss Havisham.

As the scene of *A Tale of Two Cities* shifts again to France (in chapter vii of Book II), the portrayal of Monseigneur the Marquis resumes the satiric approach of the opening chapter. His attitudes and actions in the three chapters devoted to him (vii, viii, and ix) advance the plot of the melodrama through their harmful effect upon the fortunes of Charles Darnay. The failure to identify the Marquis except by title until the very end of chapter viii, when we learn that he is Darnay's uncle, allows extension of the satiric attack to the whole class he represents. Yet the heavy-handed irony of the first paragraphs of chapter vii cannot last long: the atrocious behavior of the Marquis soon makes the narrator bitterly direct. Nor does the narration remain satirical in tone when the novel returns to France in chapter xv. Mme. Defarge and her lieutenant the Vengeance depict the ultimate development of the denatured woman, but this theme is now rendered in the serious tone of melodrama without the modulation of satiric mockery. The nightmare of terror finally demands a response too intense for even the bitterest satiric invective. For full emotional involvement, the most direct relation between reader and subject is required, and any rhetorical denunciation by the narrator would intervene.

As the denatured women become figures of horror, described without even the lightening of satirical embellishment, Lucie reverts to the simpler golden-girl type of the early novels. The anti-women are by far the most active and aggressive of their line, and the heroine, in reaction, becomes problematically passive. Yet Dickens does retain the later novels' recognition of sexuality. He renders it not in its true form, linked to the truly desirable, but in its debasement and as part of the pernicious cause. Mme. Defarge is more human than the Vengeance exactly in the degree in which we understand her motivation: she was turned into an implacable avenger by the rape of her sister. These three women represent stages of one terrible process: the sister was the immediate sufferer, Mme. Defarge is the figure of prolonged pain and resentment, and the Vengeance embodies the final, crazed violence. Because Dr. Manette protested against the original sexual abuse, he was imprisoned. The rape is in this way the motivating force for the whole plot: a single act lies behind both Dr. Manette's long imprisonment and consequent position among the Jacquerie and Mme. Defarge's overriding determination to have Darnay's blood. For the purposes of the plot, however, this first cause could just as well have been almost any other violation of human right. Dickens's choice of the *droit du seigneur* is consistent with the thematic preoccupations of his work as a whole.

Death in this novel has a special aspect of horror. It is physically real, bloody, and violent, unlike the institutional stultification and rigidity or the spiritual inertia of the satiric novels. It is also the book's central image. In the introductory description in chapter i of Book I, it is silently at work:

> It is likely enough that in the rough outhouses of some tillers of the heavy lands adjacent to Paris, there were shel-

> tered from the weather that very day, rude carts, bespattered with rustic mire, snuffed about by pigs, and roosted in by poultry, which the Farmer, Death, had already set apart to be his tumbrils of the Revolution.

In England death is the catch-all solution of lazy misgovernment, flourishing as life is held cheap:

> But indeed, at that time, putting to death was a recipe much in vogue with all trades and professions, and not least of all with Tellson's. Death is Nature's remedy for all things, and why not Legislations's? Accordingly, the forger was put to Death; the utterer of a bad note was put to Death; the unlawful opener of a letter was put to Death; the purloiner of forty shillings and sixpence was put to Death; the holder of a horse at Tellson's door, who made off with it, was put to Death; the coiner of a bad shilling was put to death; the sounders of three-fourths of the notes in the whole gamut of Crime, were put to Death. [Bk. II, chap. i]

The threat of capital punishment is the principal developing force of the plot. When the terror of the Revolution breaks out in France, death becomes omnipresent.

Through almost the whole novel, death appears as the cruel cutting down of life, with the prospect of rebirth offered only ironically: Jerry Cruncher, in his profession of grave-robber, is a "resurrection-man"; Dr. Manette is "recalled to Life" from burial, not from death. With the self-sacrifice of Sydney Carton, however, resurrection becomes quite straightforward and Christian. Between the executions of the little seamstress and of Carton, the narrator inserts the quotation: " 'I am the Resurrection and the Life, saith the Lord: he that believeth in me, though he were dead, yet shall he live: and whosoever liveth and believeth in me shall never die' " (Bk. III, chap. xv). But the evils of the novel have been set in social, not personal and religious, terms. Sydney Carton's choosing to die so that Darnay and Lucie can live a happy life is a noble act of generosity, but his vision of a regenerated world has no wider foundation than his own selfless motivation—and hope:

> I see a beautiful city and a brilliant people rising from this abyss, and, in their struggles to be truly free, in their triumphs and defeats, through long years to come, I see the evil of this time and of the previous time of which this is the natural birth, gradually making expiation for itself and wearing out. [Bk. III, chap. xv]

Carton's own moral redemption and the benefits of happiness and life he gives to the Manettes are unquestionable, but he cannot, even emblematically, expiate the sins of a whole society. The "solution" *Dombey and Son* offered was personal—and properly so, because the indictment was primarily moral. In the novels that followed—*Bleak House, Hard Times,* and *Little Dorrit*—personal solutions were the only ones possible. The problems in these novels were expressed from the beginning in personal terms: their plots were concerned with central characters seeking a way of living in the satiric world around them. Although for those who succeeded there was an implication that their individual achievements could be translated into a wider, social morality and so ultimately, perhaps, produce a better world, that implication remained tacit; what salvation the individual gained was his alone. *A Tale of Two Cities,* on the other hand, begins with problems of class difference and social abuse and expresses those problems in social terms. *Oliver Twist* did the same, but it maintained that formulation. The Workhouses can only be improved by action to reform them, and though Oliver's escape saves Oliver, there is no implication that it helps any of his companions who did not run away. *A Tale of Two Cities,* however, attempts to make Carton's sacrifice, which is a noble solution to the plot of the melodrama, the solution to the satiric setting as well. Carton's heroism does not even expiate Darnay's inherited guilt: it only frees Darnay himself from undeserved punishment. The shift of principal mode in *A Tale of Two Cities* from satire to melodrama is successful and effective; the collapse of the two into one, implied by the single act of redemption at the end, produces a sense of narrative sophistry.

A Tale of Two Cities is not primarily satiric, but it uses satire to define its norms. The foreground of the novel is a romantic tale of love and conflicting loyalties; the far more important background is a dark picture of a world that goes from inconvenience and injustice to chaos. In *Great Expectations* the integration of foreground and background is much tighter. The foreground story is the growth of Pip, but this growth is contained in the development of Pip's relations to the world about him—that is, to the background. The narration, as in *A Tale of Two Cities,* employs two different modes: satire and irony, which is somewhat closer to satire than to melodrama. Irony is the principal mode of *Great Expectations,* but the satire it contains is essential to its structure.

There are two Pips in *Great Expectations:* the growing boy, whom the novel is about, and the grown man, who is as narrator much wiser and more sober. This retrospective narrator and the reader are on a par in that they perceive equally all the irony that is turned upon the adolescent Pip. We can therefore talk about two levels of perception: the confusion and misunderstanding of the younger Pip, and the deeper realization that the reader gains from the narrator. The distance between these two levels diminishes with the progress of the novel, for Pip's growth to maturity consists of a series of recognitions that finally lead him to the position held by the narrator and the reader from the beginning. At the close of the novel, Pip the protagonist and Pip the narrator have become one.[1]

A convincing reading of *Great Expectations* can be made

1. It is also important to distinguish between Pip the narrator and Dickens the author. Thus there are elements and effects in the novel created by Dickens and perceived by the reader but never understood by Pip at any stage. One example is Pip's relation to Trabb's boy, which will be discussed in the chapter on *Our Mutual Friend.* This shade of difference in perception applies in some degree to the various relations to be discussed here as well. Certainly Pip never articulates them as Dickens enables the reader to.

with Orlick as the embodiment of the evil inside Pip.[2] Orlick may represent external evil or the evil perpetual in man, making him somewhat analogous to Rigaud in *Little Dorrit;* or he may represent the evil within Pip himself, the tendencies to cruelty and violence which Pip must conquer in his own spirit. This reading of the novel, which emphasizes the suppression of violence beneath a social veneer, must be supported by details that are read symbolically or schematically rather than dramatically. Orlick's accusation in chapter liii that Pip was responsible for the murder of Mrs. Joe, for instance, must be taken as having moral validity; certainly it is reinforced by the fact that the weapon Orlick used was the leg-iron from which Pip had helped free Magwitch. But Pip, as he is directly presented by the narrator and as he is conscious of himself, is never tempted and hardly troubled by violent instincts. What Pip tries to ignore rather than face with dignity is the squalor, illiteracy, and general unsophistication in his background, not the aggressive drives in himself. He must outgrow false pride, snobbishness, and social ambition. In his ideals of womanhood, Pip establishes a false polarity between Mrs. Joe on the one hand and Miss Havisham and Estella on the other, while the truth lies in Biddy and above all in the "womanly" Joe (see above, pp. 97–98). The error is compounded to social dimensions when he mistakes Miss Havisham for the source of his fortunes. The criminal base of the "gentleman" Pip becomes is Magwitch, whose crimes were acts of larceny and fraud (Compeyson, who had deceived Miss Havisham, is involved with Magwitch in "the swindling, handwriting forging, stolen banknote passing, and such-like" [chap. xlii]): Magwitch has no essential inner violence to conceal or control; his great concern when he joins Pip in London is that he has been and may again be "low" (chaps. xl–xlii). In this novel, the veneer of society is a thin crust, not over violence but over selfishness and vanity. The difference is critical. Though violence may ensue, society disregards not instincts of violence so much as the

2. See, for instance, Julian Moynahan, "The Hero's Guilt: the Case of *Great Expectations*," *Essays in Criticism* 10 (1960): 60–79.

humane qualities of love, sympathy, kindness, and tolerance. Pip embraces the false values of this society; bitter experience must teach him to reject them.

These values are embodied in the satiric objects of the novel. The narrator renders characters like Pumblechook and situations like the Gargerys' Christmas dinner in a strongly ironic light; before Pip can escape this same light, he must learn the moral values held by the narrator. Pip's feelings toward the people satirized may be from the start no kinder than those of the narrator, and he may even criticize them from the same standpoint (he seems, for example, immediately to understand Mrs. Pocket), but what he does not realize is that he himself shares their moral premises.

Uncle Pumblechook is a groveling, fawning, self-inflating hypocrite, in many ways reminiscent of Pecksniff. As a child Pip suffers his inquisitions and hates him thoroughly, but as an adolescent with newly acquired property he displays modified versions of many Pumblechookian characteristics. He is filled with his own importance as he orders clothes from Mr. Trabb and the other outfitters of the village, and he feels his dignity vexed by Trabb's boy, the "most audacious boy in all that country-side" (chap. xix). He condescends to Joe and Biddy much as Pumblechook did to the whole family, and he courts his "betters" somewhat more smoothly but no less assiduously. Finally, as Pumblechook nominates himself Pip's "earliest benefactor, and founder of fortun's" Pip is no less pretentious and mistaken in his own nomination of Miss Havisham for that role. Pip is the folly to Mr. Pumblechook's vice, but he never sees that Pumblechook is as much a warning as an aggravation to him.

Pip's likeness to Mrs. Pocket is even closer than to Pumblechook, but he is equally oblivious to it. He sees at their first meeting the folly of her obsession with being "grandpapa's granddaughter" and marks her as "perfectly helpless and useless" (chap. xxiii). It does not occur to him that his aspirations to become a gentleman lead to the same state of indolence or that his respect for money and class in Miss Havisham is only a counterpart of Mrs. Pocket's emulation of aristocracy. He knows that his valet Pepper is an "avenging phantom," but he never looks back from this situation to draw an analogy with the "unknown power" of the servants who hold true possession of the Pockets' house (chap. xxiii).

To Wemmick Pip stands in an almost obverse relation. The Wemmick who consistently advises Pip to amass portable property is the mechanical instrument of Mr. Jaggers and the world in which justice means profit. At home, however, he is a devoted son and ardent lover, just as precise and eccentric in these roles as he is in business but acting upon foundations of true feeling. Jaggers's Wemmick is an object of satire, a self-imposed exterior necessitated by social circumstances; the man of "Walworth sentiments," we are convinced, is the real man. Pip, unfortunately, is the opposite. In his misguided aspirations he would delight to stand in the same relation to Mr. Jaggers as Miss Havisham does; the fact of Mr. Jaggers's being his guardian is the crux of his hopes. At home he denigrates Joe, who is really a father to him, and snubs Biddy. To see things rightly, he must learn the meaning of Wemmick's schizophrenic existence (the schism is the source of his satiric comicality)—the truth of the values it strives to preserve but also the perils of such disjunction and the necessity of an integrated life.

Mrs. Joe, as devoted to her apron full of pins and needles as Mrs. Wilfer will be to her penitential kerchief and gloves, is a comic, satiric type of Dickens's recurrent termagant. Her bringing Pip up "by hand," her bullying of Joe and fawning upon Uncle Pumblechook, her masculine household dictatorship, even her strange manner of preparing slices of bread-and-butter, make her a superb anti-woman. All these qualities, however, shrink to foibles beside the sinister cruelty of Miss Havisham. Miss Havisham stops the world about her at the moment she is jilted by Compeyson. To keep her anger unabated and to nourish the indiscriminate vengeance prompted by the first waves of outrage, she forces the rigidity of her mind upon her surroundings. Only one thing does she allow to grow: Estella, by whose beauty she will torture the sex that humiliated her. Miss Havisham makes herself into the archetypical antiwoman and replaces Mrs. Joe in this role. Dickens signals this change in the severe punishment visited upon Mrs. Joe and her emergence as a harmless and pathetic figure. Mrs. Joe, mistreated by a vicious, barely human male, becomes a frightened paralytic frantic for conciliation but otherwise quietly affable; Miss Havisham, perhaps equally mistreated but at least physically unharmed, willfully confines herself to a wheelchair and cherishes her bitterness. Pip knows from childhood that his best interest is to keep out of Mrs. Joe's way; he is utterly seduced, however, by Miss Havisham.

This failure of perception extends to Pip's relations with other characters as well. His attitudes toward Mr. Wopsle and the Hubbles are endorsed by the narrator's satiric treatment of these people, but in his pretentious unease Pip mistakenly puts Joe in the same class with them. He fails to make the distinction that is crucial to the narrator (and consequently to the reader). The narrator is virtually following Fielding's prescription for the Ridiculous in his preface to *Joseph Andrews:* the only true source of the Ridiculous is affectation, which is caused by vanity and hypocrisy. As they are vain and affected, Mr. Wopsle and Mr. and Mrs. Hubble deserve the ridicule of satire; as Joe is quite the antithesis, he is worthy of respect. Pip sees not values but externals, and because Joe's manner is as awkward as Mr. Wopsle's is absurd, Pip is embarrassed by him. Chapter xxvii, when Joe visits Pip in London, combines gentle amusement at Joe's stiffness with a strong impression that Pip is a precious fool to be so aware of it. In this relation, as Pip later realizes, he himself is ridiculous.

The funeral of Mrs. Joe may be taken as a final instance of the integration of the satiric parts of *Great Expectations* with the whole of the novel. Pip, immersed in other, falsely predicated emotions, returns home for this funeral. He is properly distressed at the hollow pageantry and ridiculous pretensions of this parade of unreal figures, but he does not see its analogy to the life he hastens back to in London. The only real people with real emotions at the funeral are Joe and Biddy, but at this meeting Pip's relation to them becomes even more strained than before. That the ridiculousness he witnesses is something of which he too is culpable escapes him.

As in the primarily satirical novels, the irony that *Great Expectations* turns upon its young hero is extended generally to most of the society about him—but with important modifications. For one thing, this novel, far more than any since *David Copperfield,* is concerned with the development of a single person; thus the emphasis is necessarily less social. Furthermore, society is various. Chapter xix, the end of the first stage of Pip's great expectations, ends with the sentence: "And the mists had all solemnly risen now, and the world lay spread before me." The Miltonic echo has significance, for the world, as Pip eventually will realize, is what man chooses to make it. Pip chooses the Finches of the Grove and Satis House, blind to the goodness that can arise from the crude forge or even the hostile marshes. The extended consideration *Great Expectations* gives to individual culpability—its admission that the faults of society may lie as much in the individual beholder as in the object—is a step toward the slightly more hopeful outlook of Dickens's latest work. The society that nurtured Pip's false conception of great expectations is rendered in the same ironic light that falls upon the deluded Pip, but it is not so pervasive as only to permit escape in seclusion or pastoral retreat. This appears to be the implication of Pip's return to England after an eleven-year exile of penitence: he returns to honest work within society. Much more effectively, it is implied in the continuous presence of the enlightened Pip as narrator. In *Little Dorrit* Arthur survived the danger of satirical absorption into the satirized society and married Amy instead—and there the novel ended. With *Great Expectations,* because the protagonist is also the narrator, we have before us throughout the story evidence of what the positive alternatives may become: Pip grows up to become the sobered, critical narrator.

Yet *Great Expectations* also offers an indictment as broad as that of *Bleak House* or *Little Dorrit,* if it is read less literally; if, that is, we take Pip as the Everyman of the Victorian middle class. He is the end of the road that began with Robinson Crusoe, and his exposure is the exposure of a whole class. Such a reading is supported by the observation that the whole and "honest" society to which Pip presumably returns is barely represented in the novel. Since Joe and Biddy are really outside the urban pale, we have only Clarriker in the business world and Herbert as the private man. In an emblematic reading, this makes perfect sense: the good society will only grow up after the purge and regeneration—the novel does not show us the future. In the more literal reading, it makes only practical, novelistic sense: the good society is not very interesting, at least not in Dickens's seldom skillful attempts to present it. The emblematic interpretation also clarifies the rhythm of the final chapters. We can see two fundamental, contrapuntal movements—one of life and one of death—masterfully interwoven. The movement of death begins with Orlick's attempt to kill Pip and the recapture and injury of Magwitch (chaps. liii and liv). Magwitch, not Pip, will continue it to the end. In chapter lv the counter movement is set in Herbert's rise to partnership and the accompanying assurance that he will soon marry Clara; the same chapter contains Wemmick's marriage. The next chapter (lvi) contains the death of Magwitch, followed in chapter lvii by Pip's deathlike fever, the climax of this movement. Chapter lviii is occupied with the critical development of the life and marriage movement in the wedding of Joe and Biddy; its culmination comes in the final chapter (lix) with the appearance of little Pip. The stepchild of Joe's uncomfortable union with Mrs. Joe was Pip, whose misfortunes we have followed; at the end a new cycle is beginning, in which Joe has found a true bride and their union produced a true child. The new Pip offers a second chance.

CHAPTER 10

Modified Satire: *Our Mutual Friend*

The satire in *Our Mutual Friend* is as vigorous as that of *Bleak House, Hard Times,* or *Little Dorrit,* but it is less continuous and lacks the clear definition provided by symbols such as Chancery, Fairy Palaces, or the Marshalsea. The bildungsroman upon Bella, for instance, is relevant to the satiric theme but more fully developed than that relation alone requires. The dominant image equivalent to Chancery or the Marshalsea is not a single symbol but an amalgam: the vision of a society preying upon garbage comes only when we put together the Mounds, the waterside scavenging, the stock-in-trade of Silas Wegg, the rags of Pubsey and Co., the assorted bones and pickled bodies of Mr. Venus. Satire in this novel is pitted against the most complex novelistic developments that Dickens attempted (except Pip), making this book the preeminent example of that Dickensian hybrid, the satiric novel. Further conditions contribute to this modification, without mitigation, of the satire: satire is deflected from principals upon secondary characters; satire shares its ultimate motif with melodrama, which uses it quite differently; satire is leveled against deserving objects, not by the narrator but by characters whose position is itself somewhat assailable.

The typical late-Dickensian plot of a contest between a novelistic hero and an absurd society recurs in *Our Mutual Friend* with special variations. This book, more than any of the previous novels, divides its concern between two heroes and two struggles, but two that move in the same direction: from self-imposed separation from society to a blending of spiritual remove and dutiful participation similar to Pip's. Eugene Wrayburn and John Harmon begin equally, if differently, alienated from the world about them. Like Arthur Clennam in *Little Dorrit,* they find themselves sufficiently uncomfortable to consider withdrawing altogether. Unsure how to enter this world successfully, if at all, they both stand deliberately apart: Eugene as an idler and cynic and Harmon, more strikingly, as a dead man. The problem for both is one of morality.

Harmon meets this problem in the form of material greed. He starts his campaign of investigation (and, soon enough, amelioration) in an alliance with the Boffins. Two things must be accomplished before the unreal Rokesmith can take his place in society as John Harmon, or before Harmon can return to life: the Harmon fortune, marked by its source as sheer filth, must be cleansed; and the beautiful Bella, flawed by the same material desire that prompted the amassing of dust, must be brought to full womanhood. The satiric opponent in the first effort is Silas Wegg, and for a while he finds a reluctant ally in Mr. Venus. Wegg, uglier than anything in Dickens except perhaps Quilp (and in convincing repulsiveness far outreaching him), does all he can to keep the money base. The relative nature of money explains the apparent inconsistency of a novel that condemns the pursuit of money at all social levels and yet rewards at least one of its heroes with a considerable fortune. What is at issue is the evaluation not of things themselves but of the meanings people attach to them. The opposition in *Our Mutual Friend* is not between wealth and poverty but between satisfaction or acceptance and gnawing greed. Dickens did see money as necessary for the good life, but the satirized characters of *Our Mutual Friend* make life serve the pursuit of money rather than allow money to serve the enjoyment of life. Hence the emphasis on the wretchedness of the lives led by Daniel Dancer and the rest of Mr. Boffin's pretended literary heroes and the lengthy detail of Fledgeby's nervous stinginess not only as a host but even toward himself.

The opponent of Harmon's rescue of Bella from satiric selfishness is really Bella herself, but, as it would be impossible to treat the eventual heroine to any but the mildest satiric irony, the satire is deflected to her mother, Mrs. Wilfer. That monster of pride, however, is assisted in what unfortunate influence she has over Bella by the greed that permeates society —so again Harmon is battling a social force.

Eugene's disaffection and its causes are both vaguer and more complex than Harmon's. His development—consequently the more interesting—is toward union with Lizzie as opposed to the grimly comic fiction of union with Lady Tippins, toward real life instead of the dead mockery of life his lethargy indulges. The oneness of Tippins and Society in opposition to Lizzie is articulated by Eugene himself:

> "Honourable and staunch," said Lightwood. "And yet, Eugene—"
>
> "And yet what, Mortimer?"
>
> "And yet, are you sure that you might not feel (for her sake, I say for her sake) any slight coldness towards her on the part of—Society?"
>
> "Oh! You and I may well stumble at the word," returned Eugene, laughing. "Do we mean our Tippins?"
>
> "Perhaps we do," said Mortimer, laughing also.
>
> "Faith, we DO!" returned Eugene. [Bk. IV, chap. xvi]

The associates of Tippins are the Veneerings, the Podsnaps, the Lammles, and Fledgeby. The social climbing, snobbery, and humbug respectability characteristic of this group bore Eugene. In these respects Bradley Headstone and Charley Hexam are small fry of the same breed as the Tippins circle. The prospect of a world of Veneerings, Podsnaps, and Tippinses has sapped Eugene of the will to fight the immediate antagonists who keep him from Lizzie. Physically he has to fight Headstone, but spiritually he first has to rid himself of the Veneering-Tippins incubus. These people, therefore, are Eugene's principal antagonists and the novel's prime targets of satire.

Harmon, of course, is not concerned exclusively with money, nor Eugene with emptiness and pretension—the motives cross. The Lammles, on Eugene's side, are preoccupied with the acquisition of money in order to maintain social position; their chosen tool, Fledgeby, pursues money with the same pleasureless passion that presumably motivated Old Harmon. On the other side, in Bella (and particularly in her mother), social ambition is an adjunct of material desire; in a purely comic version, Mrs. Boffin "goes in for Fashion"; in absolute grotesque, even Silas Wegg has schemes of living high. Furthermore, as the plots are continuously interwoven, so are the themes. Thus, long before the plot brings Sophronia and Alfred across Bella's path, the reader perceives that the Lammles, though well within the Veneering world and thus far from Harmon's experience, exemplify the greed and intense material pursuit Bella believes —perhaps for a while in truth—to be hers. Similarly, Mrs. Wilfer's condescending attitudes have a clear relation to the snobbery of Tippinses and Podsnaps, as does her awesomeness to the "respectability" cherished alike by Bradley Headstone, Charley, Hexam, Wegg, and Riderhood.

In *Bleak House* Richard Carstone did battle directly against Chancery and Esther worked to relieve the disruptive effects of Chancery, Dedlocks, and Jellybys in the world about her. In *Hard Times* Louisa, Sissy in her passive way, and Mr. Gradgrind himself after the reversal struggled against the strangulation of Gradgrindery and Bounderbyism. In *Little Dorrit* Arthur besieged the Circumlocution Office, competed, though half-heartedly, with Henry Gowan, and turned against the doubtful program of his mother and Jeremiah Flintwinch, while Amy quietly resisted Mrs. General and spent her youth trying to free her family from their spiritual imprisonment. *Our Mutual Friend* differs from these three novels in that its heroes do not battle directly against their satiric adversaries. John Harmon is concerned with Bella—not with the mother upon whom satiric treatment is deflected—and with the Boffins, who in turn suffer under Wegg. His immediate contact with Mrs. Wilfer and Silas Wegg, the satiric embodiments of the forces that make society undesirable to him, is minimal. As for Eugene, Tippins's attentions turn to his friend Mortimer Lightwood more than to himself. Although he has some contact with the society of Veneerings and Podsnaps, his dealings in the action of the novel are primarily with their lower-class counterparts Headstone and Charley Hexam; with the "good" characters Mortimer, Jenny Wren, and of course Lizzie; and above all with his own apathetic self. One result of this separation of the protagonists from the satiric characters is that the satire in this novel is less prominent than in the dark novels. It is no less important—serving as the ground of the peculiar behavior of the heroes and the unifying background to the numerous strands of the novel—but its presence is not so continuous. The essence of satire is not embodied in a visible institution or system that embraces the whole world of the novel, and there is more concentration upon the positive, nonsatiric characters (the reformed Bella Harmon, Mr. Wilfer, the Boffins, Riah).

The principal satiric characters, the Veneerings and their circle, are objects of the moral indictment recurrent in Dickens's work: they are organic forms of nonlife. These particular upper-middle-class social aspirants are not only unreal but pretend to realities that are themselves insufferable. Their two-dimensional unreality is emphasized by the narrator's introductory description of them through the mediation of a looking glass, with the implication that the figures around the real table are no different from the figures in the mirror:

> The great looking-glass above the sideboard reflects the table and the company. Reflects the new Veneering crest, in gold and eke in silver . . . Reflects Veneering . . . Reflects Mrs. Veneering . . . Reflects Podsnap . . . Reflects Mrs. Podsnap . . . Reflects Twemlow . . . Reflects mature young lady . . . Reflects charming old Lady Tippins . . . Reflects a certain "Mortimer" . . . Reflects Eugene, friend of Mortimer: buried alive in the back of his chair. . . . Lastly, the looking-glass reflects Boots and Brewer, and two other stuffed Buffers interposed between the rest of the company and possible accidents. [Bk. I, chap. ii]

Eugene, we note, is buried alive in this company: he is dead in the ironic sense that if they are alive the truly living must be dead; and he is dead in the straightforward sense that he is bored to death, but even more in that he has given in to their death by apathetically consenting to join them.

The novel continues to play on the motif of death, pretended death, and living death. John Harmon is presumed dead; by allowing the belief to stand and by living under the name of John Rokesmith, he creates a situation for himself that he finds painfully ambiguous:

> "It is a sensation not experienced by many mortals," said he, "to be looking into a churchyard on a wild windy night, and to feel that I no more hold a place among the living than these dead do, and even to know what I lie buried somewhere else, as they lie buried here. Nothing uses me to it. A spirit that was once a man could hardly feel stranger or lonelier, going unrecognized among mankind than I feel." [Bk. II, chap. xiii]

The crucial distinction between Rokesmith-Harmon and the satirized figures is that he is aware of, and troubled by, his deathlike state. He finds himself spiritually very much alive but officially and somehow even physically dead. Eugene knows quite well that physically he is alive, but he is constantly threatened by spiritual death through his own lethargy. The grim comedy of the relation of life to death is set in the opening chapter of the novel. We see it first in Gaffer Hexam's exclamation at Lizzie's confession of disliking the river and the corpses they dredge out of it—"As if it wasn't your living! As if it wasn't meat and drink to you!"—and again in Hexam's defense of robbing dead men:

> "Has a dead man any use for money? Is it possible for a dead man to have money? What world does a dead man belong to? T'other world. What world does money belong to? This world. How can money be a corpse's? Can a corpse own it, want it, spend it, claim it, miss it? Don't try confounding the rights and wrongs of things in that way. But it's worthy of the sneaking spirit that robs a live man."

Of course the comedy of this is that Hexam is in fact quite right, but—as Lizzie's revulsion is meant to show—the insensitivity he displays to the presence and meaning of death is dismaying.

Even more unnerving is Silas Wegg's comfortable acceptance of a dead appendage to his own body. When the narrator first introduces him, he suggests: "Sooth to say, he was so wooden a man that he seemed to have taken his wooden leg naturally, and rather suggested to the fanciful observer, that he might be expected—if his development received no untimely check—to be completely set up with a pair of wooden legs in about six months" (Bk. I, chap. v). This reification of the human is a typically Dickensian satiric phenomenon, but nothing in Dickens's earlier work matches the relation we learn of later between Wegg and the remains of his amputated, organic leg. When he comes to ask the articulator of bones, Mr. Venus, about it, he simply says, "Where am I?" to which Venus answers unperturbed, "You're somewhere in the back shop across the yard, sir; and speaking quite candidly, I wish I'd never bought you of the Hospital Porter" (Bk. I, chap. vii). Mr. Venus himself amply contributes to the grotesquerie with his composite skeletons and proud collection of "human warious." Before his reversion to honesty, in fact, Venus's establishment seems to stand in the same paradigmatic relation to the world around it as Krook's shop held to Chancery and Wiglomeration: instead of whole, living beings, we have bits and pieces of dead bodies artificially held together. (One might note that after Venus reforms, Dickens de-emphasizes the gruesomeness of this awkward profession and makes it almost wholly a comic problem in the wooing of Pleasant Riderhood.)

The clearest ironic inversion of the meaning of life and death is Jenny Wren's. When Fledgeby's arrival calls Riah down from the roof of Pubsey and Co., Jenny urges him back with the chant "Come up and be dead!" Her version of death, however, is resurrection; it is an escape from the death-in-life of the world:

> "Oh, so tranquil!" cried the little creature, smiling. "Oh, so peaceful and so thankful! And you hear the people who are alive, crying, and working, and calling to one another down in the close dark streets, and you seem to pity them so! And such a chain has fallen from you, and

> such a strange good sorrowful happiness comes upon you!" [Bk. II, chap. v]

Here the satiric motif of death-and-life meets the theme of death and regeneration. Arnold Kettle has attempted to refute the Jungian interpretation of the image of the Thames.[1] His most convincing argument is that the one time Dickens does deal explicitly with the idea of regeneration he mocks it: Pleasant Riderhood's vague hopes that her father's "drowning" will be restorative are quickly dispelled by the revived Rogue, who returns to consciousness rather worse for the experience. But the burlesque of Riderhood does not devalue the straightforward treatment of Eugene. To some extent it even has a function analogous to that Empson suggests for the parodic plot in drama, to "anticipate the parody a hearer might have in mind without losing its dignity . . . not at all to parody the heroes but to stop you from doing so."[2] Dickens could not have made clearer the meaning of Eugene's near escape from drowning and rescue by Lizzie without the excessive explanatoriness that in other places irritates his modern readers.

With Betty Higden the usual signification of death in Dickens's satiric novels is again inverted—but this time without irony. The positive meaning that death may have for the good when life has become deadly, suggested with Jenny Wren, is extended with Betty Higden to a kind of pathos dangerously reminiscent of Little Nell. What saves it may be only that it is a short part of a very long book, but it is also helped by the fact of Betty's age and by the addresses to the "Lords and Gentlemen and Honourable Boards" interspersed, so curiously and so typically in Dickens's manner, with the sentimental passages. Betty's age quite simply makes the idea of death as relief appropriate, as it could not be for a child; the alternatives then become death in terror or death happily accepted, and Dickens enhances the preferability of the latter by surrounding the old woman with Christian reference. It is important in

1. *"Our Mutual Friend," Dickens and the Twentieth Century*, ed. Gross and Pearson, p. 222.

2. William Empson, *Some Versions of Pastoral* (Norfolk, Conn., n.d.), p. 30.

this connection to keep in mind that when Betty starts on her journey she is running away not only from Sloppy but from the "deadness," as she repeatedly describes it, that is creeping over her. She resists this living deadness while fully accepting real, natural death. The mingling of tones shows a careful manipulation of emotional effect. The Boffins first meet Mrs. Higden in Book I, chapter xvi, and their secretary soon provokes an outburst upon the Poorhouses:

> "Do I never read in the newspapers," said the dame, fondling the child, "—God help me and the like of me!—how the worn-out people that do come down to that get driven from post to pillar and pillar to post, a-purpose to tire them out! Do I never read how they are put off, put off, put off—how they are grudged, grudged, grudged the shelter, or the doctor, or the drop of physic, or the bit of bread? Do I never read how they grow heartsick of it and give it up, after having let themselves drop so low, and how they after all die out for want of help? Then I say, I hope I can die as well as another, and I'll die without that disgrace."

The rhetoric is recognizably Dickens's; its purpose is unmistakable. The paragraph that follows is equally rhetorical: "Absolutely impossible, my Lords and Gentlemen and Honourable Boards, by any stretch of legislative wisdom to set these perverse people right in their logic?" The note of sarcasm, however, particularly that of the "stretch of legislative wisdom," is discordant with what has gone before and checks its tearfulness. The alternation continues in the next two paragraphs:

> "Johnny, my pretty," continued old Betty caressing the child and rather mourning over it than speaking to it, "your old Granny Betty is nigher fourscore year than threescore and ten. She never begged nor had a penny of the Union money in all her life. She paid scot and she paid lot when she had money to pay; she worked when she could, and she starved when she must. You pray that your Granny may have strength enough left her at the last (she's strong for

> an old one, Johnny) to get up from her bed and run and hide herself, and sworn to death in a hole, sooner than fall into the hands of those Cruel Jacks we read of, that dodge and drive, and worry and weary, and scorn and shame the decent poor."
>
> A brilliant success, my Lords and Gentlemen and Honourable Boards, to have brought it to this in the minds of the best of the poor! Under submission, might it be worth thinking of, at any odd time?

Leaving the Lords and Gentlemen for a space, Dickens continues to build the pathos of the scene, focusing upon Betty until "the fine strong old face broke up into weakness and tears." This is the sentimental climax, and from it Dickens proceeds happily to undercut:

> Now, greatly to the relief of the visitors, the emotional Sloppy no sooner beheld his patroness in this condition than, throwing back his head and throwing open his mouth, he lifted up his voice and bellowed. This alarming note of something wrong instantly terrified Toddles and Poddles, who were no sooner heard to roar surprisingly than Johnny, curving himself the wrong way and striking out at Mrs. Boffin with a pair of indifferent shoes, became a prey to despair. The absurdity of the situation put its pathos to the rout.

The later Dickens can forestall the reader's rejection of excessive lacrimosity by ridiculing it himself. The narrator who confesses the absurdity of sentimental scenes fosters a sort of confidence in the reader, upon whom he can then pass off other scenes almost as sentimental: compared to Betty and her friends, the narrator is hard-nosed.

Nevertheless, it remains undeniable that for Betty Higden death carries none of the implications it has in the satiric portions of this and other novels. Yet since this death is of an old, heroic woman who dies defying the poorhouse, one of Dickens's favorite satiric butts (though in this novel a minor one), the fact that it represents peace is perhaps not as surprising as the aura of death attached to Lizzie when she meets Eugene at the Plashwater Mill. As they are about to part, "The purity with which in these words she expressed something of her own love and her own suffering made a deep impression on him for the passing time. He held her, almost as if she were sanctified to him by death, and kissed her, once, almost as he might have kissed the dead" (Bk. IV, chap. iv). In a sense the trouble with Eugene is that he cannot yet come to Lizzie in full life. What is more remarkable about the passage is its direct meaning: Mrs. Wilfer is satirized by her likeness to the Dead March in Saul (Bk. II, chap. viii), but Lizzie is sanctified as the dead. The inconsistency is further complicated when at the end of the same chapter Lizzie brings both Eugene's novelistic development and his part in the satiric plot to a climax by rescuing Eugene simultaneously from physical death through drowning and moral death through Tippins. The meaning arises clearly in the contrast to the opening scene of the novel: where Gaffer fished for the dead, Lizzie now fishes for life; so far have the cherishers of life come in the contest with forces of death. In this major motif as in the satires, death is the ultimate constriction of life; with Betty Higden and with Lizzie in the passage quoted above, it is used purely novelistically, with the simplest Christian attitudes and with a dangerous touch of sentimental fervor.

The boundary between satiric and novelistic rendering of character is equally hard to define. At one end of the spectrum, the Veneerings and Podsnaps are in absolute satire: the persistent "newness" of the Veneerings and the "fatal freshness" of the Podsnaps, the extended metaphor of Twemlow as a Veneering piece of dining-room furniture, the unabashed rhetoric of passages such as the mirror-description quoted above, transformations such as that of Mrs. Podsnap into a rocking horse, characters reduced to ciphers like Boots and Brewer. Boots and Brewer are not much of an advance upon *Little Dorrit*'s Bar and Bishop, but at one point in *Our Mutual Friend* the joke runs riot: at a dinner attended by Twemlow "were a Member, an Engineer, a Payer-off of the National Debt, a Poem on Shakespeare, a Grievance, and a Public Office" (Bk. I, chap.

ii). The same order of satire is present in Mrs. Wilfer. With her kerchief and gloves and absurd sonority, she is the novel's version of the unwomanly female, as comic and as purely satirically conceived as any of her predecessors. The Lammles, however, though they are satirically exposed, are presented in a more novelistic manner: they reveal themselves in action and dialogue with few narratorial comments or comic embellishments. Fledgeby represents a step even further in the same direction. We know enough about him to be tempted almost as much to psychological explanation as to satiric contempt. Although the narrator states that he is one of a common type ("the murky fog closed about him and shut him up in its sooty embrace. If it had never let him out any more, the world would have had no irreparable loss, but could easily have replaced him from its stock on hand" [Bk. III, chap. i]), his extreme eccentricity precludes the satiric typicality of the Veneerings or Podsnaps. The one recognizably satiric mannerism is his automatic feeling for whiskers.

Except for the descriptions of Veneerings and Podsnaps, in fact, the highly rhetorical satire in this novel is confined to its least successful parts: the apostrophic addresses in behalf of Betty Higden. The satiric figures of central concern are less rhetorically presented. Because the tone is so relatively natural, one's awareness of them as satiric is stronger in retrospect than while reading the novel.

The peculiar blend of satiric emphasis and novelistic realism is evident in the character of Bradley Headstone. The narrator introduces him in highly wrought, satirical rhetoric:

> Bradley Headstone, in his decent black coat and waistcoat, and decent white shirt, and decent formal black tie, and decent pantaloons of pepper and salt, with his decent silver watch in his pocket and its decent hair-guard round his neck, looked a thoroughly decent young man of six-and-twenty. He was never seen in any other dress, and yet there was a certain stiffness in his manner of wearing this, as if there were a want of adaptation between him and it, recalling some mechanics in their holiday clothes. He had

> acquired mechanically a great store of teacher's knowledge. He could do mental arithmetic mechanically, sing at sight mechanically, blow various wind instruments mechanically, even play the great church organ mechanically. From his early childhood up, his mind had been a place of mechanical stowage. The arrangement of his wholesale warehouse, so that it might be always ready to meet the demands of retail dealers—history here, geography there, astronomy to the right, political economy to the left—natural history, the physical sciences, figures, music, the lower mathematics, and what not, all in their several places—this care had imparted to his countenance a look of care; while the habit of questioning and being questioned had given him a suspicious manner, or a manner that would be better described as one of lying in wait. There was a kind of settled trouble in the face. It was the face belonging to a naturally slow or inattentive intellect that had toiled hard to get what it won, and that had to hold it now that it was gotten. He always seemed to be uneasy lest anything should be missing from his mental warehouse, and taking stock to assure himself. [Bk. II, chap. i]

The use of anaphora is a frequent strategy of Dickens's;[3] here the term *mechanical* makes Headstone a quintessential figure of Dickensian satire, with decency a coordinate of hollow respectability and class pretension. But although the watch and guard stay with Headstone to the end (he leaves them with Miss Peecher before he goes off to grapple with Riderhood in Book IV, chapter xv), and although he never loses his self-righteous obtuseness, he does grow in the course of the novel into something more than this satiric cipher—into the principal case of paranoia in Dickens's writings. He suffers too much for such simple satiric contempt as the passage above invites; when Charley deserts him at the worst moment, the former pupil diverts to himself enough of the reader's moral repugnance to allow a twinge of pity and even sympathy for Headstone. Yet

3. Cf. Taylor Stoehr, *Dickens: The Dreamer's Stance* (Ithaca, N.Y., 1965), chap. 1.

the development of this character is not so much at odds with the original presentation as it might appear, for the paranoia grows to murderous proportions because it is planted in the kind of mind that arouses satire. Headstone's mechanical, pigeon-holed intellect cannot deal with the irrational passion for Lizzie and jealousy of Eugene that it suddenly discovers in itself. It is also mechanical obtuseness that provokes Eugene to taunting and open contempt and that leaves Headstone writhing helplessly in the presence of Eugene's intellectual flexibility.

Characters such as Rogue Riderhood, Headstone, Charley Hexam, Fledgeby, and Wegg are not satiric in the way the Veneerings and Podsnaps are. The rhetoric that is turned upon the Veneerings and Podsnaps immediately and continuously marks them as satiric. Riderhood, Headstone, and the rest are often depicted novelistically; however, the vision of a whole society made up of people like them or of a world infested by them is a satiric one. The Veneerings and Podsnaps are caricatures treated as caricatures; the others are, in a sense, caricatures treated as characters. The effect is less immediately "satiric" but ultimately more disturbing. The technique is essentially a sort of large-scale burlesque, with the correspondence between the created world of satire and the real world it reflects not caricature for character or mock-institution for institution but world for world.

One satiric strategy that Dickens employed occasionally in his earlier novels comes into its own in *Our Mutual Friend* and contributes significantly to the effect of a relatively nonsatirical narrative tone in a highly satirical novel. That is the transfer of a good deal of satiric attack and ridicule from the narrator's voice to that of one of the characters, who thereby becomes to some extent a satirist figure within the novel. In *Dombey and Son* Philip Collins has noted one of the functions of the child Paul: "His questions are those we are too polite to ask, or too subdued to the element we work in; he has the privilege of inexperience, and thus operates much like visiting Chinamen, or a King of Brobdingnag, in Utopian satire—or like Shakespearean Fools."[4] The most obvious analogues in Dickens's work to the

4. *Dickens and Education*, p. 201.

foreign visitors of traditional satire are Martin Chuzzlewit and Mark Tapley in the United States. In the aspect of naïveté, another character who resembles Paul at times is Esther Summerson; her innocent acceptance, particularly of Harold Skimpole at his own valuation, often heightens by contrast the knavery or folly of the satiric butts she describes. The Dickensian narrator occasionally assumes the pose of *faux-naif,* generally with heavy sarcasm; on other occasions Dickens takes advantage of his fictive medium to create a character who really is naïve, who without posturing asks the same questions the narrator might ask as *faux-naif,* and whose true innocence may further emphasize the falsity that is being exposed. In *Our Mutual Friend,* however, Dickens offers a character-satirist of a line more effective and more recent in his work: the alienated cynic.

The type has its beginnings in Dick Swiveller *(The Old Curiosity Shop)* and James Steerforth *(David Copperfield),* but its first conjunction with satire is in James Harthouse in *Hard Times.* Harthouse has little to recommend him—perhaps nothing at all—and the novel's satire was fully developed without his aid. Yet he does have the combination of distance and intelligence lacking in the other characters that enables him to see through the façades of Coketown. He greets Mrs. Sparsit's boast of her Powler relations with open surprise at the name, responds to Bounderby's bluster with bored perfunctoriness, and suggests for young Tom the name "Whelp" that the narrator then takes up. He remains, however, without wit or value in himself, and the narrator calls him the "very Devil" (Bk. II, chap, viii).

Henry Gowan, who succeeds Harthouse in *Little Dorrit,* has at least the superiority of some sense of humor. He parries with Tip Dorrit when they meet at the monastery of the Great Saint Bernard:

> "These fellows are an immense time with supper," he [Tip] drawled. "I wonder what they'll give us! Has anybody any idea?"
>
> "Not roast man, I believe," replied the voice of the second gentleman of the party of three [Gowan].
>
> "I suppose not. What d'ye mean?" he inquired.

> "That, as you are not to be served for the general supper, perhaps you will do us the favour of not cooking yourself at the general fire," returned the other. [Bk. II, chap. i]

Whatever he may think of Gowan, the reader is pleased to see Tip put down. Gowan is especially qualified to debunk his own class, the Barnacles and Stiltstalkings, and does so frequently, though he is motivated rather by spite than by a sense of justice. Thus the narrator explains that "he found a pleasure in setting up Blandois as the type of elegance, and making him a satire upon others who piqued themselves on personal graces." Gowan has not taken up Blandois without seeing through him:

> He seriously protested that the bow of Blandois was perfect, that the address of Blandois was irresistible, and that the picturesque ease of Blandois would be cheaply purchased (if it were not a gift, and unpurchasable) for a hundred thousand francs. That exaggeration in the manner of the man, which has been noticed as appertaining to him and to every such man, whatever his original breeding, as certainly as the sun belongs to this system, was acceptable to Gowan as a caricature, which he found it a humourous resource to have at hand for the ridiculing of numbers of people who necessarily did more or less of what Blandois overdid. [Bk. II, chap. vi]

Yet even here there is a sense that Gowan is doing nothing worthwhile, that those he chooses to ridicule are not generally those who deserve it. Gowan's effect is more often to debase (as he does the art of painting) than justly to expose. He is, like James Harthouse, more satirized than satirizing.

A lesser character in *Little Dorrit,* whose barbs are more discriminately aimed, is Gowan's cousin Ferdinand Barnacle, the "engaging" or "airy" young Barnacle whom we first meet (without learning his name) during Arthur's second visit to the Circumlocution Office. In describing to Arthur how he will have to proceed, the sprightly Barnacle continues the satire that the narrator began in his introduction at the beginning of this chapter on the "Whole Science of Government":

> "Why, you'll—you'll ask till they tell you. Then you'll memorialise that Department (according to regular forms which you'll find out) for leave to memorialise this Department. If you get it (which you may after a time), that memorial must be entered in that Department, sent to be registered in this Department, sent back to be signed by that Department, sent back to be countersigned by this Department, and then it will begin to be regularly before that Department. You'll find out when the business passes through each of these stages, by asking at both Departments till they tell you." [Bk. I, chap. x]

The crucial difference between the airy young Barnacle and the Barnacle Junior (son of Tite Barnacle) whom Arthur encounters on his first visit, is that Ferdinand is fully aware of the absurdity of the system he supports:

> "But surely this is not the way to do the business," Arthur Clennam could not help saying.
>
> This airy young Barnacle was quite entertained by his simplicity in supposing for a moment that it was. This light in hand young Barnacle knew perfectly well that it was not . . . he fully understood the Department to be a politico-diplomatic hocus pocus piece of machinery, for the assistance of the nobs in keeping off the snobs.

It is this awareness, which amounts to satirical perception, that gives him the presence and power to manipulate the two impossible chieftains Lord Decimus and Mr. Merdle into conversation with each other (Bk. II, chap. xii). But if young Ferdinand has a true satiric perception, he has no moral basis from which to judge; his one advantage, understanding, makes his behavior all the more culpable.

The quality of wit that raises Ferdinand over the other Barnacles and his freedom from their pomposity and blindness are developed into key traits in the personality of Eugene Wrayburn. Between Ferdinand and Eugene is the intermediate figure of Sydney Carton in *A Tale of Two Cities*. Carton is the first in this line of satirist-cynics who achieves a kind of personal salvation. Two things are in has favor from the start: his alienation is given sympathetic explanation, and it has yet left his heart in the right place. Carton, the jackal, says himself to his lion, Stryver:

> "Even when we were fellow-students . . . you were always somewhere, and I was always—nowhere."
>
> "And whose fault was that?"
>
> "Upon my soul, I am not sure that it was not yours. You were always driving and riving and shouldering and pressing, to that restless degree that I had no chance for my life but in rust and repose. It's a gloomy thing, however, to talk about one's own past." [Bk. II, chap. v]

And the first time we see him it is in the act of doing a good turn to the relative stranger Darnay, whose charm, as we soon learn, can only be an irritant to Carton's sense of self-waste. If Carton is derelict in some ways, he has a humane instinct for justice and is evidently brilliant. It is clear that he has been led to dissipate his talent because he could not bring himself to compete in a world of aggressive vulgarians like Stryver. The more satire that is directed upon Stryver (see Bk. II, chaps. xi and xii), the more understandable Carton's position becomes. The relation of the two is made almost graphic in their attitudes toward Lucie Manette: Stryver's complacent self-assertion is set against Carton's beautiful silence. Yet is the talent really wasted? The narrator, in the same chapter in which he suggests Stryver's at least partial responsibility, seems to say it is:

> Waste forces within him, and a desert all around, this man stood still on his way across a silent terrace, and saw for a moment, lying in the wilderness before him, a mirage of honourable ambition, self-denial, and perseverance. . . . A moment, and it was gone. Climbing to a high chamber in a well of houses, he threw himself down in his clothes on a neglected bed, and its pillow was wet with wasted tears.
>
> Sadly, sadly, the sun rose; it rose upon no sadder sight than the man of good abilities and good emotions, incapable of their directed exercise, incapable of his own help

> and his own happiness, sensible of the blight on him, and resigning himself to let it eat him away. [Bk. II, chap. v]

Carton is not ambitious and lacks the qualities to gain what ambitions he might have had, but his abilities, at least in law, are being put to use—though they are channeled through Stryver and so contribute to the latter's glory, not his own. Dickens seems excessively condemnatory of Carton's being unkempt: his sympathy is more with the man's potential and his ultimate heroic realization of that potential than with the sensitivity that made "honourable ambition" impossible for him. To evolve the character of Eugene Wrayburn, Dickens must give to the cynical type he has created full justification for his withdrawal. He explains Eugene's by setting him against the Veneerings, the Podsnaps, Lady Tippins, Bradley Headstone, and even Rogue Riderhood; Carton is set positively only against Stryver. In negative contrast, Dickens measures Carton against the near-perfect Darnay, whereas Eugene has only the far less prominent John Harmon, who is at least capable of the subversion of an alias, to show him up. Carton has to give his life to achieve salvation; Eugene has only to give his hand.

In *Our Mutual Friend* the figure of the satirical cynic steps into the foreground. Eugene is first seen in the novel in honest disaffection from his own class, gloomily attendant at a Veneering dinner. The moral basis of value that sets him apart from the company, deeply buried as it is, is hinted from the start. Mortimer Lightwood has just told the company of the pathetically devoted marriage of Old Harmon's disowned daughter; the narrator continues:

> There is that in the indolent Mortimer, which seems to hint that if good society might on any account allow itself to be impressible, he, one of good society, might have the weakness to be impressed by what he here relates. It is hidden with great pains, but it is in him. The gloomy Eugene, too, is not without some kindred touch; for, when that appalling Lady Tippins declares that if Another had survived, he should have gone down at the head of her list

> of lovers—and also when the mature young lady shrugs her epaulettes and laughs at some private and confidential comment from the mature young gentleman—his gloom deepens to that degree that he trifles quite ferociously with his dessert-knife. [Bk. I, chap. ii]

In this role Eugene baits Mrs. Veneering (Bk. III, chap. xvii) and becomes quite Dickensian in his rhetoric upon "my respected father":

> "When my eldest brother was born, of course the rest of us knew (I mean the rest of us would have known, if we had been in existence) that he was heir to the Family Embarrassments—we call it before company the Family Estate. But when my second brother was going to be born by-the-bye, 'this,' says M. R. F., 'is a little pillar of the church.' *Was* born, and became a pillar of the church; a very shaky one. My third brother appeared, considerably in advance of his engagement to my mother; but M. R. F., not at all put out by surprise, instantly declared him a Circumnavigator. Was pitch-forked into the Navy, but has not circumnavigated. I announced myself, and was disposed of with the highly satisfactory results embodied before you. When my younger brother was half an hour old, it was settled by M. R. F. that he should have a mechanical genius, and so on." [Bk. I, chap. xii]

Eugene is, however, less actively the satirist of the upper middle class—the Veneerings and Podsnaps and Tippinses—against whom the narrator turns his own mocking rhetoric than of the lower echelons about whom the narrator is relatively restrained. The ridicule of energy when it is only a laudatory euphemism for middle-class aggressiveness attacks the morality of both Podsnap and Headstone, who in this regard are pretty much the same:

> "Then idiots talk," said Eugene, leaning back, folding his arms, smoking with his eyes shut, and speaking slightly through his nose, "of Energy. If there is a word in the dic-

> tionary under any letter from A to Z that I abominate, it is energy. It is such a conventional superstition, such parrot gabble! What the deuce! Am I to rush out into the street, collar the first man of a wealthy appearance that I meet, shake him, and say, 'Go to law upon the spot, you dog, and retain me, or I'll be the death of you'? Yet that would be energy." [Bk. I, chap. iii]

Eugene's indolence is certainly not admirable, but, as the exponents of energy in the novel turn out to be Wegg, Headstone, Podsnap, and Riderhood, his position gains sympathy if not actual approval. Still, his status at this point in the book remains ambivalent. As the dialogue continues, he and Mortimer do establish their inaction upon a moral basis: " 'Precisely my view of the case, Eugene. But show me a good opportunity, show me something really worth being energetic about, and *I'll* show you energy.' 'And so will I,' said Eugene." But the narrator immediately undercuts them: "And it is likely enough that ten thousand other young men, within the limits of the London Post-office town delivery, made the same hopeful remark in the course of the same evening." Similarly, when Eugene picks up Mr. Boffin's unwary reference to the busyness of the bees and makes havoc with that cliché (Bk. I, chap. viii), though Eugene's humor is winning and the cliché itself deserving of such treatment, his discomfiting of the innocent Boffin is unwarranted and shows a lack of human sympathy. Later in the book, when, just before a meeting with Charley Hexam and Headstone that is quite agonizing to them, he teases Mortimer on the value of earnestness (Bk. II, chap. vi), our sympathies are more with Eugene. Despite his cruelty, his mocking of Headstone—not only by word and action but by his very presence and the contrast he presents to the mechanical and paranoiac schoolmaster—is supported by the values of the novel.

Eugene himself is the satiric exposer of the society he will not enter. Like the narrator, he reduces characters to types by giving them generic names: Schoolmaster (Headstone), Mr. Aaron (Riah), Mr. Dolls (Jenny Wren's father). Only in the first instance is the derogatory implication of such a name justified. Yet the narrator too feels free to dub a fairly innocent and well-meaning character "Mr. Inspector" and to transform his assistant into "the satellite" (Bk. I, chap. iii). The appellation "Mr. Aaron" remains nonetheless offensive and contributes to the continuous qualification of Eugene's character throughout the novel. His marriage to Lizzie, however, and his attraction from the first to the good in her counterbalance his attitude toward her brother and his teacher. Eugene has more wit and finer perception than his predecessors; from righteous repudiation of Steerforth and unmitigated dislike for James Harthouse, Dickens has moved to justification and championship of Eugene Wrayburn. Eugene is as light as Richard Carstone (consider his disquisition upon domestic influences in Bk. II, chap. vi), but lightness is no longer a direct route to destruction. He begins in the same center of indifference that is the locus of Harthouse and Gowan, but he, like Arthur Clennam, finally moves beyond it to a qualified Everlasting Yea. Dickens upholds both the necessity of the progress and the legitimate grounds of the indifference. In his retreat from philistine society into a posture of boredom and indolence, in the justifiable basis of his alienation and the brilliant wit that makes the pose seductive, Eugene seems a good deal like the later Decadents. Although Dickens rejects this attitude in favor of a more orthodox vigor, he shows in Eugene a remarkable understanding of the disaffection that soon would give rise to the decadent movement of the eighties. The rejection itself should not be overemphasized: Eugene's position in the novel is much like that of the rake in a Restoration comedy, not an *honnête homme,* but still more honest than most.

A second significant succession of character-satirists is the series whose nonintellectual, instinctive perception of humbug spurs them to derisive comments or jeers. Susan Nipper's sharp-tongued resistance to Mrs. Pipchin in *Dombey and Son* shows early traces of this kind of attack. In *Hard Times* the acidic dwarf Kidderminster evinces the same refusal to be awed:

> "Nine oils, Merrylegs, missing tips, garters, banners, and Ponging, eh!" ejaculated Bounderby, with his laugh of

> laughs. "Queer sort of company, too, for a man who has raised himself."
>
> "Lower yourself, then," retorted Cupid. "Oh Lord! if you've raised yourself so high as all that comes to, let yourself down a bit." [Bk. I, chap. vi]

The narrator associates him with the misanthrope or railer but in the same sentence redeems his humanity: when Sissy leaves the Circus, all its members gather to give her a parting kiss, "Master Kidderminster excepted, in whose young nature there was an original flavour of the misanthrope, who was also known to have harboured matrimonial views, and who moodily withdrew" (Bk. I, chap. vi). The jeer in its purest form comes in the next novel, *Little Dorrit,* with the screeches of Mrs. Merdle's parrot. This bird is simultaneously an emblem of Mrs. Merdle and a satirical commentator upon her pretensions. It is introduced in the first role: "there was a parrot on the outside of a golden cage holding on by its beak with its scaly legs in the air, and putting itself into many strange upside-down postures. This peculiarity has been observed in birds of quite another feather, climbing upon golden wires" (Bk. I, chap. xx). The reference in the last sentence is clarified when its owner soon "compose[s] herself voluptuously, in a nest of crimson and gold cushions, on an ottoman near the parrot." In the conversation that follows the parrot intersperses shrieks timed for derisive meaning. The points at which it interrupts Mrs. Merdle are critical:

> "I wish Society was not quite so arbitrary, I wish it was not so exacting—Bird, be quiet!"
>
> "But . . . we must consult it. It is the common lot. Mr. Merdle is a most extensive merchant, his transactions are on the vastest scale, his wealth and influence are very great, but even he—Bird, be quiet!"
>
> "Much to be lamented, no doubt, particularly by myself, who am a child of nature if I could but show it; but so it is. Society suppresses us and dominates us—Bird, be quiet!"

> The parrot had broken into a violent fit of laughter, after twisting divers bars of his cage with his crooked bill, and licking them with his black tongue.

In *Great Expectations* Trabb's boy performs a similar function in regard to Pip. He virtually succeeds in driving Pip away from town because the latter cannot bear his mockery. Yet when Pip is saved from the lime-kiln torture by Orlick, it is through the help of Trabb's boy: as Pip's illusions are now dispelled, his satirist becomes his rescuer.

In *Our Mutual Friend* a similarly derisive effect is achieved by Lavinia Wilfer's impertinence to her mother. Lavvy is a brat, but every time she undercuts Mrs. Wilfer's majesty we are on her side. The comedy finally turns against her too, and toward the end we see her growing up to be exactly like her mother (in her maiden hysterical fit [Bk. IV, chap. v] and in her final appearance when she unites with her mother in torturing George Sampson [Bk. IV, chap. xvi]). There is another derisive satirist in this novel, however, whose judgments are never qualified by ambivalence: Jenny Wren.

Jenny is sharp-tongued like Susan Nipper, physically deformed and somewhat bitter like Kidderminster, intolerant of pretension like Trabb's boy, and instinctively perceptive of falsity like Mrs. Merdle's parrot. She is the parrot articulate and a touchstone of truth. Her instinct is such that it raises her to a sort of supernatural knowing, yet her relation to the world of the novel is analogous to that of Physician in *Little Dorrit* to the society of Merdles and Barnacles: "Where he was, something real was" (Bk. II, chap. xxv). She is honest and good, but she threatens with a primitive cruelty and vindictiveness. Her dislike of other children leads to this suggestion:

> "I'll tell you what I'd do to punish 'em. There's doors under the church in the Square—black doors, leading into black vaults, Well! I'd open one of those doors, and I'd cram 'em all in, and then I'd lock the door and through the keyhole I'd blow in pepper."
>
> "What would be the good of blowing in pepper?" asked Charley Hexam.

> "To set 'em sneezing," said the person of the house, "and make their eyes water. And when they are all sneezing and inflamed I'd mock 'em through the keyhole." [Bk. II, chap. i]

She berates her father: " 'I wish you had been taken up, and locked up. . . . I wish you had been poked into cells and black holes, and run over by rats and spiders and beetles. *I* know their tricks and their manners, and they'd have tickled you nicely.' " And she proposes as punishment for an unfaithful lover: " 'When he was asleep, I'd make a spoon red hot, and I'd have some boiling liquor bubbling in a saucepan, and I'd take it out hissing, and I'd open his mouth with the other hand—or perhaps he'd sleep with his mouth ready open—and I'd pour it down his throat, and blister it and choke him' " (Bk. II, chap ii). All these qualities combine to make Jenny strangely like the type of primitive satirist described by R. C. Elliott in the first chapters of *The Power of Satire: Magic, Ritual, Art.*[5] The relish of physical punishment, the bitterness, hatred, and abuse, and the sense of outraged justice behind these resemble the state of satire as it passed from magic to art. The weirdness of the small, twisted figure in an aureole of shining hair; the surprisingly literal truth of the reiterated phrase "I know your tricks and your manners"; the instinctive perceptivity that sees through outward show; and the wise irony of "Come up and be dead" even give her something of the supernatural aura of the magician. One might further suggest an analogy between her employment as a dolls' dressmaker and the magical use of effigies, but this occupation, with the emphasis Dickens puts upon it, also allies her with the more sophisticated art-satirist. Jenny's world of dolls, like the satirist's world of fictive characters, is created from close and shrewd observation of the "real" world. The dolls share all the follies of their models:

> "And they take no care of their clothes, and they never keep to the same fashions a month. I work for a doll with

5. R. C. Elliott, *The Power of Satire: Magic, Ritual, Art* (Princeton, 1960), chaps. 1 and 2, passim.

> three daughters. Bless you, she's enough to ruin her husband!"
>
> . . . "I finished a large mourning order the day before yesterday. Doll I work for lost a canary-bird." [Bk. II, chap. i]

Jenny breaks the comfortable barrier between the dolls and real people when she instantly ties Eugene's playful suggestion that he is thinking of "setting up a doll" to his effort to pay for Lizzie's education (Bk. II, chap. ii). Jenny is true here not to his conscious but quite probably to his unconscious motives, and she immediately announces his unfitness for the position. Another link between the two worlds is forged by the plot as both Jenny's dolls and the Lammles turn out to depend for their material existence upon Fledgeby's Pubsey and Co. The image of a doll (the Doll's house) is offered by Bella to stand for all that she hopes she has outgrown. Finally, Jenny's beatific vision of birds, flowers, and children is the ideal perception that underlies her outrage with reality:

> "I dare say my birds sing better than other birds, and my flowers smell better than other flowers. For when I was a little child . . . the children that I used to see early in the morning were very different from any others that I ever saw. They were not like me: they were not chilled, anxious, ragged, or beaten; they were never in pain. They were not like the children of the neighbours; they never made me tremble all over by setting up shrill noises, and they never mocked me. Such numbers of them, too! All in white dresses, and with something shining on the borders, and on their heads, that I have never been able to imitate with my work, though I know it so well. They used to come down in long bright slanting rows and say altogether, 'Who is this in pain? Who is this in pain?' When I told them who it was, they answered, 'Come and play with us!' When I said, 'I never play! I can't play!' they swept about me and took me up and made me light. Then it was all delicious ease and rest till they laid me down and said, all

> together, 'Have patience, and we will come again.'" [Bk. II, chap. ii]

From the roof of Pubsey and Co., she offers again this vision of beauty; the imaginative range proves her not merely bitter and twisted but creative too.

In Book II, chapter xi, Jenny spontaneously creates Mrs. Truth, a satirist's touchstone, to comment upon the allegations of Bradley Headstone. Jenny sees through Headstone and Wrayburn both and takes immediate dislike to Charley Hexam and Fledgeby. It is for Fledgeby, about whom her perception is temporarily blinded, that the extreme of her venom is finally reserved. With him she realizes the retribution she conceived for the children who laughed at her. In peppering Fledgeby she translates into action the kind of threat that was common when satire was believed to derive from the ancient satyr play:

> The *Satyre* should be like the *Porcupine*,
> That shoots sharpe quills out in each angry line,
> And wounds the blushing cheeke, and fiery eye,
> Of him that heares, and readeth guiltily.[6]

The vindication of the satirist's art comes most strongly, however, through neither Eugene nor Jenny. Mr. Boffin is preeminently the satirist as teacher; the pupil is Bella. When Boffin makes himself into a miser to teach Bella the evils of avarice, he is doing in life, with himself as material, what the satirist at least claims to do in art: presenting the ugly, without disguise and possibly even exaggerated in its ugliness, so that we will be able to recognize it for what it is. Unlike most satirists, Boffin succeeds at least with his primary object (Silas Wegg, of course, is unteachable). If we consider this success, the joy Boffin takes in his work as it calls upon all his resources of playacting ("'my grandest demonstration—I allude to Mew says the cat, Quack-quack says the duck, and Bow-wow-wow says the dog'" [Bk. IV, chap. xiii]), and the jolly and benevolent disposition so em-

6. Joseph Hall, *Virgidemiarum*, Bk. V, Satire 3, ll. 1–4, in *Collected Poems*, ed. A. Davenport (Liverpool, 1949), p. 83.

phatically his, I think we can see a certain if partial projection of Dickens's ideal self.

The beating of Fledgeby and the disposal of Wegg in a scavenger's cart are strongly reminiscent of the sentences meted out at the end of *Volpone;* Dickens's intimate knowledge of Jonson makes such influence, though it may have been unconscious, very likely. True to Dickens's own satiric vision is the fact that in the final chapter the Voice of Society is still being heard, as it was throughout the novel, in the present tense (Bk. I, chaps. ii and x; Bk. II, chaps. iii and xvi; Bk. III, chap. xvii) and is exactly what it was (Podsnappery) and where it was (dining at the Veneerings') in chapter ii of Book I. At the same time, the plot itself has left some sacred cows badly butchered: respectability, from Riderhood through Podsnap, is revealed to be a form of self-interest; education has ruined Charley as a human being (the novel simply forgets him at the end) and proved a dangerous experiment for Mr. Boffin. Raising himself through education to respectability was the great achievement of the young Dickens: here both the goal and the means are exposed to contempt. But there are counter impulses too. Throughout the book the reader has seen much (more than either hero) of what is positive: the Boffins, Lizzie, Riah, even Mr. Venus. The theme of regeneration is strong, and at the end both heroes leave their deathlike states in the conclusion that to enter society and work within it is desirable and right. Though society is far from the comfortable destiny it was for the early heroes, the Harmons and the Wrayburns can participate in it considerably more than the sympathetic characters of the dark novels. Veneering is still in power, but we have a prediction that he won't last long; the final word at the last Veneering dinner is after all Twemlow's, no longer a piece of furniture, standing up for the true gentility in himself. There is yet no vision of a reformed society, but the hope of individual regeneration is bright. The likeness of the Boffins to the Cheerybles is significant, and one must not underestimate the strength of Lizzie. As John and Eugene unite with the quintessentially feminine—Bella in being domestic and having an "Inexhaustible" baby the most fully developed of the typically Dickensian type; Lizzie in her growth out of the darkest elements of the river and her prowess upon it a more mature, less "Victorian," conception—they achieve a marvelous wholeness. In the dark novels these figures would have shown small against the urban glitter and dust of the mechanized, megalopolic civilization Dickens holds behind them. Now, though the desiccation and inhumanity are grasped as fully as ever, the balance remains suspended: the vision is certainly not serene, but neither is the satire absolute.

Epilogue

The social structures in Dickens's novels are comments primarily upon moral and psychic states, not upon economic or political orders. The satirized characters and institutions are emblems of spiritual malaise. In the earlier books the standards are touchstones, equally unreal. It is this character that makes the novels continuingly meaningful, their vision powerful whether or not historically correct. No solutions are offered beyond what is implied in the malaise, for Dickens speaks as a satirist, rendering the world he sees. Reformism is left to the journalistic writings.

In the later satires the central institutions tend toward pure symbolism. In *Bleak House,* for instance, life that is ridden with confusion, red tape, spinach, and gammon finds its emblem in the workings of Chancery—although in *Our Mutual Friend* Mortimer Lightwood's connection with Chancery is hardly significant. Imagination and fertility are basic vital principles; the statistics, the Fairy Palaces, and the mechanical jungle of Coketown render the sense of life enjoying only their mockeries. The vision of life as imprisonment within imprisonment gives rise to *Little Dorrit*'s Marshalsea. (In *Pickwick Papers* Dickens adds a footnote on the Marshalsea to say that it no longer exists [chap. xxi]; in *Little Dorrit* it is beside the point.) Life preys upon dust and sewage, as expressed in Mounds, Veneerings, and a Thames to be dredged for corpses. The thematic significance of its institutions gives each novel its ongoing value; the concretion, in characters and customs, makes it vivid.

I make this claim for the later novels only. In the earlier novels, as we have seen, there is much incidental satire, most of it social and a good part of it barely related to any thematic concern. There is also considerable evidence of the sort of phenomena that will become central to Dickens's later satiric vision.

But satiric themes and satiric tone in the early novels frequently do not coincide. These novels are often delightful, but they are not fully organic; cohesion comes with the progress toward congruity in the satire.

The satire, as I have reiterated throughout this discussion, is continuously in defense of life; its objects of attack are gradually defined as the representatives and creators of all forms of rigidity. This thematic principle can bear significantly upon our understanding of Dickens's style (I use the term here in its broadest sense). The 1841 preface to *Oliver Twist* contains possibly the most important statement by Dickens about his own literary antecedents:

> On the other hand, if I look for examples and precedents, I find them in the noblest range of English literature. Fielding, Defoe, Goldsmith, Smollett, Richardson, Mackenzie—all these for wise purposes, and especially the two first, brought upon the scene the very scum and refuse of the land. Hogarth, the moralist, and censor of his age—in whose great works the times in which he lived and the characters of every time will never cease to be reflected—did the like, without the compromise of a hair's breadth, with a power and depth of thought which belonged to few men before him and will probaly appertain to fewer still in time to come. Where does this giant stand now in the estimation of his countrymen?

Dickens referred frequently to Hogarth and owned forty-eight of his engravings.[1] Their relationship, however, is less significantly in the righteous proclamation of ugly truth than in the aura that surrounds this "truth": a combination of the grotesque and the realistic that also influenced Dickens's illustrators Cruikshank, Phiz, and Leech. Ronald Paulson observes that "Hogarth's ideal figures tend to appear as graceful curves, while the objects of his ridicule express the rigidity of straight lines, circles, or squares."[2] Affinity with Dickens's static, rigid char-

1. Harry Stone, "Dickens' Reading," (Ph.D. diss., UCLA, 1955), p. 546.

2. Ronald Paulson, *Hogarth's Graphic Works*, 2 vols. (New Haven, 1965), 1:26.

acters and the struggles against them on the part of the later heroes is surely evident. "Formally Hogarth's prints are based on the interplay or conflict of geometrical and irregular forms. At times the firm straight lines of buildings and the graceful curving towers of Wren churches stand for the order and ideals that hold society together; but at other times they suggest the straitjacketing of human vitality and the remoteness of the ecclesiastic from human needs."[3] Even the inconsistency is mirrored in Dickens: in *Bleak House* justice is perverted into the strangulation of Chancery, but amidst the anarchy of *A Tale of Two Cities* justice is the lost norm. For Dickens at his best, however, fixed forms almost always mean straitjacketings.

A more important likeness to this conflict of forms is stylistic and oblique. The geometrical form exists not in the work itself but in the reader's expectations. The irregular form is the eruptive, bursting, apparently spontaneous verbal flow that is perhaps after all the essential quality we recognize as peculiarly Dickensian. He describes Silas Wegg:

> All weathers saw the man at the post. This is to be accepted in a double sense, for he contrived a back to his wooden stool by placing it against the lamp-post. When the weather was wet, he put up his umbrella over his stock-in-trade, not over himself; when the weather was dry, he furled that faded article, tied it round with a piece of yarn, and laid it cross-wise under the trestles—where it looked like an unwholesomely-forced lettuce that had lost in colour and crispness what it had gained in size. [*Our Mutual Friend,* Bk. I, chap. v]

In this kind of elaboration, which Dickens is likely to toss off casually at any moment, it almost seems that the images have assumed a life of their own, the essentials of which are profusion and comedy. A more revealing passage is found in *Hard Times.* James Harthouse has just accepted Sissy's recommendation that he leave "immediately and finally," and he ponders despondently: " 'The defeat may now be considered perfectly accom-

3. Paulson, *Hogarth's Graphic Works,* 1:49.

plished. Only a poor girl—only a stroller—only James Harthouse made nothing of—only James Harthouse a Great Pyramid of failure' " (Bk. III, chap. ii). Then the last metaphor takes over the structure, and we find the final disposal of Harthouse dictated not by an ordered plot (even in this most ordered of Dickens's novels) but by the style: "The Great Pyramid put it into his head to go up the Nile. He took a pen upon the instant, and wrote the following note (in appropriate hieroglyphics) to his brother: Dear Jack,—All up at Coketown. Bored out of the place, and going in for camels. Affectionately, Jem."

It seems to me that Dickens's novels, the later ones in particular, are meaningful and valuable as they bring into confrontation the vital energies of life and the various forces of rigidity threatening to stop them. *Pickwick Papers* celebrates the energy, and its satire is occasional and secondary. In the later novels the proponents of life must engage in desperate struggle, and the victories are always qualified; satire dominates. As the Pickwickians disappear from the world, standards of vitality become difficult to seek. The only constant is that embodied in Dickens's own verbal style. That style is also what makes Dickens's novels not only meaningful and valuable—great though these virtues are—but fun to read.

APPENDIX A

Dickens's Conception of Satire

[See p. 5 for the text discussion that this appendix elaborates.] Chapter i of *Nicholas Nickleby* describes the sudden inheritance by Nicholas's grandfather Godfrey of five thousand pounds from his uncle Ralph:

> As the deceased had taken no further notice of his nephew in his lifetime, than sending to his eldest boy (who had been christened after him, on desperate speculation) a silver spoon in a morocco case, which, as he had not too much to eat with it, seemed a kind of *satire* upon his having been born without that useful article of plate in his mouth. [italics mine, here and in quotations following]

In chapter xvii of *The Old Curiosity Shop,* the birds begin to sing as Little Nell wanders through a cemetery. More and more join in "all this noisy contention amidst a skimming to and fro, and lighting on fresh branches, and frequent change of place, which *satirised* the old restlessness of those who lay so still beneath the moss and turf below, and the strife in which they had worn away their lives." Later (in chap. xix) two travelers are introduced to the Jolly Sandboys: "The name of the first of these new-comers was Vuffin; the other, probably, as a pleasant *satire* upon his ugliness, was called Sweet William."

In chapter xxvi of *Barnaby Rudge,* Barnaby, his mother, and Grip wait for a coach in the churchyard. Mrs. Rudge finally hears its horn:

> Barnaby, who had been sleeping on the grass, sprung up quickly at the sound; and Grip, who appeared to understand it equally well, walked into his basket straightway,

> entreating society in general (as though he intended a kind of *satire* upon them in connection with churchyards) never to say die on any terms.

Dickens sums up the aftermath of the Gordon riots:

> In a word, those who suffered as rioters were, for the most part, the weakest, meanest, and most miserable among them. It was a most exquisite *satire* upon the false religious cry which had led to so much misery, that some of these people owned themselves to be Catholic, and begged to be attended by their own priests. [chap. lvii]

From New York Dickens wrote to Forster about the editors who insisted on taking credit for having made him popular by publishing his books in their newspapers: "A splendid *satire* upon this kind of trash has just occurred" *(Letters,* I, 387). The satire was an incident in which a gentleman arrived and demanded pecuniary assistance from Dickens's secretary Putnam, was refused by a note from Dickens, and wrote back angrily that he had been the first to sell Dickens's books in New York but now thought Dickens devoid of feeling and would warn him to take care he did not repent his action.

In *Martin Chuzzlewit,* when Mary tells young Martin that his grandfather has never mentioned his name since their quarrel, Martin explodes: " 'He may once, perhaps—to couple it with reproach—in his will. Let him, if he please! By the time it reaches me, he will be in his grave: a *satire* on his own anger, God help him" (chap. xiv). Later, Old Chuffey, who has been sitting by innocently as Jonas berates his father in speech and even more in thought, suddenly exclaims: " 'He is your own son, Mr. Chuzzlewit. Your own son, sir!' " The narrator comments: "Old Chuffey little suspected what depth of application these words had, or that, in the bitter *satire* which they bore, they might have sunk into the old man's very soul, could he have known what words were hanging on his own son's lips, or what was passing in his thoughts" (chap. xviii).

APPENDIX B

Dickens and the Tradition of Satire

Some readers may be curious about Dickens's knowledge of traditional satire and his sense of relation to it. Although Dickens knew both the classic English satirists and their models, he did not see himself as the inheritor of that tradition. Some hint of felt relationship appears in the warning to Martin Chuzzlewit from his American acquaintance that is quoted at the opening of this study: " 'I believe no satirist could breathe this air. If another Juvenal or Swift could rise up among us tomorrow . . .' " (chap. xvi). Surprising as it may seem, there is good evidence for Dickens's knowledge of Juvenal. In *Dombey and Son,* when Dr. Blimber tells Paul that a " 'repetition of such allusions would make it necessary for me to request to hear, without a mistake, before breakfast-time tomorrow morning from *Verbum personale* down to *simillima cygno,'* "[1] he is referring to specific passages in Juvenal's *Satires.* More significant is Dickens's description of himself to Forster in a letter of June 1845 as traveling through Rome "always lugging out of a bag, on all occasions," a copy of Juvenal *(Letters,* I, 684). And although there is no evidence that he read it, he owned a copy of Dryden's *Satires of Juvenal and Persius.*[2]

Dickens's familiarity with Swift is more to be expected. He knew *Gulliver's Travels* from childhood. In *American Notes* he refers to the passengers on a river steamboat as Yahoos and describes the Negro car of a railway train as "a great blundering clumsy chest, such as Gulliver put to sea in, from the kingdom

1. I am indebted for this observation to a most helpful unpublished dissertation by Harry Stone, "Dickens's Reading," p. 562. The quotation from *Dombey and Son* is from chapter xiv.

2. Stone, "Dickens's Reading," p. 388.

of Brobdingnag" (chaps. xii, iv). The sight of the slaves repels him as much as humankind must have repelled "that travelled creation of the great satirist's brain . . . fresh from living among horses" (chap. ix). Three references to *Gulliver's Travels,* scattered so evenly through so short a work, themselves seem indicative of Dickens's feelings toward his works on America.

Somewhat later, in a defense of his satire on Nonconformism, Dickens cited Swift:

> Lest there be any well-intentioned persons who do not perceive the difference . . . between religion and the cant of religion . . . let them understand that it is always the latter, and never the former, which is satirized here. . . . But it is never out of season to protest . . . against the confounding of Christianity with any class of persons who, in the words of Swift, have just enough religion to make them hate, and not enough to make them love, one another.[3]

His technique, however, at least in the passages referred to here, can be called Swiftian only in that the victim is made to expose himself; Dickens's concern with the nature of religious belief does not approach the depth of Swift's. Yet it may be worth noting that all these suggestive references are from the 1840s.

In July 1839 Dickens described to Forster a periodical which he was planning on the lines of the *Tatler,* the *Spectator,* or the *Bee,* which would use Gog and Magog, reintroduce Mr. Pickwick and Sam Weller, and

> would also commence, and continue from time to time, a series of satirical papers purporting to be translated from some Savage Chronicles, and to describe the administration of justice in some country that never existed, and record the proceedings of its wise men. The object of this series (which if I can compare it with anything would be something between Gulliver's Travels and the Citizen of

3. 1847 preface to *Pickwick Papers.* The reference to Swift is to his "Thoughts on Various Subjects," *Satires and Personal Writings,* ed. William Alfred Eddy (London, 1932), p. 406.

> the World) would be to keep a special look-out upon the magistrates in the town and country, and never to leave those worthies alone. [*Letters,* I, 219]

The periodical began on April 4, 1840. *Master Humphrey's Clock* did make use of Gog and Magog and bring back Mr. Pickwick and the Wellers, but as it then turned almost entirely into *The Old Curiosity Shop* and *Barnaby Rudge,* the Savage Chronicles were never realized. Perhaps this was just as well. Some fifteen years after *Master Humphrey's Clock,* Dickens again considered inserting a few satiric pieces into his periodical and wrote to Forster: "I have rather a bright idea, I think, for Household Words this morning: a fine little bit of satire: an account of an Arabic MS. lately discovered very like the Arabian Nights—called the Thousand and One Humbugs. With new versions of the best known stories" *(Letters,* II, 622). "The Thousand and One Humbugs" appeared accordingly in the April 21, April 28, and May 5, 1855 issues of *Household Words.* On their evidence alone, Dickens would be a very sorry satirist. The humor depends largely on such "Arabic" puns as the Grand Vizier Parmarstoon and his daughter Hansardade in the Kingdom of Taxedtaurus, and the political points are neither novel nor incisive. Dickens's experiment with the beast fable, running through four numbers of *Household Words* (April 6, May 11, June 8, and August 24, 1850), purportedly written by a bad-tempered raven, was also weak; the manner given the raven is stiff, repetitive, and without the charm of the more realistic bird in *Barnaby Rudge.* In the last number the raven cites a letter from a horse who regards himself as a rational being and explains that the highest achievement of man would be to become like him. A similar failure appears in what seems an attempt in the "Proposals for a National Jest-Book" that appeared in *Household Words* for May 3, 1856 to create a persona in the manner of Swift: while the persona is clearly not Dickens, his personality is otherwise quite nebulous.

Dickens also knew much of Swift's less familiar work: in the conclusion to his "Sketches of Young Gentlemen" *(Sketches by Boz),* he casually quotes from the *Letter To A Young Lady, On*

Her Marriage. He seems to have thought of Swift and Voltaire as closely allied, praising an account by saying that there is nothing "so satirically humourous in Swift or Voltaire" *(Letters,* III, 360), and the satiric inspiration of Voltaire is seen in an article in *All The Year Round* for April 21, 1860 ("The Great Tasmania's Cargo," reprinted in *The Uncommercial Traveller)* attacking "that great Circumlocution Office on which the sun never sets and the light of reason never rises." The narrator's guide is Pangloss, lineally descended from Candide, who demonstrates that "we live in the best of all possible official worlds." The essay is not continuously satiric, however, but rather a straightforward complaint against abuse in the army. *Sunday Under Three Heads,* though Edgar Johnson speaks of its "satire upon the intolerance and narrowness of the dissenting clergy,"[4] shows early in Dickens's career (it was published in 1836) that he could not use satire, as Swift did, for political pamphleteering: his Timothy Sparks is no Drapier, and his results were not nearly so spectacular.

Dickens's familiarity with Pope is perhaps as extensive, but certainly not so deeply felt, as with Swift. The 1850 preface to *Oliver Twist* contains a reference to Pope's "Verses on a Grotto . . . at Twickenham." In a speech for the Royal Academy on May 2, 1870, Dickens quoted in reference to Maclise the phrase "In wit a man, simplicity a child" from the epitaph on Gay. A tirade on "The Noble Savage" in *Household Words* (June 11, 1853, in *Reprinted Pieces)* asks whether he (the noble savage) has ever, "improved a dog, or attached a dog, since his nobility first ran wild in woods, and was brought down (at a very long shot) by POPE?" When *Martin Chuzzlewit*'s Tom Pinch loses his way and finds himself by the Monument, Dickens has him wonder "if Truth didn't live in the base of the Monument, notwithstanding Pope's couplet about the outside of it, where in London . . . was she likely to be found!" (chap. xxxvii). In a still lighter and more telling vein, a hairdresser in the sketch "Mr. Robert Bolton" *(Sketches by Boz)* offers as collateral for

4. Edgar Johnson, *Charles Dickens: His Triumph and Tragedy* (New York, 1952), 1:147.

a loan "a book as belonged to Pope, Byron's Poems, valued at forty pounds, because it's got Pope's identical scratch on the back."

A joke printed as broadside, in an edition of five copies (reprinted in the Nonesuch *Collected Papers,* I, 110–114), describes "The Great International Walking Match of February 29th, 1868," which Dickens's friends, worried about his depressed spirits, organized during his second American trip. One of the signers of the "Agreement" that governed the match was "George Dolby (British subject), *alias* the 'Man of Ross,' " or "The Man of Ross *(alias* old Alick Pope, *alias* All-our-praises-why-should-lords, etc, etc.)." Dolby was Dickens's tour-manager; Dickens himself is named in the agreement as the "Gad's Hill Gasper." Dickens did not think of himself as an exemplar of Pope's moral ideal, and, although he quoted frequently from the *Essay on Man,* he attacked more than once what he probably took to be the central statement of Pope's philosophy. In *Pickwick Papers* the shrewd realism of Sam Weller produces the typical but incisive Wellerism on the subject: " 'Yes, sir,' rejoined Mr. Weller. 'Wotever is, is right, as the young nobleman sveetly remarked wen they put him down in the pension list 'cos his mother's uncle's vife's grandfather vunce lit the king's pipe vith a portable Tinder-box' " (chap. li). Expectedly, a later attack in *A Tale of Two Cities* is both more direct and more bitter: "Altogether, the Old Bailey, at that date, was a choice illustration of the precept, that 'Whatever is is right;' an aphorism that would be as final as it is lazy, did it not include the troublesome consequence, that nothing that ever was, was wrong" (Bk. II, chap. ii).

Dickens could, however, put Pope to more subtle—and satiric—use. Mrs. Merdle in *Little Dorrit* effuses on one of her favorite themes: " 'A more primitive state of society would be delicious to me. There used to be a poem when I learnt lessons, something about Lo the poor Indian whose something mind! If a few thousand persons moving in Society could only go and be Indians' " (Bk. I, chap. xx). A more discreet allusion in the same novel shows knowledge of the *Moral Essays* as well. Book II, chapter vii ("Without presuming to decide where doctors disagreed, it did appear to Bar . . . that this new system was . . . Humbug") is a paraphrase of the opening lines of the *Epistle to Bathurst:* "Who shall decide, when Doctors disagree,/ And soundest Casuists doubt, like you and me?"[5] Other allusions are still less obvious, though they contain some satiric point for those who catch them. Mr. Mould, the undertaker in *Martin Chuzzlewit,* in conversation with Mrs. Gamp praises his own profession: " 'We should be an honoured calling. We do good by stealth, and blush to have it mentioned in our little bills' " (chap. xix). The paraphrase is of lines 135–36 of the *Epilogue to the Satires,* Dialogue I: "Let humble ALLEN, with an awkward Shame,/Do good by stealth, and blush to find it Fame." As—aside from the difference between little bills and Fame—Allen is a true model of virtue and Mr. Mould a canting liar, Dickens's version has something of the mock heroic. Similarly, when Mr. Leo Hunter invites Mr. Pickwick to partake of " 'feasts of reason, sir, and flows of soul,' as somebody who wrote a sonnet to Mrs. Leo Hunter on her breakfasts feelingly and originally observed" (chap. xv), the sonneteer has in fact plagiarized from the *Imitations of Horace,* Satire II.i., where Pope praises the quiet retreat of his grotto: "There *St. John* mingles with my friendly Bowl,/The Feast of Reason and the Flow of Soul" (ll. 127–28).

A number of references suggest that, as Dickens knew Pope's *Imitations of Horace,* he was familiar with the model too. In the essay "Tramps" in *The Uncommercial Traveller* he uses the phrase *fruges consumere nati.* In *Pictures from Italy* he describes Albano, in the neighborhood of Rome, as a place "that certainly has not improved since the days of Horace, and in these times hardly justifies his panegyric" ("Rome"). Finally, in *A Tale of Two Cities* there is a silent allusion like the one in *Little Dorrit* to the *Epistle to Bathurst.* In chapter xiv of Book II, Jerry Cruncher is described as gazing on two streams "like the heathen rustic who has for several centuries been on duty watching one stream." The reference here is to Epistle i.2.41–3, "Rusticus expectat," in the Conington translation:

5. I am indebted for this and the three references that follow to Stone, "Dickens's Reading," pp. 399–400, 562. The commentary is my own.

He who puts off the time for mending, stands
A clodpole by the stream with folded hands,
Waiting till all the water be gone past;
But it runs on and will, while time shall last.[6]

Only Jerry had "no expectation of their ever running dry."

Dickens's satire, however, is remote from Horace's, and has little formal or conscious relation to Pope's. His work was never of the highly literary sort that would have made him mindful, as it did the Augustans, of classical precedent; indeed, his one character outstanding for her veneration of the classics is Mrs. Blimber in *Dombey and Son,* who is full of ignorant, gushing admiration for Cicero. Although there are important affinities between Pope's and Dickens's darker visions—although, too, in the "dark" novels Dickens seems to have regarded himself, like Pope, as one stripping away the false tinsel and glitter of rogues and villains—the objects of attack, the standards, the forms, and the methods that the different forms commend or prescribe amount to a separation between the two writers wide enough that Dickens himself never recognized any kinship.

A. O. J. Cockshut has pointed out the link between Dickens and the Augustans in the use of the mock heroic but also, in Dickens's crudity, the weakness of that link.[7] The reports of the "Mudfog Association" or the opening parody of *Pickwick Papers* make this painfully clear; The United Metropolitan Improved Hot Muffin and Crumpet Baking and Punctual Delivery Company *(Nicholas Nickleby)* is of the same order. Dickens's ineptitude arises to some extent from the failure of an acceptable standard. When Pope floods his text with footnotes, he also knows what profitable scholarship is; when the dunces play games, the feats to which the comparable styles contrast them are still felt as truly heroic; when Belinda and her friends are ridiculous, it is with reference to a fully appreciated elegant and delicate world. Dickens has no such positives: there

6. Pointed out by Vernon Rendall, "Dickens and Horace," *The Dickensian* 11 (July 1915): 193–94.

7. A. O. J. Cockshut, *The Imagination of Charles Dickens* (New York, 1962), p. 16.

is no feeling of a worthy learned society, even in idea, behind Mudfog; no respected parliamentary procedure to contrast the Pickwickians' imitation or the blunderings and grossness of the real Parliament they reflect; no conception in *Nicholas Nickleby,* despite the Cheerybles, of valid commercial enterprise. Dickens's strength, as even the Eatanswill election will show, lies not in the indirection of parody but in the direct attack of comic or grotesque exaggeration.

The important relations between Dickens and the Augustans, Swift in particular, do not lie in allusions or direct imitations. *Martin Chuzzlewit,* with its relatively high quantity of anatomizing of follies, while successful, is singular to the Dickens canon. Dickens was far more comfortable when he maintained his own characteristic manner. The conception of the Reverend Mr. Chadband in *Bleak House* as an Oil Works, converting food into train oil and exuding it in perspiration, may have owed something to Swift's *Discourse Concerning the Mechanical Operation of the Spirit,* but it succeeds because its development is utterly Dickensian. The striking affinities of Dickens's work to earlier satire, especially that of Pope and Swift, are in tone and atmosphere; the qualities he shares with them are largely those he and they also shared with Hogarth (cf. epilogue). Whatever he actually may have learned from his Augustan predecessors, Dickens seldom thought of himself as a satirist and was not consciously their follower.

The same may be said of Dickens's relation to Ben Jonson. Comparison has been made between his eccentrics and Jonson's humor characters,[8] but even though Dickens's knowledge of Jonson had an actor's intimacy, the case for significant influence is weak—the caricatured, two-dimensional, or "ruling passion" character is almost basic to satire. (Dickens actually uses the phrase "ruling passion" in *Pickwick Papers,* chapter i.) The method is part of a reductive vision that carries its own indictment: the avaricious man, for instance, is condemned not

8. Evelyn Simpson, "Jonson and Dickens: A Study in the Comic Genius of London," *Essays and Studies* 29 (1944): 82–92; E. M. Forster, *Aspects of the Novel* (New York, 1927), p. 67 ff.; Monroe Engel, "Dickens on Art," *Modern Philology* 53 (1955): 34; Mario Praz, *The Hero in Eclipse,* p. 174.

only because greed is evil but also because his greed has consumed all other qualities and become the whole of his character. To define the predominant humor of a character is often simultaneously to specify his characterization. Pecksniff shares with Volpone a remarkable flair for verbal expansion, but for the active, extroverted hypocrite (the passive type is the scheming Uriah Heep), the exercise of this talent is fundamental. There is, moreover, a radical difference between Dickens and Jonson in standards of character: Jonson's gulls are primarily stupid and pretentious, his admirable characters triumphant in wit (Volpone becomes a gull when he outwits himself, but Face, in *The Alchemist,* though hardly more upright, escapes punishment because he knows just when to pull up short); Dickens's butts are morally insensitive or perverse, his admirable figures honest and good. In one it is an axis of intelligence, in the other of morality.

Earle Davis has compared old Martin in *Martin Chuzzlewit* —leading on his hypocritical victim Pecksniff, then turning about and exposing him—to Volpone.[9] But Volpone himself is finally a fool, whereas old Martin is actually "good." What is close to *Volpone* is the general organization of *Martin Chuzzlewit:* selecting eccentric figures that display aspects of one satiric theme,[10] then setting them in action designed for maximum display, and bringing them together for a final scene in which the principal impostor is formally and publicly punished.[11] Crossing this, however, is an equally strong line of structure following young Martin, who in his travels through America might well be compared to Gulliver, and in the flux of his career as a whole, except for his egotistic peevishness in the earlier stages, is a descendant of Tom Jones.

Even in his darkest works Dickens's tone is consistently kinder than Jonson's, his desire to see the possibilities for human regeneration stronger, his forgiveness readier. Jonson

9. Earle Davis, *The Flint and the Flame* (Columbia, Mo., 1963), p. 164.

10. John Forster writes that *Dombey and Son* "was to do with Pride what its predecessor had done with Selfishness" *(Life of Charles Dickens,* 2:19).

11. Actually, this occurs in chapter lii, the third to last. Mrs. Gamp is also punished, and the young innocents are rewarded.

attacks in contemptuous fury or mocking distaste; Dickens's is more a suffering anger. It would be ridiculous to insist that Dickens was in no way influenced by Jonson or that he did not learn from him, but there is certainly no evidence that he ever saw himself as the inheritor of Jonsonian tradition, either comic or satiric.

Almost the obverse is true of Dickens's relations to Smollett and Fielding. Their works were central to his boyhood reading, and when he began to write novels he considered them his predecessors. The relationship to Smollett is perhaps the more obvious. In *Pickwick Papers* alone, Harry Stone notes:

> the malaprop letter, the farce duel, the traveling group, the visit to Bath, the sojourn in debtors' prison, the letter written entirely in occupational terms (in *Pickwick* the terms are coaching ones), the bucolic country scenes, the pranks, the interpolated stories, the faithful country servant remaining with his jailed master, the multiple marriages, the shrewish and man-hungry women—all of which, and much more, are to be found in Smollett as well. Of course, such items are found elsewhere in eighteenth-century literature; but Dickens from boyhood on had read, reread, and lived his Smollett, and Smollett's writings, therefore, became for him the chief example of this type of eighteenth-century writing.[12]

The list is long, but it is probably longer for this novel than for any other; as Dickens matured, he grew away from Smollett. Even from the beginning he lacked the coarseness, particularly in sexual and other physical crudity, that also separates him from Surtees, whose *Jorrocks' Jaunts and Jollities* is a model of the "Nimrod Club" novel Dickens rejected in preliminary planning for *Pickwick*. To distinguish Dickens on this basis is not mere prudishness. As Steven Marcus points out, it was only when the novel had escaped this insistent coarseness that Dickens could develop a form of greater moral and social complexity.[13] And only when he turned from picaresque organiza-

12. Stone, "Dickens's Reading," p. 220.

13. Marcus, *Pickwick to Dombey*, p. 29.

tion to more symphonic forms of structure could Dickens render in its totality his deeper satiric vision. Smollett's, he wrote in 1854, is a "way without tenderness" (*Letters,* II, 560); in his mature work, Dickens was free of both the manner and the matter of that way.

There is great distance too between Dickens and Fielding, though in a different direction. Harry Stone points out the similarity of the burlesque genealogy and mock heroics of chapter i of *Martin Chuzzlewit* and chapter ii of *Joseph Andrews;* calls Pickwick's bedroom error at Ipswich "merely a more genteel version" of Book IV, chapter xiv, of the same novel; and finds the title of chapter xxxvi of *Oliver Twist* ("Is a very short one, and may appear of no great importance in its place, but it should be read notwithstanding, as a sequel to the last and a key to one that will follow when its time arrives") generally reminiscent of Fielding.[14] All this is true, and undoubtedly much more could be found; but Dickens's tone, except in rare moments, is remote from Fielding's. Dickens may have delighted to read of but could not himself create or inhabit the essentially aristocratic world of *Tom Jones* or the humorous spoof of *Jonathan Wild.* (My use of the term *aristocratic* here is not in the sense for which, for instance, the distinction between aristocracy and squirearchy is material, but rather a less formal denotation of a certain tone determining attitudes and taste. It consists of distance, nonchalance, and a confidence that makes insistence unnecessary.) Dennis, the hangman in *Barnaby Rudge,* may, as Kathleen Tillotson suggests,[15] have derived somewhat from the irony of *Jonathan Wild,* but the attitude toward him and the atmosphere in which he is surrounded are utterly different. In the 1841 preface to *Oliver Twist,* his own underworld novel, Dickens was at pains to refute the Newgate school, of which *Jonathan Wild* is as much an exponent as *The Beggar's Opera.* As for *Tom Jones,* Dickens would be too concerned with the eventual fate of Molly to allow Tom blamelessly to love and leave her. Witness *Nicholas Nickleby*—Dickens's

14. Stone, "Dickens's Reading," p. 215.

15. In her introduction to the New Oxford Illustrated edition of *Barnaby Rudge,* p. xi.

novel closest to *Tom Jones* in situation, structure, and outcome —in which the hero not only is occupied at length with preserving the maidenhood of his sister and then of Madeline Bray but displays an almost unbearable priggishness himself. Dickens had too much "high seriousness" to write as Fielding did, much as he admired him. He did learn much from Fielding of such types as Thwackum and Square, particularly in their unctuousness and their ultimate exposure as hypocrites, but Fielding's play of fine satiric wit, moral and yet socially defined, allied to the carefree comedy of manners, is, if not inevitably of another age, certainly of another class. Dickens may have been able to appreciate the values of Squire Allworthy, but he would still ask where his money came from and how he behaved in matters of politics. Dickens, as has often been said, could create an aristocratic world only to condemn it, and although he did not especially care for Richardson, he could not have derided Pamela from the same standpoint as Fielding did. In *Kings and Desperate Men* Louis Kronenberger shows a preference for Hogarth over Fielding because Hogarth was more penetrating in his own sphere, more seriously concerned with moral issues, and therefore capable of a "sense of the tragic."[16] If Hogarth's vision can mediate between Dickens and the Augustans, as suggested above, then the range of his concerns can mediate between Dickens and Fielding. Kronenberger, in fairness to Fielding, follows his comment that Fielding, "though he might denounce injustice and corruption, never dreamt of questioning the conditions that produced them" with a note that some distinction needs to be made between Fielding the novelist and Fielding the practicing magistrate. Dickens brought the concerns of the magistrate into the novel—indeed, he was incapable of separating the two realms—and, with them, a sense of the tragic very much like Hogarth's. The differences between Dickens and Fielding mean in Dickens a loss in finesse and gentility, but they mean as well a gain in range of moral commitment and, consequently, in depth of moral concern.

A similar Victorian earnestness separates Dickens from Byron.

16. Louis Kronenberger, *Kings and Desperate Men* (New York, 1959), pp. 282–83.

Dickens's taste for Byron's work was gratifyingly modern: he disliked the "Byronic" Byron but admired to an equal degree the satirist of *Don Juan*. When a young solicitor's clerk with poetical ambitions asked Dickens for advice, he replied: "It is not the province of a Poet to harp upon his own discontents, or to teach other people that they ought to be discontented. Leave Byron to his gloomy greatness" *(Letters,* I, 279). Dickens often put Byronism to his own comic purposes. One day in September 1841, Dickens was discussing *Childe Harold* with a group of friends. He criticized the phrases "Dazzled and drunk with beauty" and "The heart *reels* with its fulness" as less suggestive of Venus than of gin-and-water, then shouted "Stand back! I am suddenly seized with the divine afflatus!" He took up a pencil, looked round for some paper, and, finding none, went to the window and wrote on the white-painted shutter:

LINES TO E.P.————. AFTER BYRON

O maiden of the amber-dropping hair
  May I Byronically, thy praises utter?
Drunk with *thy* beauty, tell me, may I dare
  To sing thy paeans *borne upon a shutter?*[17]

With perhaps greater literary inspiration, he could also use Byronism for satiric commentary in his works. The illustration for *Martin Chuzzlewit* that depicts Mr. Moddle wooing Charity Pecksniff shows a copy of *Childe Harold* lying within reach. Of course, this bit of silent commentary may have been Hablôt Browne's, but Dickens generally gave very specific instructions for the drawings and certainly reviewed them carefully before publication. Also in *Martin Chuzzlewit,* the imbecility of an American litterateur is meant to reach a climax when he asks young Martin to favor him "with any critical observations that have ever presented themselves to your reflective faculties, on 'Cain: a Mystery,' by the Right Honourable Lord Byron" (chap. xxii). And in *The Old Curiosity Shop* both the girls and the mistress herself of Miss Monflathers's school prove

17. The story is recounted by Johnson, *Charles Dickens: His Triumph and Tragedy,* I: 350–51.

their empty-headedness in their fashionable reaction to one of Mrs. Jarley's waxwork impositions. Mrs. Jarley was not above multiple uses of a single figure, and at a Private View "Mary Queen of Scots in a dark wig, white shirt-collar, and male attire, was such a complete image of Lord Byron that the young ladies quite screamed when they saw it. Miss Monflathers, however, rebuked this enthusiasm, and took occasion to reprove Mrs. Jarley for not keeping her collection more select: observing that His Lordship had held certain opinions quite incompatible with wax-work honours" (chap. xxix). On the other hand, the character in "The Boarding-House" *(Sketches by Boz)* who is tagged by his habit of constantly quoting from *Don Juan* is ridiculed not for his choice of book but because it is the only book he has ever read, and Dickens seems rather to enjoy the passages he allows Mr. Septimus Hicks to recite.

Dickens must have relished lines like the following, hilarious themselves and on a theme close to his heart: "But—oh! ye lords of ladies intellectual,/Inform us truly, have they not hen-peck'd you all?" (Bk. I, chap. xxii). These lines also illustrate a device of style that Dickens, in his own mode, shared with Byron. It is well to recollect that Dr. Johnson's famous definition of *wit* was meant to cover both the surprising thoughts expressed by the metaphysical poets and Pope's "happiness of language": "But Wit, abstracted from its effects upon the hearer, may be more rigorously and philosophically considered as a kind of *discordia concors;* a combination of dissimilar images, or discovery of occult resemblances in things apparently unlike. . . . The most heterogeneous ideas are yoked by violence together; nature and art are ransacked for illustrations, comparisons, and allusions."[18] Since the definition seeks the essential spirit behind wit, it can be extended to other modes of wit as well. As it is applicable to Pope's diction, so it also encompasses the nature of Byron's rhyme and speaks tellingly of Dickens's metaphors. The surprise, the forcing of incongruities, the yoking together of disparate elements in a configuration often comic comprise

18. Samuel Johnson, "Life of Cowley"; the edition used here is *Lives of the English Poets,* 2 vols. (London, Oxford University Press, 1952), 1:14.

a spirit common to them all. The bias of comedy allies Dickens most closely to Byron. With Dickens, the spirit is most evident in the grotesque metaphors that serve the creation of character. These characters are more frequent in the earlier novels, but where the treatment is comic and lightly satiric they persist throughout his work. A late instance is the description of the Wilfers in *Our Mutual Friend.* The family is introduced in chapter iv of Book I; the first two paragraphs identify the unfortunate Reginald Wilfer:

> Reginald Wilfer is a name with rather a grand sound, suggesting on first acquaintance brasses in country churches, scrolls in stained-glass windows, and generally the De Wilfers who came over with the Conqueror. For, it is a remarkable fact in genealogy that no De Any ones ever came over with Anybody else.
>
> But the Reginald Wilfer family were of such commonplace extraction and pursuits that their forefathers had for generations modestly subsisted on the Docks, the Excise Office, and the Custom House, and the existing R. Wilfer was a poor clerk. So poor a clerk, through having a limited salary and an unlimited family, that he had never yet attained the modest object of his ambition: which was, to wear a complete new suit of clothes, hat and boots included, at one time. His black hat was brown before he could afford a coat, his pantaloons were white at the seams and knees before he could buy a pair of boots, his boots had worn out before he could treat himself to new pantaloons, and by the time he worked round to the hat again, that shining modern article roofed-in an ancient ruin of various periods.

Then Dickens opens the third paragraph with the sentence: "If the conventional Cherub could ever grow up and be clothed, he might be photographed as a portrait of Wilfer." Nothing so far has led up to this image; in fact, the lengthy detail of dress has rather led away from such a conception. But Dickens insists upon the unlikely and apparently incongruous likeness:

"His chubby, smooth, innocent appearance was a reason for his being always treated with condescension when he was put down. . . . In short, he was the conventional cherub, after the supposititious shoot just mentioned, rather grey, with signs of care upon his expression. . . ." In spite of the disparity, the union of Wilfer and cherub is affirmed. Then the final clause reaches a climax of absurdity, causing the image to disintegrate in grotesquerie: ". . . and in decidedly insolvent circumstances." Nevertheless the metaphor has been established: Reginald Wilfer is a cherub and will remain one through the book. A logic independent of obvious reason has been established and will persist. The next step follows soon: Mr. Wilfer being cherubic, Mrs. Wilfer "was necessarily majestic, according to the principle which matrimonially unites contrasts." At the end of the chapter and the evening it describes, she retires to bed "cherubically escorted, like some severe saint in a painting, or merely human matron allegorically treated."

Occasionally in his novels and more frequently in his minor writings or in such ephemera as the poem "The Bill of Fare" (a parody of Goldsmith's "Retaliation" written in 1831 for Maria Beadnell), Dickens attempted a flippant attitude, evinced primarily in willful digressions and interjections, that seems an imitation of the Byronic persona of *Beppo* or *Don Juan*. Like almost all his conscious imitations, this generally failed. Dickens did achieve a Byronic tone (of the satirical Byron, that is) only when he produced in his own medium—the creation of character—the same comic grotesquerie that sparks Byron's rhyme.

Dickens may have caught from *Don Juan* something of this informing spirit. In the broadest terms, other kinships between the two writers—as satirists—may be found. Alvin Kernan concludes of *Don Juan* that in every case what Byron "holds up to ridicule is some attempt to restrain life, to bind and force it into some narrow, permanent form."[19] I have said very similar things of Dickens. But the tone, the attitude, the viewpoint are all radically different. And the difference may be defined, tell-

19. *Plot of Satire,* p. 205.

ingly though perhaps cruelly, as the difference between the light aristocratic and the heavily serious bourgeois. The following digression is from canto XII of *Don Juan:*

> But if Love don't, *Cash* does, and Cash alone:
> Cash rules the grove, and fells it too beside;
> Without cash, camps were thin, and courts were none;
> Without cash, Malthus tells you—'take no brides.'
> So Cash rules Love the ruler, on his own
> High ground, as virgin Cynthia sways the tides: [st. xiv]

A society ruled by cash and Malthusian principles was one of the horrors Dickens too was to depict—but to denounce rather than to mock. Compare the tone of his tirade on shares:

> As is well known to the wise in their generation, traffic in Shares is the one thing to have to do with in this world. Have no antecedents, no established character, no cultivation, no ideas, no manners; have Shares. Have Shares enough to be on Boards of Direction in capital letters, oscillate on mysterious business between London and Paris, and be great. Where does he come from? Shares. Where is he going to? Shares. What are his tastes? Shares. Has he any principles? Shares. What squeezes him into Parliament? Shares. Perhaps he never of himself achieved success in anything, never originated anything, never produced anything! Sufficient answer to all; Shares. O mighty Shares! To set those blaring images so high, and to cause us smaller vermin, as under the influence of henbane or opium, to cry out night and day, "Relieve us of our money, scatter it for us, buy us and sell us, ruin us, only we beseech ye take rank among the powers of the earth, and fatten on us!" [*Our Mutual Friend,* Bk. I, chap. x]

Beside Byron, Dickens is hysterical. Byron laughs at those who govern their lives by cash: he attacks from above; Dickens is enraged for those who are duped into converting their cash into shares and are thus deprived of the goods, in food and shelter, that cash could provide: he attacks from below. The difference again is "high seriousness." Byron could close his stanza with the marvelous tongue-in-cheek couplet: "And as for 'Heaven being Love,' why not say honey/Is wax? Heaven is not Love, 'tis Matrimony." Dickens's feelings about matrimony were not much holier, but their expression was confined to private letters. We know that Dickens read and enjoyed *Don Juan,* but his image of Byron was not of the satirist, not even of a fellow literary artist, but of the popular fop and lover. The treatment of Steerforth in *David Copperfield* is probably a fair reflection of Dickens's judgment upon the Byronic figure. In *American Notes* he describes the fancy young men of New York and then dismisses them with: "Byrons of the desk and counter, pass on" (chap. vi). Dickens knew Byron, but not as one whose work he could see in any continuum with his own.

Classical satire is a highly conscious genre, very much aware of its long tradition and very proud of it. Dickens knew the tradition, but he did not place himself within it, and his work is not satiric in that formal sense. One aim of this study, however, has been to demonstrate the necessity for less rigid generic definition.

Index

Page numbers for extended discussions are in italics.